CHALLENGES TO INDIA'S FOREIGN POLICY IN THE NEW ERA

CHALLENGES TO INDIA'S FOREIGN POLICY IN THE NEW ERA

Editor
Dr. (Mrs.) Annupurna Nautiyal

GYAN PUBLISHING HOUSE
NEW DELHI-110002

Challenges to India's Foreign Policy in the New Era

Rs. 690

ISBN: 81-212-0889-0

The views expressed in the papers are there of the authors themselves. They do not reflect the views of the editior.

Published in 2008 in India by
Gyan Publishing House
5, Ansari Road,
Darya Ganj, New Delhi-110002
Phones: 23282060, 23261060, Fax: 23285914
E-mail: books@gyanbooks.com

Laser Typesetting at : Shiva Infosystem, Delhi
Printed at : Vishal Kaushik Printers Delhi

For My Parents
Dr. K. Purohit and Mrs. Leelawati

Contents

SECTION-III: HUMAN SECURITY, GOOD GOVERNANCE AND REGION SPECIFIC ISSUES

Preface

India's foreign policy is facing enormous challenges in the new era of securing peaceful atmosphere in the sub-continent, curbing terrorism and promoting peace and human security. Under the evolving global scenario India is also confronting the task of developing a right strategy to deal with Pakistan, China, South East Asian countries and the US, the only superpower. There is no denying of the fact that India is playing a powerful role in the sub-continent but the desire of playing a leading role in the global politics has yet to be fulfilled because of various constraints. In the new era, the consolidation of the US as the most powerful nation state and its attempts to maintain this position and Doctrine of pre-emption have eroded the concept of sovereignty of the states. The selective approach of the US towards terrorism, regime change, containment of rogue states and insistence on retaining the WMD and the proliferation of nuclear weapons has increased the threat to security multi-fold. In the absence of a proper approach to deal with these challenge India's response towards these have been inappropriate with the result India has not been able to register its presence in the global politics. Moreover, in the last four years, particularly after the 9/11 terrorist attacks on the US and the happenings in Afghanistan and Iraq has not only removed the illusion of Post-Cold War peace but has also heightened uncertainty and insecurity in the world. Actually an increasingly violent and insecure world has also compelled a superpower like the US also to reorient its foreign policy goals and focus on combating terrorism and homeland security. This scenario has allowed every country to restructure its foreign policy to counter the challenges produced by the new circumstances. India is no exception to this as it is facing various challenges in the field of foreign policy in the new era. Besides developing good relations with the US without sacrificing its capacity of independent decision making, India has also to develop good relations with China and Pakistan as well as bring social cohesion and harmony in the society. It has to work towards enhancing its national interest under the present unstable and highly unpredictable world. In fact the challenges are many but the strategies to tackle these are very limited because with the disintegration of the Soviet Union, India's strategy of Non-alignment and close relations with the Soviet Union has lost much of its relevance in the present era. More so due to internal problems, and security challenges from Pakistan, India in place of playing the global role has to confine itself in the South Asia region only. There is an urgent need not only to look at the challenges being faced by India but also to suggest strategies for playing a meaningful role in the global politics.

It is hoped that this publication would be helpful in comprehending the challenges to India's foreign policy in the new era in totality. I am thankful to all the contributors for their valuable contributions. I am particularly grateful to Professor P.M. Kamath for the special write-up for this book. I am also thankful to my husband Professor Vinod Nautiyal and my daughter Jaishikha for their cooperation and help during the preparation of this book.

Annpurna Nautiyal

Introduction

The historic changes that swept the international scenario in the last decade of the 20th century have not only transformed the existing political relationships between the states but also the pattern which had governed the international system for the last fifty years. The disintegration of the Soviet Union, the growing democratization, economic liberalization and cultural globalization, development and spread of the Information Technology, environmental degradation, weapons of mass degradation have compelled the statesmen, scholars and researchers throughout the world to adopt a different approach to analyse the global scenario. These changes have also forced almost all the states to reframe their foreign policy strategies as well as to redefine their role in the world politics. India's foreign Policy is facing serious challenges in the new era. India is not only facing the challenge of securing peaceful atmosphere in the sub-continent but also achieving satisfactory economic growth, curbing terrorism, promoting peace and human security as well as to evolve a right strategy to deal with Pakistan, China and the US the only superpower. Actually there are many challenges but the strategies for confronting these challenges are limited. India is playing a powerful role in the sub-continent but the desire of playing a leading role in the global politics has yet to be fulfilled because of the above challenges. In the new era, the consolidation of the US as the most powerful nation state, attempts to maintain this position, the selective approach towards terrorism, regime change, containment of rogue states, doctrine of pre-emption, insistence on retaining the WMD and the horizontal proliferation of such weapons have eroded the security and sovereignty of the states.

In the absence of a proper strategy to deal with these challenges India's response towards these challenges have been inappropriate with the result India has not been able to register its presence in the global politics.

In the present global scenario India is facing a serious challenge of developing its relations with the US without sacrificing its capacity of independent decision making because there is no alternative to dealing with the US. As the US has the capacity to mobilize support for denying India its objectives in the world politics and the challenges being faced by India also demand the US support and good relation. Though there is no denying of the fact that the terrorist strikes on the US has allowed it to understand the problems of terrorism being faced by India in a better way and it also wants India's cooperation in defeating terrorism. The progress through the Next Steps in Strategic Partnership, the US desire of seeing India evolve as a major power of the 21st century, meeting of different levels of officials and joint defence exercises, acknowledging India as a responsible state with advanced nuclear technology are being seen as moves in the right direction and generate hope for a healthy relationship in the future. In view of China's growing clout in Asia the US also needs the support of democratic India for its strategy against China but despite the convergence of interest, the doubts still persist because of the duplicity of the US policy towards the nuclear issues, transfer of high technology, supply of arms, ignoring the cross-border terrorism being supported by Pakistan, objection to India's relationship with Iran and policy of no support to India's claim for the permanent membership in the UN Security Council which India feels is against the US declaration of helping India to become a major power in 21st century and playing a more important role in the world bodies. The geopolitical necessity of seeking Pakistan's support in its war against terrorism has forced the US to maintain equal relations with India and Pakistan. Actually the American pressures on Pakistan to end support for militant organizations and on India for negotiations with Pakistan on Kashmir and all other issues is the new US policy of parity. This means that the US wants to maintain equal relations and parallel improvement of relations with both India and Pakistan and force them to adopt peaceful means in resolving the Kashmir issue. India believes that the US policy of ignoring Pakistan's activities whether related to nuclear development or terrorism has not only emboldened Pakistan but also enhanced tensions and instability in the region and the American attitude towards Pakistan and its nuclear activities is also different in comparison to the activities of India and its scientists. India's placement along with China, North Korea, Iran, Iraq, Syria, Pakistan and Sudan, which are subjected to extra strict visa review, also reveals the US policies towards India. The approach of overlooking Pakistan's role in cross border terrorism, using pressure tactics on India for negotiations, interfering and meddling in the regional affairs is also not liked by India. But there is no choice except following the US suggestions and accepting the US role. The Indian position indicates the helplessness through which India is undergoing because Pakistan not only remains an integral part of the India-US dynamic but it was also due to the US pressures that India and Pakistan agreed to open dialogue for the resolution of problems. In view of this situation it becomes necessary to highlight the issues of convergence and divergence in the Indo-US relations in the new era and suggest appropriate strategies to deal with the US, the only superpower.

As far as the relations between India and Pakistan are concerned presently India and Pakistan are on a spree of mending relationship and have agreed not only to resume dialogue at different levels, but also the air, rail, bus links have been restored, clearly under the US pressures which considers South Asia a highly volatile region. The process of normalization of relations with Pakistan, cease fire in the LoC, and the success in SAARC and the meeting of Indian Prime Minister Manmohan Singh and Pakistani President Pervez Musharraf in New York and New Delhi, the cricket diplomacy, growing people to people contact, agreement for more CBM and also for peaceful solution of all the disputes are the positive signs but its difficult to say whether the same would be maintained in future also because still the statements whether related to Kashmir issue, Shimla Agreement, or nuclear issue which indicate towards divide keep on coming from both side moreover the cross-border terrorism has also not stopped. The relations with China are also witnessing a new high and flexibility of attitude on resolution of problems and recently both India and China have signed a joint agreement outlining eleven political parameters to make meaningful and mutually acceptable adjustments to their respective positions on the boundary but the boundary question is still a very ticklish issue which also needs to be resolved for a healthy relationship. But these gestures certainly indicate towards the opportunities and challenges in the new era for India's foreign policy.

With the end of the cold war and strengthening of the regional economic groupings and free trade zones among these groups the economic issues have gained primacy in the world politics. Although the forces of globalization and liberalization have also forced India to bring suitable changes in its economic policies and open its market to the world. India has also emerged a key player in the Information and Technology sector, but despite all the claims of economic growth India has not been able to create its place in the world markets because of the poor monitoring and management of its economic policies. In the new era the need for the regional cooperation has increased manifold because the regions, which have integrated through regional cooperation have become powerful actors in the global politics like the EU (European Union). South Asia because of its uneven growth, poverty and unfriendly relations among each other is not only the poorest but also a very volatile region. On account of the state of not so good relations among the countries of this region, poverty and deprivation, the desired growth and cooperation could not be achieved. As a peaceful atmosphere is necessary for economic growth and development therefore the challenge before India is how to maintain peace in this region. Although South Asia is a very weak player in the international politics but the cooperation among its states can make it a strong area because it has some valuable natural resources like water which could be used judiciously to increase the prosperity of the region. Since India is the largest, richest and most developed member of the SAARC and it is also the only country, which borders either by land or sea all the other South Asian countries. Therefore being the largest country the onus of guiding South Asia towards such cooperation lies with India. In view of the state of relationship which India shares with the South Asian countries the challenge before India is how to lead this area towards regional cooperation, prosperity and peace? This issue also needs scholarly analysis for a better understanding of the prospects of regional cooperation.

In the present day international scenario the safety of its people from the threat of terrorism has emerged as an important challenge for the foreign policy of every country. Due to this threat even the only super- power like the US has also to restructure its foreign policy towards combating the terrorism and homeland security has become its major concern. Although the US has also declared that the terrorists are the enemies of the mankind and it intends to deal with this threat on the global basis but the selective approach of the US in dealing the terrorism is not very helpful for India, which is facing this threat since the last one decade. The US approach of differentiating between its terrorist and other's terrorist has created havoc in India, because such approach has not only emboldened Pakistan to continue its support to the cross-border terrorism but also propagate that whatever is happening in Kashmir is not terrorism but people's struggle for freedom. Such kind of propaganda has also promoted internal terrorism in India, which has made the life of the common people very insecure. In view of the growing menace of terrorism human security has become a very important concern for India and its policy makers. Besides this the intensification of internal discords, socio-political unrests, stress and tensions related to the economic, social, political, demographical, developmental and ecological issues in the different regions of India, the widening gulf between the rich and poor, problems of population growth, poverty are increasing militancy and frustration in the different parts of the country which is also a cause of grave concern for the foreign policy makers. India has also to take into consideration the various kinds of pressures, emerging from the different regions while framing a good foreign policy because presently not only the security has become comprehensive but these issues also have a capacity to influence the external relations of a country. In view of this presently the biggest challenge for India is how to frame a policy which besides fulfilling its national interests also works for the satisfaction of the people particularly of the border regions like Uttaranchal because their continuous dissatisfaction and underdevelopment can prove costly for the safety and well being of the Indian union. In the present day world order of uncertainty and chaos the satisfaction of the units has also emerged as a challenge particularly for the federal states like India because its strength and unity lies in their satisfaction. Although Uttaranchal has become a state but the lack of proper development, good governance and the big army of unemployed educated youth, are making the people restless. It could be dangerous in view of the porous borders and influx of people from Nepal, presently witnessing the Maoist insurgency and which could be exploited by some vested interests. This situation not only warrants attention but also a very careful approach towards the border areas and its people. Actually the protection of the human rights and freedom from fear and want has emerged as a major challenge for the policy makers of every country and India is no exception to it.

In view of this the department of political science organized a two-day national seminar in October 2004 to discuss the various issues and suggest measures to overcome the challenges being faced by India in the new era. Wide ranging discussions among the participants on the issues confronting the foreign policy took place and it was felt that though the internal conflicts which prevail in Indian society are not good for India's security but the external powers should not be allowed to manipulate them. The domestic regional unrest in the forms of agitations and aggression or extremists' activities in Pithoragarh district around Indo-Nepal Border in Uttaranchal or such activities reflecting dissatisfaction of the people in any part of the country should not be allowed to be exploited by the foreign countries for their vested interests. It was also recommended by the participants that cooperation in larger and more active scale is needed from the Muslim community to tackle the problem of internal terrorism and the problems of external terrorism would require joint international efforts. It was the general observation that while joining the globalization bandwagon India must be sensitive to the inconvenience of the weaker segments of the society because following the Western liberal philosophy and economics of the *laisser-faire* blindly may lead to greater problems. India has to be cautious with the unpredictable process of globalization, which appears to be promising on the surface but underneath the problems linger. Since India and US have much common concern such as defense, combating terrorism, baring narcotic trade and commerce therefore it was recommended that the two countries should come together to address these concerns. It was also felt dialogue and discussion with Nepal without biases should be helpful in removing irritation in Indo-Nepal relations as they have common concerns too. Positive prospects were seen in Sino-Indian relations as they have common concerns like nuclear stability and terrorism. It was even recommended that India could act as a mediator in solving problems between China and Tibetan leaders. In view of the growing importance of regional cooperation it was recommended that serious attempts to strengthen SAARC should be made. Despite differences between South Asian countries India should develop healthy relations with South Asian countries. The need of joint efforts to encounter the problem of terrorism, restructuring economic, political and military policy, acknowledging the contribution of women in the politics was also expressed very strongly. Indo-Pak relations were named as the snake and ladder game due to their unpredictability but it was also necessary to maintain peace in the subcontinent therefore for establishing more goodwill the promotion of people to people relation and also through Bollywood was recommended. The participating scholars, academics and intellectuals as well as the Key note speaker Prof. Machkand Dubey (former foreign secretary government of India) felt that Indian foreign policy in the post-cold war period should concentrate on the following: restructuring political and economic system, creating a global society, mobilising resources for reorientation of foreign policy, try to gain the status of a great power in industrial development, seek to be militarily powerful, support universal disarmament and protection of global ecology. Since the present volume consists of the papers presented during the seminar, an attempt has been made by the editor to put the different views together to analyse the challenges and the solutions from a realistic angle. These papers have been divided into three sections. Section one deals with the conceptual issues, Section 2 with the problems and Section 3 consists of papers, which deal with the issues of human security, good governance and region specific issues

The opening paper of this volume by Professor Kamath, which was presented as the valedictory address of the seminar reflects in detail about the challenges being faced and on the dilemmas and need of maintaining the relations with Pakistan, China, Russia, USA and other countries. He also feels that non-alignment is still relevant in the sense as it is considered a right to take an independent decision on every issue affecting nation's interest in international arena. But he has also elaborated the requirement of US support to India for assuring the permanent seat in United Nations and determining India's status in terms of nuclear weapon power states but suggested to be careful and objective in our approach. He has also analysed the problems of the cross-border terrorism from Pakistan and China as a security puzzle for India. While accepting that there are many foreign policy challenges he has concluded that foreign policy is a means to national goals of economic development, strengthening of national security, and most important is to make India a major player in international affairs. If India maintains an economic growth rate of 7 to 8 per cent, it should not be impossible for India to emerge as a major player in world affairs

Sheel K. Asopa in her paper has stressed that the challenges to India's foreign policy, relate to the developments at the global level as well as to the geo-political realities of the region in which India is situated. Although the challenges have always been there but after the eclipse of Soviet Union their number has increased and nature has become more complex. The sole surviving superpower, America is trying to make best use of the opportunities that have come to its way after the collapse of the Soviet Union. She feels that the Unilateralism of the Superpower has come as a biggest challenge to the foreign policy of India. In the post-cold war period the US pressures on India – on nuclear issues, economic liberalisation, Kashmir problem, human rights, environmental matters have multiplied. With the eclipse of Soviet Union and the Russian Federation becoming totally dependent on the Western aid and support, India has to fend for itself. Under these circumstances India has not only to maintain its dignity but also the freedom of action for which non-aligned movement has to be strengthened.

The third paper of this section by Pramod Mishra on Changing Security Paradigms in India the UPA phase deals with the changes that are taking place in the notion of national security since the end of cold war and also discusses the new orientations on national security by the United Progressive Alliance (UPA) government headed by Manmohan Singh. He has stressed that the traditional norm of security linked with national interest and war has been modified by a large number of nations and major attention at the present juncture seems to be focused around internal security linked with terrorism, and the notion of "human security". In view of this he has advocated the need to develop a mulit-dimensional approach to security which would basically address several human related issues like sustainable development, hunger, modernization of agriculture, controlling water scarcity, flood control and social security for the marginalized and aboriginal people. He feels that the UPA Government seems to be committed to improve conditions of the vulnerable section of the society including women and also considers NAM vital to address vital issues of present era.

Madhurendra Kumar feels that in the changed international milieu though the Indian foreign policy is facing enormous challenges both at global and regional level but there are opportunities also. The Indian geopolitics offers her political economic and strategic benefits in the post-cold war period. He has stressed that the kind of independence of decision making India showed through Pokhran II and her expanding ties with ASEAN countries and Myanmar, her positive approach towards regional grouping particularly ARF, SAARC and BIMSET-EC provide ample testimony to its emergence as a significant actor on the horizon of world politics. But this new role in the post-cold war periods is beset with numerous challenges. I.D. Mishra in his paper on visualising New Dynamics of Challenges to India's Foreign Policy has focused on how to promote India's national interest in the international field and also to satisfy the aspiration of the people who constitute the major component of a state. He feels that the main aim of the Indian foreign policy if visualised from the human angle is to promote human security, sustainable development and good governance.

M.T. Desai in his paper on Indo-US Partnership in Post-Cold War Period: Strategies and Constraints has identified the reasons as to why Indo-US relations have not been so close. In his view, both the nations have different worldviews especially on the issues like clash of civilization, globalization and nuclear disarmament. In spite of these differences, both the nations have taken similar stand on some global challenges. He has highlighted that in a unipolar world, Vajpayee at least at the rhetorical level talked of India and US being 'natural allies' in 1998 but there was unease about developing deeper relationship with US. He has admired BJP for its realistic attitude in acknowledging the demands of new world order and not talking about non-alignment as a foreign policy strategy in the post- Cold War period. To S.J.R. Bilgrami the increasing domination and control of the lone superpower, the United States of America, develops the temptation to take arbitrary action in the name of international community. But he feels that the policies, overloaded with the humanitarian objectives cannot automatically become the echo of international community to the extent of justifying unilateral intervention. The arbitrary and selective character of policies and actions serves the strategic interests of major powers than contributing to the stability of the national security of developing nations. Such actions also manifest duality of divergence and convergence within the US administration, which has had its implications for the security arrangement of the countries like India, desirous of establishing cordial or expanding relations with the USA. The contradiction of divergence and convergence within the US administration, creates difficulties for India in managing her national security and dealing with its varied ingredients. Indu Singh in her paper has also discussed the issues of convergence and divergence in the Indo-US relations. The issues that have further widened the chasm between India and the US like India's decision to pursue the policy of non-alignment and US decision to align with India's major enemy; Pakistan, the Kashmir imbroglio, India's drawing closer to the Soviet Union, the communist victory in China, the US military alliances further soured their relations. She has concluded that the academic, cultural and economic ties have provided a productive contrast to their political ties. Avaneet Kumar Ghildial has highlighted the historical relationship between India and the USA and their different stands on the chronic issues like terrorism and Iraq War.

I.N. Mukherjee in his paper Transiting from SAPTA to SAFTA: Challenges and Opportunities for India has focused on the challenges of moving from SAPTA to SAFTA. He feels that the Agreement on SAFTA which would be implemented from January 2006 would provide some time for fulfilling a number of enabling conditions like the governing rules of origin; reporting to the SAARC secretariat, the non-tariff barriers to trade by each member state; and working a revenue compensation mechanism for the least developed countries. He has stressed the need for strengthening SAARC for fulfilling India's national interests. S.D. Chamola has presented an analysis of the cooperation among SAARC countries on the core economic sectors especially agriculture and complimentary trading system in the region. He has also identified several policy measures for the future especially in areas of information gap, financial transaction, and tariff barrier, fear of Indian domination by other peripheral countries of South Asia. Saroj Pathak has discussed the evolution of SAARC and evaluated the modest role played by India in the SAARC initiative. She has opined that the inception of SAARC marks the first concrete step taken by the countries of the region towards regional integration aiming at achieving collective self-reliance, acceleration of social progress, promotion of cultural development and collaboration for better understanding of each other but it has often passed through a rough weather due to the mutual problems and irritants in relation of the member nations, most important being the Indo-Pak relation. This factor has consistently cast a dark shadow over the health and progress of the SAARC. Although India being the largest and economically more developed nation in the region has special responsibility towards taking the organization forward on the path of success but India's lack of commitment, unimaginative and impractical approach towards it has not been very helpful.

Jyotirmoy Banerjee has dealt with the issue of the Cooperative Denuclearision in South Asia and the dilemmas of Indo-Pak nuclear doctrine. He has posed a question that if bitter enemies like France and Germany can turn into the leading advocates of an European Union and enjoy excellent relations today, if Japan, the only country to be nuked so far, can become a great partner of its bitter enemy, the USA, and if Russia can receive a helping hand from its diehard enemies of yesteryears like Germany and the USA, why India and Pakistan cannot bury the hatchet, even if it takes time? He has advocated the necessity of both the track one and track two diplomacy as under the prevailing circumstances the people to people approach would be more helpful in bringing the two nations closer. A great deal of cross-border interaction via seminars, symposia, publications and media coverage would be an excellent way to put pressure on the respective governments.

Pakistan has also not allowed their leaders to develop and maintain good relations with India. Cross-border terrorism from Pakistan has become the order of the day. He has concluded that even in this prevailing situation leaders of both the countries are found engaged in confidence-building measures therefore one can only hope for a new turn in place of a snake-ladder game between the two countries, but history suggests otherwise. Badruddin has opined that though the various peace agencies have been able to ensure de nuclearisation in subcontinent but Pakistan is actively engaged in nuclear bureaucracy since seventies. No serious attempt has been made to probe the illegal and illicit network of its privately held nuclear programmes. He feels that Arab countries' support to manufacture Saudi Arab's Islamic Bomb, America's willingness to supply F16s, China's eagerness to have secret deal of weapons with Pak has emboldened Pakistan. He has suggested that the best way to promote Indo-Pak Dialogue is to adopt bilateral notification mechanism to prevent underlying dilemma between the two countries.

In his paper Roop Singh Bareth has reflected that since the debacle of 1962 much snow has melted in the Himalayas and the relationship between India and China is improving after the end of cold war. The security scenario in the region has been changed vastly and economic and trade compulsions are now forcing to open up new vistas of co-operation and cordiality. He feels that the intermittent phase of 1998, when Sino-Indian relations witnessed 'a new low' has now been overcome and the 'problem solving attitude' witnessed in both New Delhi and Beijing in recent years with a deepening urge for economic and technological collaboration are sufficient enough to indicate a new phase in their relationship. Mutual trade is emerging as an important CBM in their bilateral relationship. He believes that trans-frontier economic and trade co-operation, restoring historical trade routes and opening roads to pilgrims will certainly add new dimensions in their political relationship in which 'geo-economics' will precede over 'geopolitics'. He has stressed that a new pattern of relationship seems to be in the offing in the last few years where ' prudence' and 'economics' is providing driving force to the entire gamut of their bilateral relationship.

Annpurna Nautiyal has discussed the new challenges and equations in the triangular relationship between India, Pakistan and the United States of America in the new era. She has stressed that in view of the similarity of the threat perception the US intends to develop a close cooperation with India for confronting the challenges to peace, security and stability. Bush administration's policies of favouring democracies and acknowledging India as a rising power has made India hopeful towards developing good relations with the US but the soft policies of the US towards Pakistan despite its role in promoting cross-border terrorism and nuclear proliferation has not allowed the desired closeness to develop between India and the US. Although there is a slight change in the US outlook towards India and the US has also expressed its wish to help India evolve as a major power in the 21st century but the duplicity of the US policies towards the nuclear proliferation, terrorism, refusal to support India's claim for the permanent seat in the UN Security Council, pressures on India for reviewing its relations with Iran to which the US considers a rogue state and desire to have a good working relationship with Pakistan makes India apprehensive. As India has no other option except to improve relations with the US therefore India has to tread very carefully to promote and protect its national interest in the new era.

As one of the main funding agency of this seminar, ICSSR and particulary its former charirman Prof. V.R. Panchamukhi who enaugurated this seminar who expected that the seminar while discussing the foreign policy challenges must take a note of the regional and developmental issues, because in the present world scenario the security has become comprehensive and the regional imbalances and disparities are capable of effecting the foreign policy of a state therefore papers in the third section of this book have focused on the challenges; human security, sustainable development, good governance and regional issues. In his paper D.B. Shekatakar has highlighted the changing perspectives of National Security: External and Internal Dimensions both and raised a few vital questions pertaining to aims, objectives, vision-mission of national security. He feels that the vulnerability of the state is creating problems because a large mass of humanity is unhappy, poor and is in want. He has raised a very pertinent question whether we as a society are prepared to accept western philosophy of life, which is invading us through media and the market and feels that present day terrorism is the gift of the United States of America. According to him conflicts are very much within our society and outsiders were just exploiting it. He has emphatically argued for having faith in our capabilities and qualities and should not follow the Western philosophy blindly.

Sanjeev K. Sharma in his paper has argued that the global structures of production, trade, advancements in technology and communication have brought rapid and revolutionary changes in the world order. These have also facilitated the groups and states sponsoring terrorism, which has acquired a dangerous form, to extend the reach and the organization of their subversive activities through flow of funds from abroad and foreign sanctuaries. He feels that the link between globalization, increasing poverty and the rising graph of international terrorism cannot be denied. To counter the challenge he has suggested more international cooperation among the governments to monitor flow of information, people and money across border. Nalineet Ghildial has discussed the relationship between India and Russia from the point of view of tackling international terrorism. She has opined that the end of the cold war has not resulted into an era of peace and stability rather the international terrorism supported by the advanced technology has increased manifold. N.K. Jha has reflected on the consequences of the armed rebellion and the present political scenario in Nepal for India, which is important from the point of the India's security and relationship with Nepal. He has stressed for the need of caution on the part of India as India's smaller neighbours, including Nepal, have been confronting the crisis of identity and suffering from the "big-neighbour-small-neighbour syndrome," It is therefore necessary for India to be extra cautious in extending a helping hand to Nepal lest it be misunderstood as interference in its internal affairs. He feels that while trying to persuade the King to restore democracy in Nepal, the Indian establishment must develop discrete contacts across Nepal's political spectrum. Even the Maoists need not be neglected. India can take the cue from China, which has developed an across the board contact with the political class of Nepal. Indian foreign policy establishment should also undertake initiatives to win the confidence of the Nepalese people directly. This can include low cost options such as opening of primary schools, health care centres or other institutions for providing humanitarian relief, preferably with the help of non-governmental organisations. This will help Nepal to weaken the Maoist appeal and earn the good will of the Nepalese people to India.

Vijay Kumar has discussed the problems of the human security from the perspective of the refugees and stressed that the end of Cold War and the emerging third world political, economic and social realities demand a fresh look at the refugee problem. As these countries have in the last decade faced mass displacement of millions of people not only due to liberation struggles, revolutions, coups and counter-coups but also due to man-made environmental disasters, natural calamities and short sighted development policies of their own governments. The new circumstances which make them migrants, economic refugees, environmental refugees or refugees of development projects. Although these displaced people do not qualify to be called refugees because unlike political refugees they are not pushed out of their own states but are compelled to leave their homeland because of the weakness of the state to protect their rights. In view of this he feels that a new perspective is required for analyzing their problems.

While dealing with the issue of environmental security Narottam Gaan has stressed that since the late 1970s the emergence of the non-military issues including rising poverty, rapid population growth, spread of infectious diseases, and environmental degradation has forced the scholars and analysts to redefine security in non military terms which is opposed to the realist understanding and definition of security. The realist framework of national security revolved around the state, nuclear and military power. But the non-military issues particularly the environment has the potential to not only to threaten the human security but if treated rightly it can also become an entry point for wider regional cooperation based on mutual trust, harmony, and cooperation rather than on legacies of distrust and dispute.

T.K. Mishra in his paper on The Task of Good Governance in the Corporate Sector has expressed his opinion that the corporate sectors in place of taking a long-term view for the benefit of the society and following the norms set by the state are working against the norms established by laws for their own selfish and short term profits. He feels that high standards of corporate governance are not only significant for the sustenance of companies but also for making the success ever lasting. Values combined with vision can help companies not only to weather storms of changes but also charge them adequately to scale new heights. To him good governance is an attempt to replace price-based governance to value based and a cooperative environment based on mutual-trust and in tune with clear benchmarks of values synthesizes good governance. He has stressed that it is about ensuring fairness to all the stake holders' i.e. customers, employees, investors, the government and the socilarge and is participative, transparent, promotes equity and equality, aims to develop and mobilize resources for social purposes.

References

Barry Buzan: South Asia Moving Towards Transformation: Emergence of India as a great Power. *International Studies*. Vol. 39, No.1, January-March 2002.

V.P. Dutt: India's Foreign Policy in the New Era. *World Focus*, Vol. 24, Nos. 10-11-12, Issue, October-December 2003.

S.D. Muni and C. Raja Mohan: Emerging Asia: India's Options. *International Studies*. No. 3, July-September 2004.

Gautam Adhikari: Washington and Delhi: Estranged No More, *Current History*, Vol. 103, No. 672, April 2004.

List of Contributors

Professor P.M. Kamath, Professor of Political Science (Retd.) Mumbai University, Honorary Director, Vidya Prasarak Mandal's Centre, For International Studies, Mithenagar Road, Mulad (East) Bombay.

Professor (Mrs.) Sheel K. Asopa, Professor of Political Science (Retd.), 7-JHA-37, Jawahar Nagar, Jaipur– 302 004 Rajasthan (India).

Dr. Pramod Mishra, Reader in Political Science Fellow, Developing Countries Research Centre, University of Delhi, 57-E Mauraya Enclave, Pitam Pura, Delhi-110088.

Dr. Madhurendra Kumar, Reader in Political Science, UGC Research Awardee, Department of Politcal Science Chaudhary Charan Singh University, Meerut (U.P.).

Professor M.T. Desai, Professor of Political Science (Retd.), 38/297 Saraswati Nagar, Near Azad Society, Ahmedabad-380015.

Professor S.J.R. Bilgrami, Professor of Political Science Jamia Milia Islamia, New Delhi.

Dr. (Mrs.) Indu Singh, Reader in Political Science M.K.P. P.G. College, Dehradun, Uttaranchal.

Dr. A.K. Ghildial, Reader in Political Science S.M.J.N. (P.G.) College, Hardwar, Uttaranchal.

Professor Indra Nath Mukherji, Professor of South Asian Studies School of International Studies, Jawaharlal Nehru University New Delhi-110067.

Professor S.D. Chamola, Professor of Economics and Business Management (Ret.) Senior Fellow (ICSSR) CCS Haryana Agricultural University, Hisar.

Dr. Saroj Pathak, Reader in Political Science Kalindi College University of Delhi, New Delhi.

Professor Jyotirmoy Banerjee, Professor of International Relations, Jadavpur University, Kolkata.

Dr. Badruddin, Reader in Political Science, P.E.S. College of Arts and Science, Goa University Farmagudi Ponda-Goa 403401.

Dr. Jitendra Narayan, Professor of Political Science L.N. Mithila University Darbangha (Bihar)-846008.

Dr. Roop Singh Bareth, Professor of Political Science University of Rajasthan, Jaipur (India).

Professor Annpurna Nautiyal, Professor and Head Department of Political Science HNB Garhwal University, Srinagar Garhwal, Uttaranchal-246174.

Lt. Gen. (Retd.) D.B. Shekatkar, PVSM, AVSM, VSM, Chhatrapati Shivaji Chair Professor, Department of Defence and Strategic Studies, University of Pune, Pune-411 007.

Dr. Sanjeev K. Sharma, Reader in Political Science and Editors, Indian Journal of Political Science, Ch. Charan Singh University, Meerut.

Ms. Nalineet Ghildial, Lecturer in Political Science M.V. (P.G.) College, Satikund, Kankhal, Hardwar, Uttaranchal, India.

Dr. Nalini Kant Jha, Professor and Head Department of Politics and International Studies, Pondicherry Central University, Pondicherry-605014.

Dr. Vijay Kumar, Professor of Political Science T.M. Bhagalpur University, Bhagalpur-812007.

Dr. Narottam Gaan, Reader in Political Science Kendrapara College, Kendrapara.

Dr. T.K. Mishra, Reader in Commerce Deshbandhu College (E) University of Delhi, Delhi-110017.

I.D. Mishra, Head, Department of Political Science DDU Gorakhpur University, Gorakhpur-273009.

SECTION-I
CONCEPTUAL ISSUES

1

Challenges to India's Foreign Policy in the New Era: Need for a Holistic Approach

P.M. Kamath

When we speak of the new era, as the setting for the discussion on challenges to India's foreign policy, it becomes necessary to clarify the salient features of the new era. While one can list many such features but the two are most outstanding: first, the United States (US), "Lone Super Power", as Samuel Huntington calls it-dominates the world politics today. The end of bipolarity in international politics has forced India to bring about drastic changes in its foreign policy. The bipolarity of power in 1947, in which a nascent Indian nation, as a newly independent state plunged to operate, provided a degree of maneuverability to our policy makers. Policy of nonalignment was an intellectual coup on the part of Pandit Nehru. India under non-alignment at least until Nehru's death in 1964 drew political and economic mileage from it. But our subsequent foreign policy makers could not go beyond non-alignment and were unable to reflect and adjust to changes in the international scene. Thus for instance, on 8th August 1991 when Gorbachev was facing a coup by hardcore communists in Moscow, the then Indian Prime Minister (P.M.), Narasimha Rao fumbled in his response and said that it was a warning to all those—in this case Gorbachev—who pushed hard for change.[1]

It was really hard for the policy-makers to change their commitment to 'non-alignment.' Since Narasimha Rao, all Prime

Ministers have sung in the praise of it. It was only Atal Behari Vajpayee as the P.M. since 1998 who was able to bring about a perceptible change in the directions of Indian foreign policy without totally abandoning it. In fact non-alignment is not relevant today in the sense it was in the context of a bipolar world. But in another sense, non-alignment is still relevant as the crux of non-alignment— is that it claimed a right to take an independent decision on every issue affecting nation's interest in international arena. In the initial years of non-alignment there was no guarantee on the way in which India would respond to a crisis. On the other hand, it was reasonable to expect the aligned nations in Western Europe to go along with the US while Eastern European nations toed the Soviet Union's line.

But with the end of the bipolarity, not only the nations of Eastern Europe have won their freedom to take their own independent decisions; even nations in the West are also asserting their right to vote against the US in the United Nations (UN). France and Germany have become increasingly assertive of their right despite being in the NATO (North Atlantic Treaty Organisation) alliance. America may not like it,[2] but these two nations have clearly expressed their opinion against the US invasion of Iraq without a specific authorization from the UN. Second aspect of the international setting in the 21st century is the fact of overwhelming influence of globalisation as a process of conducting all kinds of interactions. Though India was forced by the economic circumstances to embrace globalisation in a big way in June 1991, there has been no looking back on it by any political party despite their opposition to it while in opposition.[3] In the economic field, Liberalisation, Privatization and Globalisation (LPG) became the buzzword in the dialogue of the developed nations and India.

But once India launched herself on the process of globalisation she could not say that she accepts globalisation in economic sphere but other spheres of international relations are out side the influence of globalisation process. The LPG as an acronym also means liquefied petroleum gas. And an important attribute of it is that once it comes out of its cylinder it occupies all space in the house not merely in kitchen. Likewise, once a nation embraces economic globalisation, it cannot escape globalising impact on social issues, national commitment to human rights or questions of national security under the garb of national sovereignty. Bill Clinton set in the process of globalisation in 'other' matters, when in 1993 he asserted promotion of human rights as a part of the US national security. Speaking at the American Society of Newspaper Editors, Annapolis, Maryland, Clinton had said: "During the Cold War, our foreign policies largely focused on relations among nations. Our strategies sought a balance of power to keep the peace. Today, our policies must also focus on relations within nations, on a nation's form of governance, on its economic structure [and] on its ethnic tolerance[4].

Beginning from there the sole surviving super power has fine-tuned above claim to intervene into others internal affairs into a doctrine of humanitarian intervention during the Clintonian eight years in the White House. His successor George W. Bush, Jr. has added his own doctrine of preemptive intervention—its extreme expression is evident in the US War against Iraq in 2002. In view of this background, it is pertinent to discuss the main challenges faced by Indian foreign policy in the new era. Two major regional issues are India's relations with Pakistan and China.

Pakistan and Cross-border Terrorism

India is the fulcrum of South Asia as all other South Asian nations have common borders with India while not all have common borders with one another. This has created scope for Pakistan to encourage terrorist groups bred and based inside the country to operate against India in pursuit of its political goal of causing secession of a province of the Indian Union as a revenge for her role in the birth of Bangladesh from the ruins of erstwhile East Pakistan. Pakistan first tried with Punjab as an experiment in the use of terrorism as an instrument of state policy. Then it was the turn of Jammu and Kashmir (J&K). Terrorism was raised to the level of *Jihad* in pursuit of remaining exercise of completion of historic partition of India on religious grounds. For a power-usurper like General Musharraf, terrorists are the Kashmiri freedom fighters and Kashmiri blood runs into veins of every Pakistani. It took two efforts on his own life by Pakistani terrorists in December 2003 for Musharraf to realise that uncontrolled encouragement to terrorists could turn against him as well. He had promised under American pressure in January 2002 not to permit Pakistan's territory to be used for terrorist activities against India. In June again he extended a promise to India through Bush emissary, deputy secretary of state, Richard Armitage.[6] But as his Foreign Minister, Mohammad Kasuri used to say that Pakistan couldn't be expected to control every bird that flies over the borders much effort was not made by Pakistan to check the cross border terrorism. Yet, Atal Behari Vajpayee in pursuit of his efforts to establish peace made one more try to reach out to Pakistan's Musharraf. Meeting in the sidelines of the South Asian Association for Regional Cooperation (SAARC) summit in Islamabad, Musharraf again promised in January 2004 not to permit territory under the control of Pakistan to be used for cross-border terrorism. On October 27, 2004 Pakistan TV showed Musharraf addressing a gathering of elite wherein he said that global perception is that Pakistan is behind happenings in Afghanistan; Pakistanis might call it as a freedom struggle, but global perception is that Pakistan is promoting cross-border terrorism in Kashmir. He stressed the need to curb domestic extremism; he wanted Pakistan to be known as a moderate Islamic progressive nation and not to be seen as an illiterate backward Islamic rogue nation. If it really turns out to be a reality, Musharraf deserves a Noble Peace Prize![7]

China as a Security Puzzle

China is another neighbour, which provides a challenge to Indian policy makers. China as a one-party state has been always aspiring to emerge, as a superpower. It understands only the language of power. Indian nuclear tests in May 1998 asserted Indian search for a major power status in international affairs. While China considers the US as a global threat to her aspirations, it also considers India as a regional threat.[8] As a state committed to 18th century doctrine of power grows in direct proportion to the possession of territory, is constantly in search of territory in its vast neighbourhood. It has turned South China Sea into a China Lake by claiming Spratly Islands and Paracel Islands. [9] However, after India conducted nuclear tests in May 1998, there have been remarkable changes in the Chinese approach to power politics. India having told the world powers that she considered China as a potential security threat and citing that perception as a rationale for her nuclear tests, has improved relations with it since then. After June 2003 visit of Indian PM to Beijing, new trading routes have been opened in Sikkim which has been shown as a part of Indian territory; China has also agreed to work with India in the UN to move towards a multipolar world. India and China have also upgraded their border negotiations to the level of special representatives—National Security Adviser from the level of officials. While increasing trade is an attraction to both the sides, the ultimate challenge to Indian policy makers is their ability to find an amicable solution to the border dispute.

Russia Alone or Part of a Triangle?

Russia even after the disintegration of the Soviet Union continues as a friend fully supportive of Indian foreign policy goals in international relations. India undoubtedly has tried to diversify her arms procurement from Russia. Now she buys them from the US, Israel and France. Yet, Russia continues as the main arms and arms technology provider. There are many areas where these two are continuing to cooperate in co-production of weapons as in the case of BrahMos missiles. There is also cooperation in joint production of Sukhoi fighter planes in Nashik. Both are also cooperating in fighting international terrorism. Now and then, India and Russia both have come under the pressure of the US over the question of their record of human rights. They are on the same side in opposing unilateral use of force by the US as in the case of Iraq or unilateral intervention in other's internal affairs. The two are also working to achieve a multipolar world. But Russia also wants to develop an India-China-Russia strategic triangle to confront the threat from the sole superpower and the idea of strategic triangle becomes quite vocal whenever these nations perceive a threat from the sole superpower. But none is willing to take on the US directly, collectively or severally.

US— Sole Superpower

India had major difficulties in the 1990s in adjusting to the status of the US as the sole superpower, with which every one desired to maintain friendliest relations. Until the disintegration of the Soviet Union, US had perceived India as leaning more towards the Soviet Union in international affairs.

The US policy makers did not resist their temptation to draw a comparison between the nature of their relations with India and Pakistan. Thus for instance, Walter Slocombe, under Secretary of Defence while addressing Asia Society on 6th June 1995, stated: "There should not be any unrealistically high expectation from the visit next fortnight of a high level Indian defence delegation to the United States. Arms sales and technology transfer are not on the agenda for the talks. Though cooperation in the defence research has been identified as an area of bilateral interaction between the two countries, it will not be an area of immediate results. It will develop only step by step. India and the United States have an opportunity to work together, which was not available a few years ago, but with Pakistan it is a matter of reviving a dormant relationship. With India we have to build up from scratch."[10]

True to the spirit of the above-mentioned statement, President Bill Clinton exploited India's internal and external security concerns whether related to her alleged violation of human rights, or status of J&K, or the question of nuclear non-proliferation in the region. After India's nuclear tests, Clinton wanted China to be a party to resolve Indo-Pak Kashmir tangle. Though Clinton was highly critical of Indian nuclear tests in May 1998, during his visit to China in June 1998 he offered missile technology to it. It was only during the NDA regime in New Delhi and after Musharraf establishing military dictatorship in Pakistan in October 1999 that there was better appreciation of Indian concerns in the US. Clinton's visit to South Asia in March 2000 helped the two sides to clear many cobwebs in the bilateral relations. Bill Clinton admitted existence of the threat from the cross border terrorism to Indian security, Pakistan government's encouragement to promote terrorism and need to create a regional climate conducive to the promotion of democracy.

Accession of George Bush to power in January 2001 really brought India and US closer to one another as never before. One of the reasons for that was the US natural inclination of competition with China and perception of India as a counterweight against Chinese power. Even before Colin Powell was confirmed as Secretary of State, he spoke of India as a strategic partner. India also responded well by extending India's support for the US plans of Nuclear Missile Defence (NMD) systems. It was the September 11 terrorist attack on the US economic nerve centre (World Trade Centre) in New York and politico-military (Pentagon) power house in Washington, DC, that really brought the two closer together to fight against international terrorism. India's unconditional support to the US war against terrorism was also appreciated by the US. Though it drew a lot of domestic criticism, it in turn helped the US to bring a 180-degree turn around by General Musharraf. Until then Pakistan was one of the three very close supporter of Taliban regime in Afghanistan.[11] Pakistani military regime not only disowned its role in the growth and development of the Taliban but also extended its help to fight against Taliban, Al Qaeda and uncrowned king of terrorists—Osama bin Laden—lest India might move closer to the US.

This created tensions and ups and down in India's relations with the US as the US was fighting with the help of Pakistan its war against terrorism while India was fighting her war against terrorism which was primarily promoted by Pakistan from across the borders. Pakistan-based terrorists were involved in the attack against the Legislative Assembly in J&K in October 2001, and the Indian Parliament in December of the same year. The US played a moderating role on Pakistan to make it see that it cannot fight against terrorism in its west while promoting it in the east.

India-US cooperation in their wars against terrorism has strengthened military cooperation as well. India-US joint military exercises have helped to build up political goodwill. In July 2003 Air Forces of the two sides held joint air exercises in Ladakh. This was surely an indication of the US dilution of its contention that J&K is a disputed territory. India has also successfully secured Phalcon aircraft from Israel—which were denied to China only a year ago— enabling Indian air force to have airborne early warning capability. The US government that said it has to begin from the scratch in 1995 within ten years had signed "Next Steps in Strategic Partnership" in transferring dual use technology. India has also been promised with Patriot missiles. India has also pressed for Arrow missiles, which Israel has agreed to sell, but needs US clearance for the sale, as they are the licensed manufacturers. India has to build on the present to develop a mutually beneficial relationship with the US. Despite occasional hiccups in India-US bilateral relations, India has derived considerable gains in her war against terrorism.

India needs to pursue its close relations with the US as the sole super-power with which every nation wants to remain close. India aspires to be the Permanent member in the UN Security Council whenever it is expanded. Other Permanent powers in the UNSC like Russia, France, UK and even China are in favour of India sitting as a permanent member. But the US has not indicated its mind on the issue, obviously trying to extract maximum price for its support. American public and think tanks are also in general in favour of India entering the UNSC as a permanent member. Indian policy makers also have to work in close cooperation with the US despite its commitment with other major powers in the world like Russia, China, France, EU which all favour the emergence of a multipolar world. There are two important issues on which India needs continued cooperation of the US. One is Indian claim for a Permanent seat in the UNSC and second, Indian status as a Nuclear Weapons State. The US has not indicated its stand on reforming and restructuring the UNSC though other permanent members of the UN,–United Kingdom, France, Russia and China have one way or the other indicated their support to Indian entry into the UNSC as a permanent member. US stand on the issue will influence general trend in the UN General Assembly. Equally important is the question of the accommodation of India into the exclusive nuclear club. Will the nuclear weapons states take initiative to amend the NPT to include India? Or will that begin with the inclusion of India in the Nuclear Suppliers Group? India has been basically a status quo nation on the issue of nuclear weapons development, deployment and even on destruction under a possible nuclear disarmament agreement. Indian record in the area of nuclear non-proliferation has been widely recognised.

National Security Council

These policy options need innovative initiatives without being bogged down with the past baggage on the foreign policy postures. Are we prepared to make foreign/national security policy in a world where the US dominates global politics and economics? Indian policy making has been ad hoc in best of the times responding to a crisis rather than proactively deciding on an issue. As stated earlier, in 1991 Narasimha Rao surprised India watchers by his observation on Gorbachev's reformist zeal. Some of us including this author have advocated creation of a National Security Council (NSC).[12] At last the BJP-led NDA government in 1998 created it. But the government has left it on paper without ever using it. The argument is that the NSC is an advisory body and not the decision-making mechanism for which there is the Cabinet Committee on Security (CCS). If so why the government should constitute another advisory body around the NSC in the form of National Security Advisory Board consisting of retired officials found in Delhi? This is hard to accept unless government insists on its right to demonstrate its capacity for muddled thinking.

More importantly, the NSC requires a very skilled, intelligent and dedicated supporting staff to prepare the policy makers to arrive at the right decisions by studying all available options on a policy. The government has made since the establishment of the NSC, Joint Intelligence Committee (JIC) to act as its secretariat. However, important the role of intelligence in policymaking might be, but policymaking is much more wider than mere analysis of intelligence. In short intelligence is not foreign policy or national security. Equally important is the role of a National Security Adviser (NSA) as a coordinator and facilitator. While the NDA government preferred to have a part time NSA, when it appointed Prime Minister's Principal Secretary to the post, United Progressive Alliance (UPA) had J.N. Dixit as its full time NSA. But after his untimely death, government by appointing a former chairman of the JIC –an intelligence man— has given importance to demote the role of the NSA, rather than enable him to play an active role in shaping the government's foreign policy.[13] But government's foreign policymaking since the establishment of the NSC has continued to show age-old phenomenon of ad hoc nature of policymaking.

Conclusion

To conclude, foreign policy challenges are many. But one

should note that foreign policy is a means to national goals of economic development, strengthening of national security, and most important is to make India a major player in international affairs. If India maintains an economic growth rate of 7 to 8 per cent, it should not be impossible for India to emerge as a major player in world affairs. The NDA was a coalition led by the BJP while the United Progressive Alliance (UPA) led by the Congress Party, which has single handedly, ruled at the centre for nearly 45 years is now making an experiment in coalition politics. The NDA did not suffer from ideological contradictions internally though the Telugu Desham by being outside the government while being a part of the coalition sought undue concessions from the centre. But there were no ideological contradictions.

But the UPA suffers from ideological contradictions apart from pulls and pressures from coalition politics. Prakash Karat, Member, CPI(M) Politburo, observed that the NDA government was "almost fully committed to globalisation including the US imperialistic hegemony all over the world and our foreign policy was radically reoriented by the NDA government to suit the global interest of the US."[14] Thus such pulls and pressure emerging from within might lead the present government to reorient its foreign policies. Then the great goal of making India a fourth great power as Nehru envisaged in 1954—next only to the US, Russia and China might suffer and might even reduce it to a fourth grade power. To guard against that is the biggest challenge to the policymakers.

Notes and References

1. Narasimha Rao's statement placed India on the side of forces opposed to Gorbachev's reforms. It did not help India to maintain traditional close relations with that country. Our relations did not improve even under the Gorbachev's successor Boris Yeltsin. See P.M. Kamath, "Emerging International Order and the Policy Making Process in India," in P.M.

2. He was addressing a Workshop on the Common Minimum Programme at the Indian Institute of Public Administration (IIPA), New Delhi. See IIPA Newsletter, October 2004.

3. Krishan D. Mathur and P.M. Kamath, *Conduct of India's Foreign*

Policy (New Delhi: South Asian Publishers, 1996), p.153.

4. During May 1994 election campaign Dr. Manmohan Singh said in Mumbai that as far as economic policies are concerned there is no difference between the Congress and the BJP. See P.M. Kamath.
5. *Department of State Dispatch*, Vol. 41, No 14 (April 5, 1993).
6. For details see P.M. Kamath: *New World Order: Who Orders and Whose Benefit?* Kousar J. Azam (ed.) *Rediscovering America: American Studies in the New Century.* South Asian Publishers, New Delhi, 2001, Particularly pp. 236-42.
7. See Bob Woodward, *Plan of Attack* (New York: Simon Schuster, 2004), pp. 132-37.
8. Lally Weymouth, "Voices From a Hot Zone," *Newsweek*, July 1, 2002, p. 21.
9. See P.M. Kamath, "Introduction" in P.M. Kamath (ed.), *India-Pakistan Relations: Courting Peace from the Corridors of War* (New Delhi and Chicago: Promilla & Co., Publishers, 2005), p. 28.
10. See Ross H. Munro, "Eavesdropping on the Chinese Military: Where It Expects War—Where It doesn't," *Orbis*, Summer, 1994.
11. P.M. Kamath, "US-China Relations the Clinton Administration: Comprehensive Engagement or the Cold War Again?" *Strategic Analysis,* Vol. 22, No. 5 (August 1998), pp. 703-04.
12. Other two were Saudi Arabia and United Arab Emeritus.
13. See pp. 18-20, note 1. Also P.M. Kamath, "Foreign Policy making in India: Need for Committee System to Strengthen the Role of Parliament," *Strategic Analysis*, Vol. 12, No. 2 (May 1987), p. 232.
14. Eventually, it might prove to be in the interest of effective foreign policy making by limiting him to the role of a coordinator and facilitator rather than an activist adviser to the Prime Minister. Only time will tell. On the desirable role of NSA see, P.M. Kamath, *US National Security: Struggle for Supremacy in Policy Making, 1969-1989* (New Delhi: Shipra Publications, 2003), pp. 172-78).

2

Aspects of India's Foreign Policy: Challenges and Response

Sheel K. Asopa

The challenges to India's foreign policy in the new era are formidable and manifold. They relate to the developments at the global level as well as to the geo-political realities of the region in which India is situated. The challenges have always been there. They are inevitable too. However, after the eclipse of Soviet Union their number has increased and nature has become more complex. The sole surviving superpower, America is trying to make best use of the opportunities that have come to its way after the collapse of the Soviet Union. To understand the nature and possible implications of these challenges it is worthwhile to see them against the backdrop of basic premises of India's foreign policy as laid down by the first generation leadership of independent India.

Foreign policy of every country in some or the other way relates to its history, traditions, culture, people's aspirations, moral, ethical, spiritual values and philosophy of life. It is truer in case of India. The philosophy of Vasudhaiv Kutumbakam has made India a Universalist nation. It relates the well-being of the nation with the well being of the peoples of the world. Nehru's thinking was deeply embedded in it. He believed that "India's long march to freedom and the world wide movement against imperialism have been so intermingled in historical perspective that it would be difficult to separate one from the other." At the Brussels meet of the oppressed in 1927 he realized that "India's destiny was closely linked with the liberation of all the oppressed peoples of the world". Support to all those nations which were struggling against colonialism, imperialism and racial discrimination became the hallmark of India's foreign policy. The policy of non-alignment and later the NAM (Non-Aligned Movement) emerged out by this thinking. India's overall approach as articulated by Nehru called for independence of decision making on issues of national and international concern, self reliance, non-interference in each others internal affairs, respect for sovereignty and territorial integrity of other nations and preservation of peace by promoting tolerance and peaceful co-existence. Non-alignment initially emerged in the context of cold war politics of bipolarization in the post-Second World War period. The decolonized States desired to retain their independence of judgement by keeping away from the conflicting power blocs and their politics. Nehru, Nasser, Tito and Sukarno were the key exponents of the policy of non-alignment.

India's global role began much before independence. Nehru convened an Asian Relations Conference at Delhi in 1947, which sought to draw guidelines for the post-colonial Asia. A later conference in 1949 worked for Indonesia's independence. The Bandung Conference held in 1954 strengthened the Afro-Asian unity and drew the agenda of action in international politics. The NAM (1961), which began with 25 members, has now grown into an organization of 113 countries. India played its role during the Korean crisis in tune with the basic principles of its foreign policy. It helped in resolving the question of prisoners of war and provided medical assistance. The first Geneva Agreement on Indo-China was also the result of India's diplomatic skills and efforts. India has participated in almost all peacekeeping operations of the United Nations. The border conflict with China in October 1962, India's wars (1948 and 1965) with Pakistan, its military intervention in East Pakistan in 1971 and the creation of independent Bangladesh were not understood by many nations in Asia in correct perspective. Notwithstanding these set backs, India under the leadership of Indira Gandhi continued to work for solidarity of the NAM. India gave tough resistance to monopolistic economic policies of the West and in the North-South dialogue presented the South's demands effectively. The New International Economic Order (NIEO) was India's answer to the New Economic Order (NEO) of the West. Indira Gandhi strengthened the foreign policy by liberating it from Nehruvian emotionality and idealism. She took pragmatic stand on various issues of international politics. Without permitting any adverse impact on policy of non-alignment India could develop a strong relationship with the Soviet Union and withstand all kinds of pressures from the United States and its allies in the West. India's foreign policy started drifting away from its basic premises during the post-Rajiv Gandhi period. The Iraq-Iran war, Soviet occupation of Afghanistan, the Sino-American rapproachment, the deteriorating situation of Palestinians – all posed serious problems before India and put its role in the Third world to test. The way India handled the Iraq-Iran war and later the Gulf-War in the United Nations and outside reflected its diplomatic and political weaknesses. It lost grip over the NAM and failed in mobilizing a strong resistance to the policies of the United States and its allies in the UN. The US succeeded in hijacking the UN Security Council and could get several anti-Iraq resolutions passed by the Council in quick succession without giving time to Iraq to respond to them and permitting the non-aligned and regional groupings to activate their conciliatory diplomatic channels in Iraq and Kuwait.

The collapse of the Soviet Union, which was becoming more and more visible during the Gulf War, came to India as a shock. Despite having a huge diplomatic mission in Moscow it could not foresee what was coming. The demise of Soviet Union put the Indian foreign policy in utter disorder. It could not timely respond to the friendly overtures of the Central Asian Republics, which were desperately seeking India's support in the initial phase of their independence. The withdrawal of the Soviet Union from Afghanistan instead of giving relief to India generated several new problems for the country. The Mujahideen and other militant groups who have been fighting against the Soviet forces in Afghanistan were diverted by Pakistan to India to carry on secessionist and terrorist activities in the State of Jammu and Kashmir and Punjab. The collapse of the Soviet Union disturbed the Third World countries and they could not muster strength to resist the dictates of Pax Americana and co-operated in the US-led military coalition's attacks against Iraq. They provided financial assistance, over flying facilities, air bases for stationing troops and refueling services to American forces in West Asia. India however remained busy only with the evacuation of Indian nationals stranded in the war zone (Iraq and Kuwait) and did nothing to provide even moral relief to Iraq.

The "New Era" or the era of "Unipolar World Order" began with the Gulf War (1991) when almost entire world supported the war efforts of the United States-led coalition forces. The United Nations was made to pass anti-Iraq resolutions introduced by the United States. In fact, Russia, China and even Japan supported the United States. India, however, succeeded in remaining away from taking part in any of the activities related to war. But its incapability in organizing a collective resistance to the US action against Iraq in the Untied Nations was the biggest set back to its image as a leading nation of the Third World. It put the entire Third World in total disarray. The Unilateralism of the superpower has come as a biggest challenge to the foreign policy of India. In the post cold war period the US pressures on India – on nuclear issues, economic liberalisation, Kashmir problem, human rights, environmental matters have multiplied. With the eclipse of Soviet Union and the Russian Federation becoming totally dependent on the Western aid and support, India had to fend for itself. The US having emerged victorious in the cold war was all set to assert its supremacy with vengeance, especially in the Third World. Francis Fukuyama, in his article titled "The End of History" published in National Interest (Summer 1989) wrote: "What we may be witnessing is not just the end of the cold war or the passing of a particular period of history as such: that is the end point of mankind's ideological evolution and the universalization of western liberal democracy as the final form of human governance". Commenting on the status of Third World in the New World Order (NOW) Fukuyama said, "What are the implications of the end of history for international relations? Clearly, the vast bulk of the Third World remains very much mired in history, and will be a terrain of conflict for many years to come. Let us focus for the time being on the larger and more developed states of the world that after all account for greater part of world politics. Thus in the NWO world was seen as divided between the "West and the Rest".

In the Post-World War II period the world order was decided at the Potsdam and Yalta. In the post-cold war period it has been decided singularly by the United States. During the cold war period the US accumulated tremendous military power to provide security to its NATO allies in Europe, the SEATO and CENTO allies in Asia and safeguard their economic interests, especially in matters of energy supply to the developed countries of Western Europe and Japan. With the Soviet challenge vanished, the US emerged as a 'hegemon' or a 'superpower'. The neo-conservatives in the US Administration asserted that no country should be allowed to challenge America's power in any part of the world. A memorandum prepared in 1991 by Paul Wolfowitz, US Deputy Defence Secretary, proclaimed the "right to prevent any country from achieving military balance with the USA" and warned the US "not to tolerate any challenge in this area". In the NWO, the military alliances of the cold war period became redundant. The United Nations has been made ineffective–effective only when American interests are at stake. The old pattern of 'hegemony' has been replaced by political and military supremacy of the United States in the world. Its new objective is to redraw the map of the world especially in the areas where America's vital interests are involved. The US attention at the moment is focused as West Asia (Iraq, Iran and Syria) and Central Asia (establish control over oil and natural gas and the pipelines). America is now capable of achieving all this alone. Coalitions are sought when needed. In fact, the superpower status of the United States draws the nations of the world to join it even without invited. The incident of 9/11 has made a serious impact on the US foreign policy as well as on the foreign policy of the countries of the world at large. Earlier, the US did not take the terrorism-related threats to the security of the nation seriously. In fact, the major terrorist outfits like the Mujahedeen, Taliban and the Al Qaeda and their leaders have been raised by Pakistan under the US patronage. But the 9/11 has shattered it badly. The United States sought assistance from all countries of the world in fighting against terrorism in Afghanistan. This was a test case for India too which was also named along with Russia,

America and Israel as targets for future terrorist attack. The US-led war in Afghanistan revealed the weaknesses of India's foreign policy. India, without giving a thought to the nature and extent of its participation in the anti-terrorist campaign of America in Afghanistan and without bothering about its implications for the country, voluntarily offered all logistic help to America. Some knowledgeable people have revealed that India had expressed its readiness not just to give logistic support but also to provide the staging ground for the military operations. India did all this in utter disregard to basic principles of its foreign policy in order to please the United States. However, in view of geopolitical requirements of the war, India's help was not needed by the United States. Pakistan having geographical proximity with Afghanistan and being conversant with the Taliban and Al Qaeda network's strategic points and support bases was more useful to America. India's offer was totally uncalled for. This deviation, however, proved fatal as at other occasions India was pressurized to participate in military ventures of the United States in West Asia. The massive support given by the UN and the countries of the world emboldened the United States to extend its military campaign to Iraq as well. The Afghan war allowed the US to strengthen its defence in Central Asia. It acquired air bases in Central Asian Republics in addition to the US controlled bases in the West Asian Countries like Saudi Arabia, Bahrain, Qatar, Kuwait and Oman and stationed troops and warplanes there as a preparatory step to its war against Iraq.

Oil has always been a major factor in determining America's West Asia policy. But the military venture in Iraq was mainly aimed at deposing Saddam Hussain and destroying his military power, which had become a threat to security of America's allies (Saudi Arabia and Israel) in West Asia. Besides, the US wants to redraw the map of the region according to its own national interest. At a later stage of war India was asked to provide troops for America's military action against Iraq. The Indian Parliament had already passed a resolution seeking withdrawal of all foreign forces from Iraq. Hence, it was logical to reject the US request for troops. But the foreign policy makers of India hesitated in refusing the US request and tried to pretend that the matter was under consideration. The public opinion was totally opposed to India's involvement in the war against Iraq. Finally under pressure from the opposition parties and the public opinion, India conveyed to the US "its inability to spare troops in view of its own security concerns". The United States had branded the nuclear countries like Iraq, Iran, North Korea as "evil states'. Of this triangle of evil states, Iraq has been destroyed by the US action although neither the US could find any weapons of mass destruction (WMD) nor could break the will of the Iraqis to stand against the United States. It was a futile war fought just to pamper the superpower ego of America. Iran and Syria are now seen as next targets of the US military venture in West Asia. In these two cases too, India is faced with tremendous pressures from the United States. Ever since India and Iran concluded strategic partnership agreement in 2003, the US pressures on India are increasing. It is alleged that Indian scientists are helping the nuclear programme of Iran. A couple of scientists have been blacklisted and a few more expected to be added to that list. India has strongly refuted the charges and asked for evidence to prove them. Syria too, has been blamed for permitting the Islamic militants and terrorist groups to enter Iraq from its territory. India is pressurized to restrain Syria. These pressures are coming despite the fact that India during the last five years did not spare any effort to please the United States. The Pakistani scientist A.Q. Khan has secretly proliferated the nuclear secrets to several countries and organizations yet no action has been taken against Pakistan, which is openly shielding him. Pakistan has been given the status equal to a NATO ally as a reward for its help during the Afghan war. On the other hand India has been harassed for having relations with Syria and Iran. Unfortunately India has subjected itself to such humiliations by deviating from the basic premises of its foreign policy.

The other areas related to foreign policy of India which demand immediate attention from the MEA and the government of India are: revival of NAM and restoring the unity of non-aligned countries in the United Nations and outside; to make the SAARC function properly; to see the Oslo Accord (1993) implemented and safeguard the rights of the Palestinians to have a homeland of their own in the territories assigned to them under the Oslo Accord; to make the Arab countries take up the

Iraqi affairs under their control and settle the future of Iraq according to the wishes of the Iraqi people; to resist American pressures on Iran and muster diplomatic strength to restrain the US from embarking upon another military venture – against Tehran; revive the status of the United Nations as an organization representing all countries of the world and not just being the custodian of interests of the superpower and its allies.

The United Nations needs to be strengthened. First of all the sanctity of the UN Charter should be restored. The UN mandate must be binding. Preference should be given to pacific settlement of international disputes and all regional, non-aligned and bilateral channels should be allowed to bring peace between the estranged states before referring the matter to the Security Council. The main function of the Security Council is to prevent war but lately it is being seen that Security Council is being used for sanctioning war under pressure from the superpower, notwithstanding the disapproval by one or two permanent members of the council. 'Veto' seems making sense only when used by the superpower the recent US-led coalition's military action against Iraq was not endorsed by France and Russia.

The Indian foreign policy needs to take up these issues, debate them in the non-aligned and bilateral fora and prepare world public opinion in favour of a world order based on justice and equality striving for world peace.

3

Changing Security Paradigms in India: The UPA Phase

Pramod Mishra

Since the end of cold war, one clearly notices a paradigm shift in the notion of national security. The traditional norm of security linked with national interest and War[1] has been modified by a large number of nations and the UN and its agencies have provided the right direction and major attention at the present juncture seems to be focused around internal security linked with terrorism, and the notion of "human security". Today one needs to develop a multi-dimensional approach to security which would basically address several human related issues like sustainable development, hunger, modernization of agriculture, controlling water scarcity, flood control and social security for the marginalized and aboriginal people. The paper will briefly highlight the changing notion of security especially in the developing world. Thereafter, it will evaluate the new orientations on national security by the United Progressive Alliance (UDA) government headed by Manmohan Singh.

Recent literature on national security strongly supports the thesis that the issues related to security cannot be effectively addressed without due focus on factors as societal, political and economic.[2] Security is not just the absence of war or preparedness for war. It has non-military dimensions at economic, diplomatic, environmental and social-political level. The meeting of a group of experts on non-military aspects of security in Tashkent in May 1990 used the following operational definition of security:[3] Security is a condition in which states consider that there is no danger of military attack, political pressure or economic coercion, so that they are able to pursue freely their own development and progress. The security of individuals and communities of which states are constituted is ensured by the guarantee and effective exercise of individual freedom, political, social and economic rights, as well as by the preservation or restoration of a livable environment for present and future generations, Security education, housing and public health are ensured on a permanent basis. An adequate protection against dangers to security may be defined in national, inter governmental, non-governmental or global terms. An important area of debate is the place of the people as the referent unit in security. As underlined by the UNDP: [4] "The concept of security has for too long been interpreted narrowly: as security of territory from external aggression, or as protection of national interests in foreign policy or as global security from the threat of nuclear holocaust. It has been related more to nation-states than to people...Forgotten were the legitimate concerns of ordinary people who sought security in their daily lives. For many of them security symbolized protection from the threat of disease, hunger, unemployment, crime, social conflict, political repression and environmental hazards".

The concept of national security must take into account the present day realities. Both the perceived and actual threats are important in national security perceptions and approaches. In present times, the main sources of conflict are of an intra-state nature. In this context it is pertinent to take note of the recommendations of the Report of the commission on global Governance, according to which "..Security must be broadened from its traditional focus on the security of the states to include the security of people and the planet".[5] It further says: "All people, no less than all states, have a right to secure existence and all states have an obligation to protect those rights."

From National Security to Human Security

The shift from the 'national security' to the 'human security' paradigm is of historic importance. The object of security changes from the state to the individual; the focus changes from security through armaments to security through human development; from territorial security to food, employment and environmental security.[6] The fundamental components of human security, the security of people against threat to life, health, livelihood, personal safety and human dignity can be put at risk by external aggression, but also by factors within a country including security forces, Over the course of the 20th century, 30 million people were killed in international wars, 7 million in civil wars and an additional 170 million by their own governments. In his Millennium Report, Secretary-General Kofi Annan has emphasized on providing freedom from fear, freedom from want to the mankind as well as a sustainable future. A recurring theme in his report is the importance of making the transition from the culture of reaction to the culture of prevention. This is even more fundamental for the attainment of human security than for national security, as even a cursory glance at threats to human security will show.

Manmohan Singh Government's New Emphasis on Comprehensive Security

As highlighted in the CMP, the UPA Government supported by the left parties will have six basic principles for governance.[7] These are as follows: (I) to preserve and protect social harmony and to enforce the law without fear or favour, to deal with all obscurantist and fundamentalist elements who seek to disturb social amity and peace. (II) To ensure that the economy grows at least 7-8 per cent per year in a sustained manner over a decade and more and in a manner that generates employment so that each family is assured of a safe and viable livelihood. (III) To enhance the welfare and well being of farmers, farm labour and workers, particularly those in the unorganized sector, and assure a secure future for their families in every respect. (IV) To fully empower women politically, educationally, economically and legally. (V) To provide for full equality of opportunity, particularly in education and employment for the Scheduled Castes, Scheduled Tribes, OBCs and religious minorities and (VI) to unleash the creative energies of our entrepreneurs, businessmen, scientists, engineers and all other professionals and productive forces of society. The UPA makes a solemn pledge to the people of our country to provide a government that is corruption-free, transparent and accountable at all times, to provide an administration that is responsible and responsive at all times.

The UPA Government will ensue that all delays in the modernization of the armed forces are eliminated and that all funds earmarked for modernization are spent fully at the earliest. The UPA will set up a new Department of Ex-Servicemen's Welfare in the Ministry of Defence. The long-pending issue of one-rank, one-pension will be re-examined. The UPA Government will make the National Security Council a professional and effective institution. The UPA Government is committed to maintaining a credible nuclear weapons programme while at the same time it will evolve demonstrable and verifiable confidence-building measures with its nuclear neighbours. It will take a leadership role in promoting universal, nuclear disarmament and working for a nuclear weapons free world.

The UPA has been concerned at the manner in which POTA has been grossly misused in the past two years. There will be no compromise in the fight against terrorism. But given the abuse of POTA that has taken place, the UPA Government will repeal it, while existing laws are enforced strictly. The UPA Government will take the strictest possible action without fear or favour, against all those individuals and organizations that spread social discord disturb social amity and propagate religious bigotry and communal hatred. The law of the land will be enforced effectively.

The UPA Government will pursue an independent foreign policy, keeping in mind its past traditions. This policy will seek to promote the multipolarity in international relations and oppose all attempts at unilateralism. The UPA Government will give the highest priority to building closer political, economic and other ties with its neighbours in South Asia and to strengthen SAARC. Particular attentions will be paid to regional projects in the area of water resources, power and ecological conservation. Dialogue with Pakistan on all issues will be pursued systematically and on a sustained basis. The UPA will support peace talks in Sri Lanka that fulfill the legitimate aspirations of Tamils and religious minorities within the territorial integrity and solidarity of Sri Lanka. Outstanding issues with Bangladesh will be resolved. Intensive dialogue will be initiated with Nepal for developing water resources to mutual advantage. Trade and investment with China will be expanded further and talks on the border issues pursued seriously. Relationships with East Asian countries will be given a fresh thrust. The UPA Government reiterates India's decades-old commitment to the case of the Palestinian people for a homeland of their own. Steps will be taken to withdraw Indian mercenaries from Iraq, while further recruitment for this purpose will be banned. Even as it pursues closer engagements and relations with USA, the UPA Government will maintain the independence of India's foreign policy position on all regional and global issues. The UPA is committed to deepening ties with Russia and Europe as well.

The UPA Government will fully protect the national interest, particularly of farmers, in all WTO negotiations. Commitment made earlier will be adhered to even as efforts are mounted to ensure that all agreements reflect our concerns fully, particularly in the area of intellectual property and agriculture. The UPA Government will use the flexibility afforded in existing WTO agreement to fully protect Indian agriculture and industry. The UPA Government will play a proactive role in strengthening the emerging solidarity of developing countries in the shape of G-20 in the WTO.

CMP Focuses on Wide Range of Social Security for Different Target Groups

The UPA Government is firmly committed to ensuring the welfare and well-being of all workers, particularly those in the unorganized sector who constitute 93 per cent of our workforce. Social security, health insurance and other schemes for such workers like weavers, handloom workers, fishermen and fisherwomen, toddy tapers, leather workers, plantation labour, beedi workers etc. will be expanded. The UPA rejects the idea of automatic hire and fire. It recognizes that some changes in labour laws may be required, but such changes must fully protect the interests of workers and families and must take place after full consultation with trade unions. The UPA will pursue a dialogue with industry and trade unions on this issue before coming up with specific proposals. However, labour laws other than the Industrial Dispute Act that create an Inspector Raj will be re-examined and procedures harmonized and streamlined. The UPA Government firmly believes that labour-management relations in our country must be marked by consultations, cooperation and consensus, not confrontation. Tripartite consultations with trade unions and industry on all proposals concerning them will be actively pursued. Rights and benefits earned by workers including the right to strike according to law will not be taken away or curtailed.

The UPA will urge the States to make legislation for conferring ownership rights in respect of minor forest produce, including tendu patta, on all those people from the weaker sections who work in the forests. All reservations, quotas, including those relating to promotions, will be fulfilled in a time-bound manner. To codify all reservations, a Reservation Act will be enacted. The UPA Government will launch a com prehensive national programme for minor irrigation of all lands owned by dalits and adivasis. Landless families will be endowed with land through implementation of land ceiling and land redistribution legislation. No reversal of ceilings legislation will be permitted. The UPA administration will take all measures to reconcile the objectives of economic growth and environmental conservation, particularly as far as tribal communities dependent on forests are concerned.

The UPA Government will immediately review the overall strategy and programmes for the development of tribal areas to plug loopholes and to work out more viable livelihood strategies. In addition, more effective systems of relief and rehabilitation will be put in place for tribal and other groups displaced by development projects. Tribal people alienated from land will be rehabilitated. The UPA Government is very sensitive to the issue of affirmative action, including reservations in the private sector. It will immediately initiate a national dialogue with all political parties, industry and other organizations to see how best the private sector can fulfill the aspirations of Scheduled Castes and Scheduled Tribes youth. Eviction of tribal communities and other forest dwelling communities will be sought for protecting forests. On the Food Security, UPA will work out, in the next three months, a comprehensive medium-term strategy for food and nutrition security. The objective will be to move towards universal food security over time, if found feasible. The UPA Government will strengthen the Public Distribution System (PDS), particularly in the poorest and backward blocks of the country, and involve women's and ex- servicemen's cooperatives in its management. Special schemes to reach food grains to the most destitute and infirm will be launched. Grain banks in chronically food-scarce areas will be established. Antyodaya cards for all households at risk of hunger will be introduced. The UPA Government will bring about major improvements in the functioning of the Food Corporation of India (FCI) to control inefficiencies that increase the food subsidy burden. Nutrition progammes, particularly for the girl child, will be expanded on a significant scale.

Keeping the Promises: New Challenges

On June 24, 2004 when the Prime Minister Manmohan Singh delivered his first address to the nation, he said: "My Fellow Citizens, I speak to you with a deep sense of humility, fully conscious of the sacred responsibility entrusted to me. You have assigned the task of governance of our country to the United Progressive Alliance and its supporting parties. You have delivered your verdict and the verdict is clear. You have sought a change in the manner in which this country is run, a change in national priorities, and a change in the processes and focus of governance. You have expressed concern for the poor and disadvantaged sections of our society and for minorities and backward regions to be at the heart of all policies of the Government. As I share with you the priorities of our Government, I am reminded of the Father of our Nation, Mahatma Gandhi who had said that his mission in life was 'to wipe every tear from every eye'. Think of the poorest person you have ever seen."[8]

New Strategy on External Security and Foreign Policy

The Indian Prime Minister while highlighting the foreign policy strategy said: [9] "We will maintain a credible minimum nuclear deterrent, along with a policy of 'no first use' in our nuclear doctrine. India is a responsible nuclear power and we will continue to work to prevent proliferation of weapons of mass destruction. At the same time, we remain committed to the goal of universal nuclear disarmament. No objective in the development agenda can be met if we do not reform the instrument in our hand with which we have to work, namely the government and public institutions. Clearly, this will be my main concern and challenge in the days to come. We will maintain our tradition of an independent foreign policy, built on a national consensus and based on our supreme national interests. We will expand our network of international relationships preserving solidarity with traditional allies and strengthening new partnerships. We will work with like-minded nations for an equitable, multi-polar world order, which takes into account the legitimate aspirations of developing countries. We desire to live in a neighbourhood of peace and prosperity. We will actively pursue the composite dialogue with Pakistan. We are sincere about discussing and resolving all issues, including Jammu and Kashmir. We recognize that resolution of major issues requires national consensus and accommodation of public sentiment in both countries. It is self-evident that terrorism and violence would cast a dark shadow over this process. With our other South Asian neighbours, it will be our sincere effort to jointly realize the vast potential for cooperation and to ensure mutual security, stability and development. In our relations with China, we are encouraged by positive developments, which we are committed to strengthening. Bilateral economic cooperation has shown remarkable growth and diversification. We shall carry forward the process of discussion to resolve the boundary question from the political perspective of our bilateral relations. As two of the world's great democracies, our strengthened relationship with USA is a fact of considerable importance. The transformation of our relations with USA has been supported by the expansion of economic links and people-to-people ties, including the presence of almost a million people of Indian origin in that country. We will welcome the expansion of cooperation, between the two Governments to include new and mutually beneficial areas, particularly high technology. The strength and vibrancy of our partnership with Russia has withstood the flux of the post-Cold War world. We will accelerate the diversification of our relationship, particularly in defence, high technology, space and nuclear energy, while intensifying economic cooperation. We have traditionally strong relations with the countries of Southeast and West Asia, based on cultural affinities, economic interaction and a vibrant Indian expatriate community. We aim to build upon these. While speaking of West Asia, I must share our deep concern about developments in Iraq and the suffering of the people of that country. It is our earnest hope that democracy will be restored and full sovereignty transferred to a truly presentative government of Iraq. India is committed to participate in all endeavours aimed at bringing stability and to ensure the well being of the Iraqi people. We will also strengthen our bilateral relations with developing countries of Latin America and Africa. Similarly, strong ties with the nations of Central Asia are of importance for our international trade, as well as for our strategic and energy security".

PM's Concerns on Internal Security

Manmohan Singh has shown his great empathy for internal and human security.[10] Internal security remains an important challenge. Terrorism posses a grave threat to the unity and progress of our nation. We shall combat it with all the resources at our command. There shall be no doubt whatsoever about our resolve to deal with this insidious threat to our nation. The Government will continue the process of dialogue with the Hurriyat and all other groups in Jammu and Kashmir. The Government is willing to talk with all disaffected groups, provided they shun the path of national security to create greater synergy between our intelligence agencies, closer coordination between internal security structures, more efficient civil-military interface and more effective harnessing of technology to nation security management.

There has been a neglect of the interests of the farmers in recent years and this is reflected in a significant slowing down in agricultural growth in the past five years. Farmers in many parts of the country have faced distress and there has been no helping hand. CMP of the United Progressive alliance is committed to giving a "New Deal" to rural India. Agriculture must receive the priority attention it deserves. Public and private investment in agriculture has to be greatly increased. A key concern in recent years has been the lack of access to credit. Our Government is already addressing this issue directly by pursuing policies that improve the farmer's access to affordable credit. Agricultural research, training and extension also require much greater attention. I would like to see the emergence of new centers of excellence in sharper focus on expanding opportunities for gainful employment, if efficiently implemented, can greatly assist in achieving this objective. The Indian farmer has also suffered from too many controls and restrictions. There are still far too many internal barriers to trade that must go. We must also re-examine those aspects of our policies that prevent a creative interaction between farmers and agro-industries. I would like to see the creation of a "Single Market" across the country for both manufactured and agricultural produce. With the introduction of value-added taxation, this integration of the Indian market will be further enabled.

A striking feature of development in our country has been the rapid increase in urbanization. There are now more than 30 cities with population of more than one million. The rapid and unplanned growth of these cities has contributed to increased urban pollution, crime and absence of the required infrastructure like access to drinking water, sanitation, road, and footpaths for pedestrians and public spaces, parks and greenery is making life in urban India a living hell for many. Most of the responsibility for this rests with States and Municipal Governments. It will be our effort to give special attention to policies that can encourage urban development and urban renewal. We will actively seek public private partnership in building urban infrastructure in a planned manner. Higher rates of economic growth, urbanization and the modernization of agriculture will continue to increase the demand for energy. This demand can only be met with new investments, increased efficiency and rational pricing. Even as we plan to make more efficient use of conventional sources of energy, we must invest in the development of non-conventional sources.

Water has emerged as a critical and contentious issue across the country. Even access to safe drinking water remains a problem in many parts of our country. Water management policies have to be so formulated as to address the needs of farmers and weaker sections, especially women, as well as those of city dwellers. We will have to find innovative, cost-effective and community-based solutions. Groundwater replenishment and management rainwater harvesting require close cooperation between Government, Panchayati Raj Institutions and non-governmental organizations. The Government will reserve the neglect of public investment in irrigation, addressing the specific problems of each river basin, in an environment and people-friendly manner. We need new thinking in health policy. While the Government will continue to help in the growth of private and community-based health and medical care, there is a crying need for the reform of public health and hospitals. We will make public hospitals more efficient and accessible, through public-private partnership aimed at offering affordable and humane health care. We need community based and public health-oriented solutions for tackling communicable diseases epidemics, especially HIV/AIDS and disability management and population stabilization.

Consensual Approach on National Security through Consultations with Allies and Opposition

In a bid to forge a political consensus ahead of the India-Pakistan Foreign Minister level talks on September 5-6, 2004 Prime Minister, Manmohan Singh, held a breakfast meeting with his predecessor Atal Bihari Vajpayee, on September 3, 2004. The Prime Minister conveyed to Vajpayee the "marginal results" attained in the talks process since the United Progressive Alliance Government took over. He also consulted Vajpayee on strategy and tactics and informed him that his Government was fully committed to dialogue process and hoped that it would yield positive results. Vajpayee is said to have told Manmohan Singh that the two countries should try and evolve ways to move beyond the stated positions. Some attention was focused on contentious issues such as Siachen, Sir Creek and Jammu and Kashmir.

In Retrospect

In this paper, we began with the hypothesis that the classical paradigm of security is not relevant to the present day world. As we have further analyzed in the context of India, the Manmohan Singh government has outlined a more comprehensive view of security. Although several promises have been made in the CMP in May 2004, the UPA Government is certainly facing several challenges at the implementation stage and only rhetoric will not satisfy the rousing expectations of the people especially on matters of social and economic security as well as environmental protection. Even on the strategy of containing the rising insurgencies in the Northeast and Naxal affected areas in Bihar, Jharkhand, Andhra Pradesh and Orissa, the Manmohan Singh government has launched no major initiatives. As regards the issue of external security, it is more or less continuing the policy of Vajpayee government. No major breakthrough with Pakistan over Kashmir is visible. There is no doubt over the fact that the UPA government is more focused on the economic diplomacy as reflected from the PM's recent tours of Southeast Asian countries. India's strategic partnership with the US government has also been further strengthened during Manmohan's September tour to Washington.

Notes and References

1. One of the major spokesmen of the traditional notion of security writes: "A nation has security when it does not have to sacrifice its legitimate interests to avoid war and is able, if challenged, to maintain them by war". *Encyclopaedia of the Social Sciences* (1963), Vol. 7 (New York: Macmillan).
2. Archana Upadhyaya: National Security Issues in South Asia: Perceptions and Perspectives in Mahavir Singh (ed.), *Asia Annual* (2002), Shipra, 2002, p. 96.
3. Har Vir Singh: How to Counter Insurgencies. *IDR*, 14(4), 1999, p. 25.
4. Thomas Homer-Dixon: The Virulence of Violence: Small Arms, Many Wars, Large threats. *Washingon Post,* February 4, 2001.
5. Anindita Dasgupta: Small Arms Proliferation India's North-East: A case study of Assam, *Economic and Political Weekly*, January 6, 2001, p. 62.
6. Ramesh Thakur: Security in the New Millennium; paper presented at the ICSSR – hosted *International Conference on Asia and the Emerging Global Order*: New Delhi, 2-3 October 2000. See also Global Action's website <www.globalaction.org>.
7. See the complete text of CMP released on 27 May 2004 as reproduced in *Strategic Digest*, Vol. 34, No. 6, June 2004.
8. *Hindu* June 25, 2004.
9. *Ibid.*
10. *Ibid.*

4

Challenges Before India's Foreign Policy in the 21st Century

Madhurendra Kumar

The world in the twenty-first century is remarkably different from the cold war period. Unprecedented transferences have taken place in the contemporary international politics. The end of ideological rivalry and strategic competition between the superpowers which had tremendous role in accentuating conflicts across the world generated new hope for building a peaceful and co-operative world order. Instead there is a great deal of uncertainty in the emerging global order. New conflicts and issues have surfaced in the forms of ethnic conflicts, refugee problem, environmental degradation, terrorism etc. These have posed variety of challenges before the community of nations. After the 9/11 terrorist attack on world trade tower global peace and international security has received a severe jolt and global terrorism has emerged as a formidable challenge for international peace and security.

In this international milieu though the Indian foreign policy is facing enormous challenges both at global and regional level but there are opportunities also. The Indian geopolitics offers her political economic and strategic benefits in the Post-Cold War period. The kind of independence of decision making India showed through Pokharan II and her expanding ties with ASEAN countries and Myanmar, her positive approach towards regional grouping particularly ARF, SAARC and BIMSET-EC provide ample testimony to its emergence as a significant actor on the horizon of world politics. But this new role in the post-cold war periods is beset with numerous challenges.

The foremost challenge before Indian foreign policy has emerged in the shape of questioning the doctrinal foundation of the foreign policy. The end of bipolarity and disintegration of the Soviet Union, emergence of the USA as the sole superpower, made the very foundation of non-alignment irrelevant. Indian foreign policy planners and executors were compelled to rethink and review their strategy. In fact, the entire foreign policy perspective stood in sharp disarray. This was not owing to factors beyond India's control and fluidity of global scenario rather it was more due to lack of strategic and political foresightedness of those who discharge the conduct of our foreign policy.[1] But India, soon-readjusted herself in the new global order and carved out a significant place as an emerging power in the 21st century with a new orientation and vision towards global as well as regional issues. If the post cold war international milieu posed challenges to India it offered opportunities too for accruing optimum strategic and economic gains by playing an efficacious role in the community of nations.

With the end of the disintegration of the Soviet Union a common concern was expressed regarding the policy of Non-alignment. It would be worthwhile to recall here that the chief Architect of India's foreign policy Pandit Jawaharlal Nehru. 'Drew the parameters and set the tone' for India's foreign policy in the shape of providing doctrinal base of Non-alignment. During his stewardship India carved out a position of a natural leader of the newly independent Afro-Asian states and chose to pursue an independent path in the surcharged atmosphere of cold war bloc politics of the East and West. This stance has been seen not only logical in terms of India's Idealistic commitment to eradicating colonialism and racism and preventing a military confrontation between the superpowers rather to a great extent it was a realistic strategy in the prevailing circumstances. The only viable option left for her to safeguard her national interest in the bipolar world was to pursue non-alignment. Justifying the rational of this policy Pandit Nehru observed: "India is too big a country. India is going to be and is bound to be a country that wants in world affairs ..while remaining quite apart from power blocs, we are in a better position to cast our weight at the right moment in favour of peace and meanwhile our relation can become as close as possible in the economic or other domain with such countries with whom we can easily develop them."[2] There were valid reasons for Nehru to oppose bloc politics of cold war. First, India believed that the cold war was excessively militarized with nuclear overtones. The bombing of Hiroshima appalled Nehru but while giving green signals to Homi Jahangir Bhabha to develop nuclear capability, he was vehemently against nuclear weapons and its testing deployment and stockpiles. Secondly, division of globe in to hostile camps meant less attention to Afro- Asian and Latin American states. Joining any camp was tantamount to going back to the days of colonialism and was detrimental to the economic development of these newly independent states of the third world including India.[3] Hence, India chose to pursue an independent path and decided to adopt the policy of non-alignment as the cardinal basis of foreign policy. In due course of time this foreign policy strategy suited other Afro-Asian states too and from strategy, non-alignment culminated into a movement in the years that followed.

Non-alignment indisputably gave prestige and influence to India in the world and the consistent commitment to NAM is a striking feature of India's foreign policy. Many swinging criticism were leveled on non-alignment propounded by Nehru. Demystifying the misgivings pertaining to India's position on Non-alignment, Pandit Jawaharlal Nehru maintained in the Lok Sabha on June 12, 1952. "I submit that so far as our policy is concerned in spite of the fact that we deal largely with the United Kingdom and the USA. We buy our things from them and we have accepted help from them. We have not swerved at all from our policy of non-alignment with any group. We stuck to our policy ever though we had to deny ourselves the offered help. There have been times when one word from us would have brought us many of the good things of life. We preferred not to give that word...not a few individuals but millions in this country. If any time help from abroad depends upon variation howsoever slight in our policy. We shall relinquish that help completely and prefer starvation and privation to taking such help and I think the world knows it well enough."[4]

Thus, choosing non-alignment was a principled choice of the foreign policy makers of India. This attitude served India's Interest till the death of Nehru. Non-alignment remained the sheet anchor of foreign policy in the post Nehruvian era also albeit with a pragmatic tilt under the stewardship of Mrs. Indira Gandhi. Even during the Janata Party regime in 1977, India did not depart from this policy. It proves the fact that Nehruvian perspective served India's interests well during the cold war period. But In the Post-Cold War period when the very context of bipolarity ceased to exist, realist critiques question the validity of non-alignment as a doctrinal base of Indian foreign policy and put a question mark on its relevance in the post-cold war period. As C. Rajamohan has opined that in the post-cold war period Indian foreign policy needs to "cross the Rubicon of nuclear morality and indecision as well as non aligned third worldism and anti- west paronia. The change in global scenario amounts to changing the philosophical premise of India's engagement with the external world."[5] The developments in the International arena emphasize the need for a fundamental rethinking in India's foreign policy.[6] Thus seeking justification for the continuation of non-alignment is a fundamental challenge for India's foreign policy in the post cold war period.

What is overlooked while dismissing the relevance of non-alignment is that the core of our foreign policy is autonomy in decision-making. In the changed situations also India should not give up this autonomy. Besides this India should also avoid too much attachment as "in a world where there are no blocs to be aligned with or non aligned from the small or medium power still has to avoid too much identification with any big power or even the sole superpower. So, in present circumstances non-alignment stands for diplomatic autonomy and economic and technological engagement with all the nations of the world."[7] India may pursue a policy of continuity and change to cope up with the momentous challenges unleashed by the changed politico-strategic context of the Post-Cold War world, which is reflected in the conduct of India's foreign policy. Because except India's look east policy and India's decision to opt for a nuclear weapon capacity there is no marked departure in India's approach to her external relations.

There are, of course some dramatic changes in the bilateral relationship with countries like USA. These changes are not due to India's response to the Post-Cold War order but due to change in the American strategic stance after the 9/11 and India's post-May 1998 nuclear status, her economic growth and widening market. India's status as an important emerging power has forced the American policy makers to not only to review its relationship with India but also to forge close bilateral ties with her. India acquired a new face in the beginning of 21st century with her vibrant economy and geopolitics. It was increasingly becoming the emerging trade partner with the United state. So India came to be viewed as important to the United States. At the same time India's position at a geo-strategic nexus between central southwest and South-East Asia was also gaining significance. In the eyes of Washington, India could counter balance assertive China. Thus, Indian and America strategic balance could be served by a strategic balance in Asia that prevented China from dominating the region.[9] Washington also signaled that its strategic goal in South Asia was no longer steered by cold war considerations. Now it was more interested in addressing the problems of terrorism, the expansion of democracy and developing an equitable global economic order which could be addressed in a cooperative spirit.[10] Thus, we find that the post-cold war order and September 11, attacks reinforced a perception of a broader political and strategic similarity of interests pulling India and the United States together. It was made clear by the Bush administration that the United States wished to engage India in a strategic dialogue that encompass the full range of global issues.[11]

The movement and progress through the next steps in strategic partnership initiative (NSSP) is also noteworthy, as it is believed to lead towards significant economic benefits for both countries and improve regional and global security. It may be mentioned here that earlier in January 2004 both the USA and India agreed to expand co-operation in three specific areas viz., civilion nuclear activities, civilian space programmes and high technology trade. In addition, the two countries agreed to expand their dialogue on missile defense. These areas of co-operation are significant landmarks in transforming Indo-US strategic partnership in the Post-Cold War period.[12]

So, it is evident now that US India relationship has progressed remarkably in the post-cold war period. However there are points of departures as well; particularly on issues such as humanitarian intervention, American practice of linking human right issue with her economic aid policy, Nuclear and missile programme and India's quest for a permanent seat in the Security Council of the United Nations. Inspite of these differences both are expected to be engaged in closer relationship. The degree to which the two actors can act upon in a relationship between the sole superpower and rising India will be a major determinant of India's role in the world politics during the decades to come.[13] It would be possible because the end of cold war has removed those irritants between New Delhi and Washington that earlier marred co-operative ties. Today, neither Indo-Soviet connection is a factor nor US-Pakistan relationship determines India's strategic utility for the USA. In fact this kind of partnership is not at the expense of India's foreign policy autonomy witnessed during recent years.

Another domain of opportunity for the Indian foreign policy is growing interaction with the European Union. Recent formal endorsement of Indo-EU's strategic partnership is recognition of India's vibrant democratic institutions, growing economic power and increasing clout on the regional and International stage. The most significant aspect of this partnership is that India is only the fifth country besides the USA, Canada, Russia and China with whom the EU has established such equation. This partnership launched in January, 2005 is a culmination of steady enhancement of relations from trade and investment to wider political issues over the years.[14] Although differences persist with regard to trade barriers market access, protection for intellectual property and subsidies yet partnership in the areas of development co-operation science and technology and education has witnessed substantial progress. Bilateral trade between India and EU has also doubled over the last decades.[15] This expanding relationship between India and EU may be attributed to shared values of democracy, secularism, multiculturalism and decentralization as both sides have evinced strong identity of views on vital importance of multiculturalism and world-wide peace keeping and leveraged this common ground to evolve positions consistent with International law. This approach finds reflections in a document released by EC which says that "EU and India should hold continuous dialogue on organizational and institutional restructuring and reform of the United Nations in particular."[16] It is obvious now that broadening contours of relationship is replete with immense possibilities of evolving into a more matured relationship.

Besides these pragmatic engagements with the USA and EU, power correlates in Asia are also marked with remarkable shifts in the Post-Cold War period. As a result, two major actors of Asia i.e. India and China have moved forward to address their mutual differences for normalization of relationship. In fact, one major challenge India faced in the Post-Cold War period was to manage the uncertainties with the immediate neighbours rather than setting grandiose global goals.[17] Learning lessons from the past it was very much desirable on the part of India and China to concentrate on mending their mutual ties and finding a solution to the territorial disputes which marred bilateral relationship in the past. As the absence of a normal neighbourly relationship has been a geopolitical reality; so in the post-cold war period both countries realized that past acrimonious relationship cannot be good to the future of Sino-India relationship. Now they are on the threshold of paradigm shift leading to close co-operation and purposeful negotiation on boundary question and other nettlesome issues such as Tibet and Sikkim. India has maintained its official position that Tibet autonomous region is part of the territory of PRC. Further reiteration of the policy of not allowing Tibetans including Dalai Lama to indulge in anti-China political activities to a great extent helped allay uneasiness and apprehensions on the Chinese side. Similarly Chinese recognition of Sikkim as integral part of India has greatly minimized the mutual misunderstanding. Now there is a need to look beyond Tibet and Sikkim and India and China must resolve their boundary dispute once and for all.[18] As a result of this approach, further shift in Chinese policy vis-a-vis India could be noticed in its neutral posture during the Kargil war. 'This posture of neutrality may have been due to a whole range of global regional and bilateral equation of China with major power and particularly the USA. Nevertheless it was a tangible strategic gain for India. Credit for this transformation goes to India's sustained initiatives and diplomatic deftness in handling her policy towards China. At the same time, stable coalition government, rapid growth rates in economy and successful nuclear tests has also enhanced India's bargaining position. Now it is high time for India to derive optimum strategic and economic dividends from the newly found bonhomie with China.[19] Striking headway in the fields of maintaining peace and tranquility in the border area, on confidence building measures in the military spheres, growing co-operation and exchange between parliament political parties, mass media and academic communities, expression of identical views on international issues and pursuing a co-operative approach in UN and WTO for safeguarding the interests of the developing countries,[20] expansion of trade relationship[21] and consensus reached by them that both sides should in no way allow their historic baggage to stand to the all round development of relationship and neither country would see the other as threat speak volumes of India-China rapprochement in the 21st century. The more they would develop their trade and commerce, exchange of technology, promotion of joint ventures and other allied economic activities greater would be the impulse for pacific relationship[22] leading to common views and positions on unfolding strategic scenario in the aftermath of the cold war.

Managing cordial relationship with her neighbours such as Pakistan, Bangladesh, Nepal, Sri Lanka is another important challenge India's foreign policy faces in the Post-Cold War period. So unlike past India's diplomatic task in the next few years should be directed more towards neighbourhood rather setting grandiose global goal she must evolve a strategic framework for dealing with its small neighbours in the post-cold war period. The need for a such framework is felt in view of the fact that forces hostile to India get safe havens for operation from these countries. Similarly India cannot afford to ignore the challenges emanating from a nuclearized environment. So neighbourhood diplomacy needs to be accorded highest priority in Indian foreign policy projections as longstanding irritants in relationship with its neighbours impinge quite crucially on India's security. Further allowing internal problems to prolong would prove counterproductive for India's long term interests in the region. Being the largest power in the region it is incumbent upon to set the tone for creating a congenial ambience to address the nettlesome issues to find solutions. It would help dispel the misgivings in the perceptions of small neighbours vis-à-vis her. Greater bilateral dialogue as well as multilateral engagements with SAARC countries would be quite advantageous.[23] India's recent initiative to evolve a framework for resolving the long-standing bilateral problems on the basis of mutual confidence and co-operation has evoked a positive response.[24] constructive engagement in the shape of confidence building measures in Indo-Pak and India-China relationship shows some silver lines. Now the most arduous task before the managers of Indian foreign policy is to evolve a strategy to carry forward the composite dialogue process with Pakistan to its logical end. One must not be complacent over the newly developed bonhomie between India and Pakistan which has paved the way for people to people contact and opening the bus service between New Delhi and Lahore and Srinagar to Muzaffrabad. The signals from Pakistan suggest that if India would not handle Kashmir issue sincerely then the peace process would have no utility. Hence pragmatic path would have to be a sustained effort[25] on the part of India to engage Pakistan for securing a solution of cross-border terrorism, drug trafficking and the core issue of Kashmir.

Similarly, in view of the deepening crisis in Nepal amidst a growing confrontation between the Monarchy and political parties, the rising menace of Maoist, insurgency India will have to rethink its policy towards its northern neighbour. India's actions must be designed to ensure that a productive dialogue starts between the king and the political parties and early ceasefire between the Royal Army and Maoist.[26] In the wake of recent political crisis in Nepal India must strive to check state failure in Nepal as its strategic implications would be disastrous. King Gyanendra's overtures towards Beijing and Pakistan need to be taken seriously in diplomatic circles. In the context of our southern neighbour, one notices that significant changes have taken place in Indo-Sri Lanka relationship in the post-cold war period. Initiatives of New Delhi and Colombo have succeeded in ending mutual misperceptions. Inspite of the fact that Sri Lanka has been one of India's assertive neighbour and its cultivated threat perception vis-à-vis India clouded the bilateral ties in the past, new trajectories in the form of growing defense co-operation, free trade agreement, practical and compassionate approach to deal with the fishermen issues and India's keenness in ending the impasses in the peace processes are visible indicators for the betterment of relationship. Both from political and economic point of views the two countries are coming closer with regular high level visits and interactions. As of now, India has become one of the biggest investors in the island. Despite apprehensions, the free trade agreement has helped enhance the quantum of trade.[27] The two countries concluded a comprehensive Economic partnership Agreement also. Now the main task before New Delhi and Colombo is to provide continuity in co-operation and strengthening their ties in a spirit of beneficial bilateralism. "The best thing that has occurred in Sri Lanka politics is the convergence of wishes and intentions on the part of all parties that relationship with India should be maintained at a special level of excellence." It is a remarkable breakthrough for New Delhi.

So for as India's relationship with Bangladesh is concerned, a serious diplomatic attention is needed in the present context because though thirty-three years. ago India helped the liberation of Bangladesh from Pakistan nevertheless the relationship between India and Bangladesh have not been so smooth. There are three major areas of discord (i) separatists in the Northeast operating from well entrenched camps in the territory of Bangladesh (ii). illegal migration (iii) Dhaka's blocking the access of India to Chittagong port while Bangladesh wants duty free access to Indian market for improving its balance of trade. Besides these factors fundamentalist orientation in Dhaka's polity also causes concern for India because these elements not only vitiated the co-operation between the two countries after the emergence of Bangladesh rather they still constitute an obstacle in the way of India-Bangladesh amity and co-operation.[28] The initiatives taken by both sides in the shape of foreign secretary level talks in 2003 yielded positive result both agreed to implement the previously arrived procedures for stopping illegal cross border movements of the people. What is needed on the part of Bangladesh is concrete measures to dismantle the insurgents' camps operating from its soil. At the same time, India must impress upon Bangladesh that strong bilateral relationship would be beneficial for the common men in both the countries. There is also a need of a specific policy framework on the whole range of issues such as military assistance, supply of arms, training of security forces and defense co-operation with neighbours like Bangladesh.[29]

Apart from paying due attention to strengthening the ties with neighbouring countries, India, being a significant power in this region, has a tremendous role in boosting SAARC and enabling this regional organization to become a forum for mutual growth and consultation. It would be worthwhile to mention here that through regional arrangements the countries of Europe as well as those of South East Asia has accrued benefits and sometimes did away with the negative fallouts of globalization. Regional groupings are essential to enhance our bargaining position vis-à-vis the developed countries in the world trade organization (WTO). The solidarity shown by the south Asian countries at the Seattle, Doha and Cancun round of negotiations over the issues of agriculture and agricultural subsides, leaves little doubt that in the age of globalization the only meaningful way to assert our position is through SAARC. The initiative taken by India at the SAARC Council of Ministers Meeting in Islamabad on July 23. 2004 for setting up a South Asian parliament to deliberate the issues pertaining to regional co-operation endeavours setting up of a SAARC infra structure fund, SAARC high Economic Council and her offer in the field of community service were endorsed by the other members of the organization. It reflects keenness of the SAARC countries to carry forward the idea of co-operation to the optimum level. It also shows that India can effectively lead the SAARC in the attainment of its objectives and must try hard for SAFTA to come into force. It must be noted that greater south Asian solidarity is quite essential for the progress and prosperity of the people of this region.

Unlike the days of cold war there is amazing metamorphosis in India's attitude towards South East Asia which is reflected by the deeper involvement, co-operation and collaboration with Association of South East Asian Nations in the Post-Cold War period. Indo-ASEAN interaction has substantially increased during these years.[30] In fact, the prologue to foreign policy shift was written with the enunciation of India's Look East Policy in the 1990s. This was in fact a beginning of real politics in India's policy towards South East Asia in 1991. During the cold war period India and ASEAN drifted apart but 'look east policy' sought to reconnect India economically to this region. As India's economic reforms unfolded, there was no let up in the pace of diplomacy towards the region. It has seen steady gains. Neither the Indian Nuclear test of 1998 nor the economic crisis in East Asia in the 1990s came in the way of rapid expansion of India's relationship with region. The close cooperative and multifaceted partnership which India- ASEAN have fostered encompassing the political, security, economic, scientific and technological, human resource development, social, cultural and other areas of mutual interest, now provides a solid foundation for taking this partnership to build up a solid ground for mutual interactions in the years to come.[31] India became a sectoral dialogue partner with ASEAN in 1993.[32] In recent years this partnership has been further reinforced by regional co-operation. It found expression in the creation of multilateral grouping such as BMSTEC (The Bangladesh, India, Myanmar, Sri Lanka, Thailand Economic cooperation) and ARF. The broad vistas of gainful synergy in India-South East Asia relationship would prove quite helpful to Indian diplomacy to counterbalance China in this region.

In view of the changing geopolitics in the aftermath of the cold war India has tried to engage Myanmar also along with the South East Asian countries. It is certainly a strategic gain for India. The main driving force behind India's Myanmar policy is to improve trade and commerce and to stimulate economic growth in the North Eastern states, combat drug trafficking from the notorious golden triangle.[33] Region and to secure support of Myanmar in checking insurgency in the North Eastern segment of the country. Besides it, in view of the growing Chinese influence in this area and her consistent quest for access to the Indian Ocean, India could no longer afford to ignore Myanmar in the conduct of her foreign policy. Apart from strategic benefits there is tremendous potential for mutually beneficial economic ties. Expanding bilateral trade between the two countries from $ 87.4 million in 1990-91 to $ 323.43 million in 2001-02 buttresses this fact.[34] In the Post-Cold War period another area which drew the attention of the world community for being the hub of global terrorism was Afghanistan and Central Asia which are also crucial from strategic and trade point of view. In the context of the growing Chinese overtures vis-à-vis central Asia, the scenario of both confrontation and co-operation will have consequences for India. In fact, the emergence of predominantly Muslim and multiethnic and multi-religious council of Asian Republic (CAR) has added a new dimension to the geopolitics of the entire Asia. It lies at the strategic junction between the two nuclear powers Russia and China and at the interface between Russia and the Islamic world. It shares borders with Afghanistan which is a major source of spreading religious fundamentalism in the region. It may be pointed out here that so long as Kashmir remains an issue India cannot afford to ignore the developments taking place in the central Asia. Because these developments tend to impinge upon ethnic dimension of Kashmir issue. Further, given the growing interests of the USA, China and Iran in the oil and natural gas of this area[35] New Delhi must take cognizance of these developments for safeguarding her economic, security and geopolitical interests in the years to come. We must bear this fact in mind that central Asia is a transit route for the continent. Throughout history Central Asia lived in mutual economic symbiosis with neighbouring India, China, Iran and Europe. Today these old ties need to once again be strengthened as trade and economic relations between India and CAR remain the most unsatisfactory aspect of an otherwise potentially beneficial relationship.[36] Hence, there is a need on the part of New Delhi to make sustained endeavours to take advantage of her stakes in the Central Asia.

Indian has also deep rooted interest in the geopolitical dynamics of West Asia due to her need of oil from this region. Strategically also this area is crucial. Any destabilization or conflict in this area will have security implications for India therefore Indian diplomacy must be conducted with skill in view of its own large Muslim population. In economic sphere there is a need to broaden trade interactions and co-operation in joint ventures with the countries like Iran, Turkey and Egypt in the West Asia.[37]

Now, it is evident that India's unfolding geopolitical postures provide her an opportunity to come out with an independent role in the post-cold war world based on pragmatic assessment of her national interests. The foregoing account of her role as an emerging power in the post-cold war period shows that India has not only successfully engaged China and Russia, it has opened a new chapter in Indo-USA relationship and has also successfully broadened its ties with Asian states too. It has sought to co-operate with other big states of the global south in negotiating fora like the World Trade Organization (WTO). During the September 2003 WTO ministerial meeting in cancun it was instrumental in forging a block of 21 developing countries opposed to the retention of the European Union and the USA of huge farm subsidies. Led by India, Brazil and China, the so-called G-21 blocked a new round of trade liberalization on the areas of investment and competition. The feeling that worked behind the South-South solidarity aimed at deepening co-operation in multilateral trade negotiation including reforms of the UN Security Council, development, defense and technology.

Finally it may be concluded that India has made remarkable headway in evolving its foreign policy assuring its emergence as a power with effective presence at global level.[38] Now in the post-cold war period the changing matrix of power equations at global as well as regional level provide a favourable ambience for India to reassert its geopolitical position in global politics in the 21st century. However, the success of foreign policy would very much depend on adapting to changes in the wider international milieu and also how it handles the challenges of economic growth, political stability and regional peace in the 21st century.

Notes and References

1. Achin Vanaik: India's Place in the World. In Partha Chatterjee (ed.) *Wages of Freedom, Fifty Years of the Indian Nation State*, Oxford University Press, Delhi, 1998, p. 61.

2. Nehru's address to the Indian council of world Affairs in 1949 as quoted by Norman D. (ed.) Nehru, *The First Sixty Years*. Vol. 2, Bodley Head, London, 1965 Vol. 2, p. 70.

3. Stephen. P. Cohen: *India Emerging Power*, Oxford University, Press 2001, p. 272.

4. Sumit Ganguly (ed.) *India as an Emerging Power*. Frank Cass, London, 2003, pp. 1-6.
5. Quoted by A.K. Damodaran: *Beyond Autonomy: Roots of India's Foreign Policy.* Somaiya Publication, Mumbai 2000, p. 131.
6. James Chiriyankandath: Realigning India, Indian Foreign Policy after the Cold War, *Round Table*, Vol. 93, No. 374, p. 201.
7. A.K. Damodaran *op. cit.*
8. S.D. Muni: Evolution of India as the US Natural Ally, *Mainstream* Vol. XLII, No. 29, July 10, 2004. p. 14 also see Tresita 'C' Schaffer: *Rising India and U.S. Policy Option in Asia*, A Report of the center for strategic and International studies (CSIS), p. 23.
9. Bruce Vaughn: Indian Geopolitics, the United States and Evolving Correlates of Power in Asia. *Geopolitics.* Vol. 9, No. 2 Summer 2004 p. 447.
10. Stephen P. Cohen, No. 7, p. 291.
11. *The Times of India*, July 21, 2001.
12. http/www.meanndia.inspeech/2004/09/175 soi.htm.
13. Stephen P. Cohen, No. 7, p. 298.
14. *The Hindu* January 28, 2005.
15. Chris Patten: E.U. and India – Natural. Partners, *The Hindu*, February 17, 2004.
16. *The Hindu*, June 23, 2003.
17. C. Rajamohan: Needed Regional Focus, *The Hindu*, April 22, 2004.
18. *The Hindu*, June 30, 2003.
19. Swarn Singh: *China South Asia, Issues Equations and Policies*, Lancer, New Delhi, 2003 pp. 340-41
20. Hua Junduo: Partners not Rivals. *The Hindu*, Wednesday, June 11, 2003.
21. China-India bilateral trade and economic co-operation have grown rapidly in recent years. Now India is China's largest trading partner in South Asia. The two way trade reached $ 4.946 billion in 2002 up to 37 per cent from the previous year. Wen Jiabao. We will never seek hegeomony, *The Hindu*, June 24, 2003.
22. V.P. Dutt: It is time for *Detenle* with China, *The Hindustan Times*, Lucknow, June 22, 2003.

23. Nancy Jetly: *India's Foreign Policy, Challenges and Prospects*, Vikas Publishing House, New Delhi, 1999, p. 19.
24. *Ibid*, p. 20.
25. C. Rajamohan: Needed a Regional Focus, *The Hindu*, April 22, 2004.
26. *The Hindu*, April 14, 2004 and *The Hindu*, February 2, 2005.
27. *The Hindu*, October 23, 2003.
28. C.B. Muthamma: Control the Hostility graph in South Asia, *South Asian Politics*, Vol. 2, No.1 May 2003, p. 14.
29. Wasbir Hussain: Dealing with Neighbours, *The Hindu*, May 20, 2003.
30. A. Laksmana Chetty: Evolving India-South East Asia partnership in the Post-Cold War era. *Dialogue*, Vol. 5, No. 1, July-September 2003 p. 132.
31. C. Raja Mohan: Look East Policy Phase Two, *The Hindu*, October 9, 2003.
32. Kripa Sridharan: Regional Perception of India and ASEAN in Frederic Grare and Amitabh Matto (ed.) *India and ASEAN*, Manohar, New Delhi 2001, pp. 72-75 also see *The Hindu*, November 11, 2004.
33. Golden Triangle signifies Myanmar's Geostrategic location by the trijunction of East, South East Asia and South Asia.
34. Udai Bhanu Singh: Perspective on Myanmar-India Relations, *Dialogue*, Vol. 5, No. 3, January-March 2004, p. 113.
35. Meena Singh Roy: India's Interest in Central Asia, *Strategic Analysis*, Vol. 24, No. 12, March 2001, p. 2275.
36. *Ibid.*, p. 228.
37. Nancy Jetly-No. 23, p. 23.
38. Chiryankandath No. 6, pp. 199-211.

5

Visualising New Dynamics of Challenges to India's Foreign Policy

I.D. Mishra

Promoting national interest is the basic objective of foreign policy. It carries with it the interest of the nation and works for it. From this perspective national interests projecting India as a nation are to be worked out, for their protection and promotion. Protection from within as well as from outside is then the crucial problem for the State and its interests. As these challenges have tendency to weaken the state structure and its identity, the question is what are those challenges and how should they be worked out? It puts forth two basic questions, first, what are the nature of challenges and second, how to resolve them? An overall implication is that foreign policy cannot escape these challenges.

An analysis of the foreign policy practice and its discourse may help us raise such questions which have been sidelined so far. Foreign Policy in the centre of discourse rests upon the state and its elements. It is this basic presumption which appears to have been missing in foreign policy discourse. The state engages itself through its foreign policy in bilateral and multilateral relations which fall within the jurisdictions of international relations and international politics respectively. Since the bilateral relations have prevailed over multi-lateral relations in India's foreign policy, it has resulted into imbalance performance, unsuitable to global politics in the era of globalization. This emerging challenge to India's foreign policy needs to be assessd for reducing the space of imbalance as far as possible between the two broad areas of its performance.

The above discourse may be engaged from different angles. We are talking about foreign policy as an isolated issue. But treating it as an isolated issue is a mistake, as it gives way to many errors responsible for challenges to foreign policy. Foreign policy is a composite whole signifying the whole state-reflecting its constituents and components, problems and prospects, aspirations and ambitions, and process towards resolutions and achievements. Thus foreign policy corresponds to state and nothing else. The state in simple terminology consists of four elements-territory, population, government and sovereignty. Each of these is a significant sub-structure of state system and hence, needs to be explained from the angle of foreign policy system.

Territory as the crucial factor in the state formation is highly vulnerable for interference. Most of the foreign relations including India's have moved around this factor. Territorial interference, an issue of grave concern for India's foreign policy ever since independence has been streamlined through out the course of foreign policy. Aggressions in the past by neighbour countries over Indian territories, have led India to counteract it possibly through negotiations and peaceful means, albeit diversion of its policy and energy to strengthen it by physical force of armanents and nuclear weapons are also on record. Apparently the nature of our bilateral relations with neighbours has been widely determined by territorial issues rather than the other important factors like population. It is why the disputes over boundaries or lands either with China or Pakistan have exclusively been the factors of concern in our foreign policy. This is the beginning of the imbalances in foreign policy sector overlooking the rest of the three elements of the state.

The question at our hands is why not the foreign policy rests on population centre. Population as the most crucial and lively element of the state structure is itself a major objective. Hence, the place of population in the foreign policy making process below than the rank it desrves could affect its over all performance. At least China's foreign policy with ideological orientation is in better assertive position than India and Pakistan. Foreign policy guided by ideology has been watchful in protecting its territory than those with uncertain ideological securities. The Chinese ideology doew not allow any alien ideological intervention. It restricts the options for any alternative system of ideology and thus protects the ideological think tank from invasion. Its area of action within the whole of state territory keeps the ideological plus territorial sovereignty intact. Since her ideology itself is a system of social economic objectives based on Marx-Mao doctrine, criticism against ideological sovereignty in its foreign policy sector is less heard of from the inner Chinese social system.

The case of India is a different one. Since it has an ideology without any fixed centre, it is much more flexible in its behaviour than that of the Chinese ideology. Liberal ideology, with supporting freedom, free economy and democracy allows interference to itself. The Indian ideology having adopted the above brand is too flexible to keep it intact as Chinese one. Hence, the problem before the foreign policy is how to keep the ideological sovereignty intact so that it could be made effective and assertive. Since independence, its foreign policy was much more activated on the problem of territorial security than the problem of its population and social security at large. Although the situational compulsion behind such activation could have been the strong reason in the past, but its continuity along with the previous lines may not be in the long interests of the state. Foreign policy has to emphasise in its curriculum the more urging centre rather than sticking to conventional annoying issues. It has to be activated for people's cause in global perspective, at least within the range of multilateral relations.

But arguing other way leads towards another emerging challenge. There are global risk factors which are ahead of national security systems therefore, the foreign policy guaranteeing security cannot escape such risks. We have opened our risks to global risks for elusive global security. Since the guarantor of global security is not the total community of states within global perspective, but a small organised groups of state and its leaders, global security steers back to state security and overpowers it and all its components. Thus how to reset national security within global security is indeed a perplexing task before foreign policy system.

The need is therefore to review India's foreign policy from angles different from the previous and traditional one. It is this pretext that the state and its constituents have figured throughout the present discourse. While framing the foreign policy, population as the top priority factor be necessarily explored about its basic structure in terms of basic needs and demands. Giving due consideration to it would be an eye opener in the foreign policy making sectors that crucial concerns remain neglected or remain little concerned. For utilization of knowledge, labour and skill of the total popultion, elevating their human dignity and status, their satisfaction is a great concern we are fighting for. Capability development is not the monopoly of elite class, nor the system should be as such to encourage the opportunity only for the elite class. Otherwise the system becomes prey to faulty procedure to narrow down the opportunities for the deprived population. India has two sides of this problem. First, the oppotunities remain contained to elite class, which in turn represents the whole mass. Opportunities cannot be represented either by the same group or by the other rather it should be made accessible to every one. This is rising problem on both hands creating insecurities and dis-advantages among the required organised mass structure for the whole state. The jobless mass looses its confidence, faith in the state existence and its governance. Therefore, seeking co-operation from other states capable of providing assistance to create conditions for opportunities accessible to every Indian be underlined as emerging areas in foreign policy. The basic support to population such as fooding, clothing, shelter, health and education and overall securities be guaranted either through indiginous resources or through resources driving from other states. These emerging challenges from population sector have high intake of issues influencing the state system including the foreign policy process.

'Government' is another important element of state. It implements constitution, enacts and executs Laws. Its duty as implementor of the constitution has wide notion. The constitution in totality including its ambitions and aspirations is to be realized through proper implementation. It means that the Government bears an obligation on its part to be fulfilled without giving any space for contrary conditions. The government frames the foreign policy and tries to pursue it in its best possible manner. But its best possible performance in foreign policy sector depends on its stability. The stability depends on its overwhelming majority and support. In the era of Coalition Polities, the stability is clubbed with risk of the parties in Coalition Government. This situation gives rise to instability factor affecting the durability of government. Thus a weak government cannot be assertive in foreign policy as the government of the single majority Party government can do. For example, question of India's relation with Pakistan, Bangladesh, China, US and others, the Government has been trapped rather in more ticklish problems than it should have the capacity to mould the House towards a definite approach to them. This is why the collective body of the parliament is found divided in its approach on many occasions and the parties in opposition always awaiting the situations for the collapse of government on any account including the foreign policy issue. The efficiency of foreign policy performance is highly affected in such situation.

The preceding decade in coaltion politics era had such condition as challenges to India's foreign policy. Hence, it is apprehended that the coalition government in Parliamentary system is generally a non-sustainable ground for strong leadership in all matters including the foreign policy issues. This has affected the leadership capacity and its assertiveness in foreign policy sector. Hence, the question is how to avert, or at least minimise the challenge. One alternative could be to strengthen the leadership for strengthening foreign policy. First, people's cause should be brought to the centre of foreign policy in governing international and diplomatic relations. Secondly, people's concern of countries in bilateral relations be adequately and properly explored, understood and represented. The task before the foreign policy is to make it possible and convenient to create situations for dialogues between peoples by means of ascertaining effective framework. Such peoples, factor may provide strength to leadership and their assertiveness to promote people's interest in foreign policy.

Thus, it gives strength to the argument that effective foreign policy depends on effective leadership, supported by the majority party in the Parliament. Its effectiveness depends on its dynamism and assertiveness in relation to its commitment to carry out the constitution. Foreign Policy system, therefore, requires constitutional commitment as well as vision to readjust itself in the changing dynamic by driving support to national interest.

The fourth, essential element of state is Government. In this era of globalization, the notion of state sovereignty is in question. Free market economy and globalization have opened the avenues for instrusion in the state process. State's inability to cope with the rising demands especially that of economic nature is becoming unavoidable factor for interference. No boundary as such exists to stop the global process from entering the state jurisdictions in one way or the other. This new dynamic of challenges to India's foreign policy stands by and therefore needs strengthening its boundary of sovereignty by self-reliance approach.

Presuming India, therefore, a prospective partner in global politics is desired to redesign the preamble of its foreign policy to be introduced to the community of nations. This preamble should highlight the people's analogous concern over the globe at large. Their voices should make a chorus of the common cause.

To attain this objective nation's participation in the common international interest programme needs to be ensured through effective foreign policy. It raises then, a most important point, i.e. how to bring India close to its interests and make them familiar to the world at large, for support and solution. Two points emerge in this context. First, what is that national interest that India should be close to it. Second, how to make them familiar to the world at large so that the foreign policy could inculcate interest in external powers for external support and help. Against the above backdrop the basic national problem India is facing is the increasing population with paucity of meaningful resources, which has been resulting in to terse situation for India to emrege as self sufficient nation. Thus, the two problems of national interests are crucial for exploring the new dynamics of challenges to India's foreign policy. First, the inproportionate population growth is causing the multifacted problems in terms of its density, resources, ethnicity, faith and religion, caste and sex and in return is inbreeding conflicts within the national interests. Second, population on these lines gives space to the vulnerable external problems. Terrorism and external intervention could be well illustrated to defend the above points. What is in between these problematics, is first, the question of human security. This question involves a very generic issue in its centre. It is right to life demanding adequate resources and opportunities for self exploration, aggrandizement and development leading to self satisfaction and happiness. This, however, is subject to satisfaction and happiness of the whole nation. Thus, satisfaction and happiness both individual and national in their complete harmony underlie all states activities and policy formulation.

Satisfaction and happiness are concerned with individual, society, nation and the world at large. The challenge to foreign policy is how to evlove its effectiveness in visualizing the inherent and forthcoming problem.

Hence, the above aspects of foreign policy involves three basic questions of human security, sustainable development and good governance. These are equally important as they are interrelated to each other. However, of all the three, human security is more important, and hence, an objective of the whole governance either political and administrative, or national and foreign which need to be achieved through sustainable development and good governance. Our foreign policy modality, due to its lapses on these accounts has not so far brought above points to its centre. Hence a modest attempt to highlight these issues have been made from foreign policy perspective.

Sustainable development and 'good governance' preferably used in context of eco-system based development and good governance includes both the managerial and administrative aspects of governance under the tutelage of political governance. But the question is what is to be managed and administered and how to be managed and administered. The key issue of political governance is human security and the content of human security covers broad areas that provide sustenance to all aspects, concerned with human life. 'Safe human' is the central point of these concerns. It become sustainable only when it is inter-linked with 'capable human'. The 'safety' and 'capability' are to be made workable. It is the concern of the foreign policy to see what aspects of safety are required to be included in foreign policy agenda. One thing is obvious from the above statement that 'workable safety' results into 'workable capacity'. Both paradigms of workable safety, and workable capacity help define the human security'.

'Sustainable development' provides protection to 'safe and capable human'. It encourages to enhance human capacities through providing workability of individuals for self reliance, self-development and happiness in complete harmony with the nature and complete whole. Good governance in the present refers to developing the capability, skill and technique to manage the problems and converge them into suitable conditions for sustainable development. 'Goodness' is ethical confined to moral human behaviour. Principles of moral behaviour have basis in Nature and complete whole. This system of relationship leading to the whole decides the principles of morality that binds the units and individual together for their full realization. These sub-categories of whole may be thus, for example, the social whole, Political whole or even greater sub-category such as the whole of the life of world.

In short, to sum up the challenges to India's foreign policy may be visualized from the above perspective of human security, sustainable development and good governance. Searching more questions in these areas may need appropriate foreign policy to answer them. It is these aspects of national interests which need protection and promotion. Placement of these issues in foreign policy sector may reduce bilateral tensions and may drive global support and sympathy, the sympathy and support of the whole mankind to such issues irrespective of the barriers–racial, ethnic, territorial, ideological and others.

SECTION-II

PROBLEMS

6

Indo-US Partnership in the Post-Cold War Period: Strategies and Constraints

M.T. Desai

The end of cold war created conceptual and actual vacuum for policy markers as well as intellectuals regarding formulation of foreign policy, both in US and India. Much depended on the perception about what the world looked like in the Post-Cold War period and whether the new world offered more opportunities or imposed more constraints and also what were the goals that each sought to achieve from and in relation to other and what strategies could be adopted to achieve these goals.

The similarity or difference in worldview of policy makers in the two countries could help create harmony or result in discord. What was the world map alike in Post-Cold War period? A lot of substantial the oretical work has come out in US regarding nature of Post-Cold War period, although not much has been done in India. Different alternative models have been presented in US. Fukuyama talked of End of History? End of communism would result in stable world of democratic states and fault line would fall between democratic and non-democratic states. Huntington talked of coming clash of civilizations where US and Europe would join hands together. Kennedy and Kaplan felt that fault line would fall between developed and developing countries. Thomas Friedmann felt that the new world order would present countries which favoured globalization and those resisting globalization. Mearsheimer felt that Post-Cold War period would result in instability, again a result of multipolarity of Pre-Second War period. Charles Kupchan felt that all these maps of different world order are a product of single fundam ental feature of world. America's preponderance of power, where the US happens to be the only pole in the world. According to Kupchan, all the models capture an element of current international system but 'miss the mark when identifying the key fault line of future'.[1]

Unipolarity is the super structure and determines primary forces that shape the international system. When the structure itself determines stability and dampens competition, secondary forces do so as well. For example forces like globalization, humanitarian intervention, war against terror are US led or US encouraged efforts or acceleration has taken place because of US Kupchan feels that unipolarity is not likely to last for long. According to him the main challenge 'is to bring together an increasingly divided world'. America may be interested in preserving unipolarity but would not be able to do so. Its ability to project power on a permanent basis suffers from certain limitations: Its willingness to pay the price, domestic opposition to international involvement, ability to manage crisis in different situations; and nationalistic resistance against Americanism in different forms and most important resistance to preponderance of American power itself, which may express itself in the form of local discontents.

Broadly speaking US had two strategies open in the Post-Cold War period for achievement of its goals (a) to act unilaterally (b) (1) to act in a genuine multilateral way with collective decision making or (2) at least taking assistance of others. One wonders whether (b) (1) would be possible. The real option today is between (a) and (b) (2). That is the issue in present presidential election. It is difficult to have (b) (2) without (b) (1).

Where does India figure in it? During Cold War the US and India mostly turned out to be on the opposite sides. India did not share the anti-communist or anti-Soviet worldview of the US, which distrusted India's policy of non-alignment because of the suspicion that it was pro-Soviet. The American critics had its counter parts in India as well. US friendship with Pakistan and then with China did not improve matters. India became a champion of 'anti-Superpowerism, and advocate of "Third Worldism" anti-west paranoia' and often 'anti-Americanism' India put faith in multilateralism and NAM. Its preference for Socialistic Model of Society and state control of economy did not create a stable basis for Indo-US economic cooperation.

End of Cold War changed many things and created many options for policy makers in terms of foreign policy in a unipolar world. C. Raja Mohan refers to several options, which were reflected in Indian policy during 1990s.[2] The options included bandwagoning with US; active pursuit of multipolar world; making NAM more relevant to new times and building a new partnership with US as part of multi-directional engagement of major powers. The last option was preferred (of course dominant emphasis was on engagement with US). This resulted even in talk of US and India becoming 'natural allies.' The close association between India and US cannot be attributed entirely to the end of Cold War. The 1980s itself reflected a realistic Indian foreign policy. India was seen as an important market even before end of Cold War, which accelerated this process. Changes in India's economic policy were partly necessitated by domestic needs but reflected pressures of US dominated international financial institutions. S.D. Muni gives credit for positive changes in Indo-US relations to India's post-1998 nuclear status and compulsions of 9/11.[3] He also raises the important issue of change at 'whose initiative?' He suggests that dynamics of power was responsible. One can give credit to BJP elite for bringing about changes. Future of Indo-US relations under new dispensation will provide some clues regarding relative merits of factors responsible for change in Indo-US relations. An important issue is how much benefit and costs has India received in this new phase of Indo-US relations? How much of it could be attributed to the policy of ruling elite and how much to the structural constraints and opportunities is also a matter of debate.

Several areas of cooperation or potential areas have been mentioned in Indo-US relations. How much has been achieved in these areas and to India's benefit is a matter of discussion. Indian foreign policy has definitely become more pragmatic and old brand of anti-Americanism is no anvil. However, it has not been possible to embrace US whole-heartedly and for the good. In fact preventing the world domination by a single power has become one of the major themes of India's foreign policy. On its own part India has always wanted a share in international governance. The 1990s has resulted in active efforts by India for a permanent membership of Security Council of UN. Negatively, India has resisted efforts by great powers to prevent it from acquiring components of great power. On the contrary even in the Post-Cold War period, a key feature of US grand strategy has remained 'containment of second tier of major powers, existing or aspiration, unless they are willing to bandwagon with the US as subordinate allies.[4]

The record of cooperation in different areas in Indo-US cooperation has not been very encouraging. Democracy has been mentioned as an area of cooperation, which could not only bring two countries together but together, they could spread the cause of democracy. As Robert Hathway has said, "The two countries appear to have different ideas on what their shared allegiance to democracy means."[5] India may attach importance to democracy but would loath to spread the cause of democracy in other countries. It would consider, form of government, as an internal affair of a country. However, India has favoured democratization of international relations. It does not favour control of world policy by one or a few. But when at community of democracies in Warsaw in July 2003, Washington lobbied to show a videotaped message from Burma's opposition leader Aung San Suu Kji, India expressed its opposition because it was cultivating better ties with military junta. May be India became cautious after Nehru's criticism of Nepali Monarch's dismissal of elected government of Koirala which spoiled Indo-Nepal relations considerably. Thus democracy can become a cementing factor, if other factors are also working in that direction.

Strengthening of economic cooperation is mentioned as potentially a very important bond in improvement of Indo-US relations. In the immediate aftermath of the end of Cold War, India was mentioned as one of the ten important emerging markets. However, it is also an area, where progress has been least satisfactory.[6] While the US is still India's largest trading partner and source of foreign investment, two way trade between two countries still represent less than 1 per cent of total US commerce. Trade between India and US in 2002 totaled $ 14.40 billion, but that between China and US was $ 116.20 billion. Americans feel that pace of India's economic reforms is slow. Accordingly to a widely noted 2001 Index of Economic Freedom, India ranks 133 in the list of 155 countries surveyed. US exports to India grew only by $ 1.2 billion in 1990s. Even a modest increase in economic cooperation could not become a catalytic agent for substantial relationship between India and US. Two countries have different views on issues like North-South relationship and priorities of World Trade Organization. US trade representative Robert Zoellick publicly stated that India was a "troublesome country in building a consensus for new international trade negotiations."

Events of 9/11 seemed to inject new substantive content in Indo- US relations. The euphoria that followed Bush's declarations of Global War on Terrorism has lost momentum. Even in US there has been no agreement on nature of threat and solution of problem. As far as India is concerned it believes that global war must be truly global and that US cannot have partnership with others only for protecting US interests. Both have complaints against each other, for not doing enough about fighting terrorism. US feels that India's main focus has become cross-border terrorism in Kashmir and that it is pressurizing Pakistan, though it cannot forsake Pakistan which is useful to it in its battle against terrorism. US also feel that India should appreciate that its war in Afghanistan has created better environment (strategic) for India. One wonders whether even India would be interested in fighting a global war on terrorism except in a limited way. Partly it is also because although terrorism poses a collective threat, terrorists target individual countries.

The active role the Indian community in US has started playing in US politics has created expectations that it can tilt US towards India. Although the community has played a positive role, it has not shown political maturity on certain occasions.[7] To take an example, some community activities berated several of allies on capitol hill for including Pakistan in a South Asian fact finding trip. It has also not learnt to demand political accountability. For example some members of Congress promised economic aid at the time of earthquake in Gujarat in 2001 and later on voted against economic aid.

The Post-Cold War period has witnessed improvement of military relations. This has been mainly in the field of intelligence sharing, joint military exercises and cooperation in space. But sale of military technology and technology with a duel use by the US has been problematic. Even recent agreement has been described as being doubtful. Some opposition parties have criticized military cooperation with the US in the post-Cold War period. Cooperation in the field of civilian nuclear technology has also had many irritants. Possible use of India card against China has been often mentioned. Cold War provided examples of Indo-US cooperation for this objective. Anxiety about China taking place of Russia has also strengthened this kind of speculation. But China is the place for US investment. Ever since US established relations with China, there is more talk of Engagement of China, rather than its containment. India also does not feel any imminent threat from China. Moreover, now India is also militarily more confident and nuclear. Its relations with China has improved, the border remains frozen and if China pursues a moderate course, New Delhi has no incentive to become a US a card for Containment of China.

This overview of issue wise cooperation between India and US does not give a very optimistic picture. There are problem areas in all spheres. Besides, India cannot become what UK and Israel are to the US. Moreover, position of government trying to toe the US line would be far more difficult in India. Further, there is not enough convergence of interests. The values of two have been different. During Cold War the strategic interests of containing Soviet Union governed the US policy more and India favoured the opposition to Colonialism and Neo-Colonialism, Fabian Socialism, Group of 77, NIEO, NAM. Post-Cold War period has been accompanied by ideology of globalization in various spheres. The US has favoured it in economic, cultural and political sphere. Since the desire for markets, avenues for capital investment have guided the US policy therefore it has advocated free trade. It has also advocated democratization abroad, humanitarian and military intervention. In practice this has resulted in violation of Westphalia system. However, its national interests have tempered the advocacy of ideology. There it has conveniently favoured Westphalia system. India on the other hand has favoured Westphalia system consistently with few exceptions. India does not favour international actions unless authorized by properly constituted authority. It believes in sanctity of Article 27 of UN charter (domestic jurisdiction). The end of Cold War has not changed India's adherence to this ideology.

Close Indo-US relations cannot come without a price. US pressure on Narashima Rao's government resulted in postponement of nuclear test. US pressurized India to not to cross the line of actual control in Kargil War and it also prevented 'Operation Parakram' from leading to all out war. It is also hoped that the US will pressurize Pakistan to stop cross border terrorism. The paper has discussed various strategies open to the foreign policy makers of India in the post-Cold War period, the possibility of Indo-US partnership, the various areas in which the Indo-US cooperation is possible and also constraints in the cooperation.

Notes and References

1. Charles A. Kupchan: *The End of the American Era*, Alfred A. Knopf, New York, 2003, p. 57.
2. C. Raja Mohan: *Crossing the Rubicon: The Shaping of India's New Foreign Policy*, Viking, 2003, p. 49.
3. "S.D. Muni: Evolution of India as the US Natural Ally", *Mainstream*, July 10, 2004. p. 14.
4. Baldev Raj Nayar and T.V. Paul: *India in the World Order: Searching for Major Power Status*. Cambridge University Press, 2003.
5. Robert Hathway: The US-India Courtship in Sumit Ganguly (ed.) *India as an Emerging Power*, Frank Cass, London, 2003, p. 25.
6. Robert Blackwill: US-India Economic Relations, The Mission Piece,

An Address to the Federation India Chamber of Commerce and Industry, p. 3.

7. Robert Hathway: *op. cit.*, p. 27.

7

Divergence and Convergence within US Administration: Its Impact on National Security of India

S.J.R. Bilgrami

The increasing domination and control of the lone superpower, the United States of America, develops the temptation to take arbitrary action in the name of international community. The policies, overloaded with the adjective 'humanitarian' cannot automatically become the echo of international community to the extent of justifying unilateral intervention on its behalf as if carrying the spirit of Rousseau's "General Will'. Such arbitrary and selective character of policies and actions serve more the strategic interests of major powers than contribute to the stability and the national security of developing nations. Such arbitrary actions manifest duality of divergence and convergence within the US administration, which has had its implications for the security arrangement of the countries like India, desirous of establishing cordial or expanding relations with the USA.

Divergence and Convergence

There is an inherent contradiction of divergence and convergence within the US administration, which creates added difficulties for India (which enjoys reciprocal relationship) of managing her national security besides dealing with its varied ingredients. The examples of such contradictions are as follows:

In the wake of nuclear tests, conducted by India and Pakistan in 1998, the USA imposed sanctions on both the countries. Two extreme viewpoints emerged in the US administration. Gilman Benjamin, Chairman of the House of International Committee, said: "The strongest possible deterrents, short of military action, are needed in South Asia to ensure against any move from weapon testing to weapon development". But Stuart E. Eizenstat, Under Secretary of State for Economic Business and Agricultural Affairs, pointed out: "Sanctions are not a panacea and they are not cost free".

Undeterred by frequency and volume of sanctions and few supporters among its allies, the USA did impose costly unilateral economic sanctions on India and Pakistan. Senator Connie Mack exposed the 'duality' of the US policy on the floor of the Senate on July 16, 1998 by observing "It is a strange logic behind rewarding inappropriate actions by the Chinese Communist party leaders while simultaneously sanctioning the democratic leaders in India. There is something inherently wrong with sanctioning a democracy legally acting in its perceived national interests while rewarding a single party communist state which threatens regional security in violation of international law". He further stated: "India did not sign NPT, not only because it was discriminatory, but also the treaty meant that China, the internally oppressive and undemocratic, occupying force on India's border, would be permitted to have nuclear weapons whereas India, fearful and insecure, would be denied to such weapons". Senator Mack also pointed out that India had never been a proliferator of nuclear weapons and missiles, but China, a nuclear power, had proliferated time and again. In fact some estimates indicated that 90 per cent of China's sales of weapons went to states bordering India and the Chinese weapons technologies to Pakistan being of particular concern. Despite the record, India has been denied the same nuclear and technical cooperation, which the US has accorded to China. India and China both have commercial electricity needs that are among the largest in the world. The US signed a nuclear cooperation agreement with China but it continues to maintain restrictions on nuclear power agreements with India. Such 'Duel-Containment' and 'Duel Balancing' manifest in respect to Iran and Iraq what we see in respect to India and Pakistan.

While throwing weight around to a greater degree, see the element of convergence in the statement of Colin Powell before the Senate for hearing on his nomination as secretary of state: "There were too many of them (sanctions). They often did not work and what was more, they gave America a bad name. The repeated use of sanctions as a foreign policy weapons shows a degree of American hubris and arrogance that may not serve our interest all that well". Christina Rocca, Assistant Secretary of State, in charge of South Asian Affairs, Senator Robert Blackwill, and the Foreign Relations Committee Chairman Joseph Biden all expressed their opinion that sanctions do not constitute a viable strategy in pursuing America's non-proliferation goal. These restrictions have outlived their usefulness and are no longer in the interests of the US.

Despite such realization, between 1992 and 1996, the United States imposed or threatened economic sanctions sixty times against thirty-five different countries, affecting 42 per cent of the world's population. These sanctions are estimated to expect an annual cost of close to $20 billion in lost exports. This shows not only the frequency but also the centrality of military or economic intervention as the core of US foreign policy. Whether the state of divergence or convergence, the accustomed imperialist attitude persists. For instance the Wall Street Journal, the spokes media for the US multinationals, that control the US government agenda, headlines: "US hits India and Pakistan with sanctions". Note the master-slave language of 'hits' and 'sanctions'. Again "the senate voted unanimously to exempt agricultural products from US economic sanctions aimed at punishing Pakistan and India". What an oxymoron! Senate is seeking trade from those to be punished. In the same way see the 'patronizing' and 'offensive' coverage by CNN and BBC on Washington's decision to lift sanctions: "President has 'rewarded' India for its contribution to the fight against terrorism". The phrase 'sanction', whether inflicted or lifted (divergence or convergence), conveys not only the imperialist attitude but also hopes to produce the myth of US 'Rights' and 'Means' to punish or reward others. It is a myth because USA has neither right nor the means to punish or even to reward, which, given with political expediency, becomes, ultimately, a bribe. It is this situation of divergence and convergence, which causes difficulties for countries, seeking cooperation with the USA, in managing their national security. But before discussing the impact, the 'National Security Arrangement' is to be elaborated.

National Security Arrangement

National security covers, broadly, two aspects: Multi-dimensionality and Institutional arrangement.

(1) **Multi-dimensionality**: National security is not a unidimensional phenomenon dealing only with military or defense matters. It has multi-dimensional facets related to international governments, food security, social cohesion and energy security. The focus, however, in this paper is on the defense, military and political dimensions of security. The significant ingredients, affecting the international security situation have been the following:

The first consideration of any nation's security arrangement is the fact that the US has consolidated itself as the most powerful nation-state and has declared its intention to retain this position of influence in all dimensions of global relations. The post 9\11 campaign of the US is though global but has been selective, focused on specific US concerns and not fully responsive to India's concerns. The new world economic order sought to be established under the WTO regime has not been successful because the broad commitments on the basis of which India and other developing countries adhered to the WTO have been modified to the disadvantage of developing countries. New concepts in inter-state equations–'regime change', 'punitive and pre-emptive peace making', 'containment of rogue states have eroded the sovereignty, security and the principle of non-interference in the internal affairs of individual countries. The insistences of legally recognized nuclear weapon states on retaining their WMDs and not agreeing to structure a time-bound programme for non-discriminatory elimination of WMDs have resulted in the horizontal proliferation of such weapons. Instead of structuring international arrangements for equitable utilization of the world's energy and natural resources, the major powers seem to be attempting to gain privileged utilization of resources. The security environment in India's immediate neighbourhood remains tense because of terrorism, political uncertainties in Iraq and Afghanistan, and the threat of religious extremism. Transfer of technologies and development inputs like investment are being subjected to political and security conditions stipulated by major world powers. The role and effectiveness of UN and its agencies stand marginalized.

(2) **The Institutional Arrangement**: The institutional arrangement rather than ad hoc dealing is a pre-requisite for the effective coordination among all the ingredients of the national security system. The institutional arrangement, set up by the government, is a four-tier system: Cabinet Committee on National Security (CCNS); the Strategic Policy Group (SPG); the National Security Advisory Board (NSAB); National Security Advisor (NSA). These institutional arrangements have not been functional. The recommendations made by various experts groups after the Kargil conflict has still not been implemented despite the passage of four years.

This confirms the fact that the national security cannot be viewed through the narrow prism of purely military context. It has political, economic, social and developmental dimensions. It is necessary to formulate and implement a comprehensive multi-dimensional national security policy, which will cover vital aspects of energy security, food security, good governance and countering the centrifugal trends affecting the country. The institutional arrangements made by the government have been cosmetic. In substance, national security is not underpinned by systematic institutional arrangements. The National Security Council (NSC) established in 1999, has not functioned with institutional cohesion.

The NDA government in its resolution of April 16, 1999 spelt out the role of the NSC by emphasizing that "The central government recognizes that national security management requires integrated thinking and coordinated application of the political, military, diplomatic, scientific and technological resources of the state to protect and promote national security goals and objectives. National security in the context of nation needs to be viewed in terms of internal security, economic security, technological strength and foreign policy. The role of the council is to advise the central government on the said matters". Seven broad areas were identified for the council to deal with: (i) external security, (ii) security threats involving nuclear energy, space and high-technology, (iii) trends in the world economy and economic security threats in the areas of energy, foreign trade, food, finance and ecology, (iv) internal security including counter-insurgency, counter-terrorism and counter-intelligence, (v) pattern of alienation emerging in the country, specially those with a social, communal or regional dimension, (vi) security threats posed by trans-border crimes such as smuggling and traffic in arms, drugs and narcotics, and (vii) coordination in intelligence collection and tasking of intelligence agencies so as to ensure that intelligence is focused on areas of concern for the nation.

After defining and elaborating its role, the NSC was unable to hold even a single meeting, at least to sort out procedural issues. Its basic role, national security management, requires an assessment of future threats and challenges to our national security in each of the areas and detailed planning to maximize our advantages and to limit damage to our interests in each of these areas. The NDA government never did such assessment of security management. It did not think highly about the need for assessments. It simply restructured the Joint Intelligence Committee (JIC) and renamed as NSC Secretariat (NSCS). The gazette notification said the erstwhile function of JIC relating to intelligence, analysis and assessment should continue to be performed by the NSCS. The result of avoiding the autonomy of assessment process is that every cabinet minister, high official, both civil and military, comes out with their own individual assessments on cross-border infiltration and increase or decrease in terrorist violence, often contradicting each other. Different ministers identify different countries as adversaries and friends. But assessments are highly professional exercises in which intelligence from different sources and even publicly available information are evaluated carefully to arrive at a balanced judgement.

It was realized that it was not the intelligence failure but failure in intelligence assessment and which led to the creation of Joint Intelligence Committee. But over a period of time this assessment body lost its effectiveness because intelligence agencies ignored the assessment body because in the administrative culture, it is presumed all wisdom is concentrated in the governmental bureaucracy. The Kargil Committee had suggested separating the two posts of principal secretary to prime minister and national security advisor. But Prime Minister Atal Bihari Bajpayee retained both the post combined because he did not want to face two contradictory advices and then having to make up his own mind. That is why NSC got stuck at the beginning.

During NDA government, important national security decisions had been taken by the prime minister and his principal secretary in consultations with the deputy PM without utilizing the CCNS, the SPG and officials of the NSAB. There had neither been systematic inter action between the SPG and the NSAB, nor any regular inter action between the NSA and the NSAB. It is necessary to appoint a separate NSA. The present arrangement of the principal secretary to the PM functioning, also as the NSA should be discontinued. Regular meetings of the CCNS should be institutionalized. It should be ensured that there should be institutional interaction between the NSA, the SPG and the NSAB. Necessary connectivity between the intelligence agencies of the government and the NSAB should be ensured. The new Government has recently reconstituted NSAB, which advises National Security Council (NSC). Modernization of the functional capacities of the intelligence agencies with appropriate modern technology should be ensured. The recommendations made by the expert group to reform the intelligence agencies post-Kargil, which have been hanging fire for the last four years – should be speedily implemented. It will ensure not only efficiency but also accountability by the intelligence agencies. It is imperative to develop national security on the basis of coherent perceptions through consistent consultations and consensus among the parties without claiming partisan credits. It should be the process of continuity, acknowledging the foundations laid in the past on which the future should be built. Only then the national security system will be able not only to resolve the multi-dimensional issues but also withstand the external pressure.

Impact

Multi-dimensionality of national security and lack of institutional connectivity has not only created mismanagement within but also sluggishness and reactive attitude. It is unable even to realize the implications of divergence and convergence behaviour consistently found within the US administration. That is why relations with the US have been characterized by submissiveness, without ensuring requisite levels of reciprocity. India's response to the challenge of terrorism directed against the country has been ineffective due to the advice given by the USA, particularly manifested in India not responding to the attack on its Parliament and the families of defence personnel.

Indian policies towards Pakistan have also been full of contradictions, ambiguities and impulsiveness. Vajpayee's 1999 visit to Lahore was followed by Kargil, which led to a break in communications with Pakistan and also the Pakistan-sponsored terrorist attack on Parliament. India's response to this attack was cosmetic and theatrical. Instead of taking effective punitive action against terrorists across the LoC, India withdrew its high commissioner from Islamabad and suspended all air and transport linkages with Pakistan. To compound the matter more India deployed more than 500,000 troops on the LoC and the border with Pakistan as an exercise in coercive diplomatic pressure. But this exercise proved futile and expensive with India nearly spending $ 8 billion. India exhausted all its national security and diplomatic options at one go without adhering to the requirements of a measured response to a critical development.

After giving unconditional support to the US without stipulating reciprocity, India complained to the US about utilizing Pakistan as a major partner in the exercise. This complaint was immature, given Pakistan's capabilities of being useful to the US. In sum the NDA government not only failed in ensuring national security but also could not combat terrorism effectively. It succumbed to the terrorists during the Kandhar hijacking. Despite the peace initiative with Pakistan, terrorism continues in J&K.

In short, national security requires the diversified linkages, the institutional connectivity and external divergence and convergence over the policy issues. It is a matter of comprehensive management, which requires a greater skill than the Commander-in-Chief of an army. No ad hoc or peace-meal arrangement is permissible while dealing with security issues. National security matters cannot be allowed to be the victims of party-rivalry. Security cannot be compromised on 'National Divergence'; it stabilizes itself on 'National Convergence; it flourishes on 'National Consensus'. It is a matter beyond partisanship. The US Senate Intelligence Committee's report on the pre-war assessment of Iraqi weapons points out, no doubt, about the failure of American Intelligence Agencies. But at the same time, this report is America's great strength. Its mature institutions are able to apply corrective measures with great rapidity. Unlike Kargil report, this was not written by former officials, but by politicians – members of the US Senate, who are present in the panel in proportion to their party strength. Yet they have come out with unanimous report that says the US intelligence, in the run up to the war, was "deeply flawed". It could not establish that Saddam Hussein had WMDs, was developing nuclear arms and that he was an imminent threat to the US. According to Senator John Rockefeller IV, the Senate would not have authorized the war with a vote of 75, "if we knew what we know today". The report rebuts the assessments of the US National Intelligence Estimate of 2002 used by the Bush administration to publicly justify the case for an invasion. The committee charged intelligence agency officials with no encouraging analysts "to challenge their assumptions, fully consider alternative arguments, accurately characterize the intelligence reporting, or counsel analysts who lost their objectivity". Though no body was directly pressurized but as Rockefeller talked that "there was an environment of intense pressure".

The US efforts came at a time when questions were being asked about the efficacy of the Indian intelligence services. Indian politicians, of all parties, could learn a lesson or two from the manner in which the US Senate dealt with the issue. There is partisanship, but in the interest of rehabilitating vital national security institutions, both sides have moderated it and shown remarkable objectivity to examine the problem and recommending solutions. The divergence\convergence is a sign of maturity as well to which nations become easily prey if they lack such maturity in security arrangement. While establishing relations with the USA, India has to assess the perfectibility, the maturity, the connectivity, the diversity, the multiplicity, and the balancing ability of her own security arrangement. For such a gigantic task, parties should learn to go above 'status-quo partition' and administration should indulge in serious 'home-work'. Only then the National Security Arrangement can withstand its dilemmas within and duality without.

Notes and References

S.J.R. Bilgrami: *The Dynamics of Sanctions in World Affairs*, Altlantic Publishers, New Delhi, 2004.

J.N. Dixit: Frayed Security Blanket, *Hindustan Times*, March 17, 2004.

K. Subrahmanyam: *Artificial Intelligence*, 71-6-04.

Hindustan Times: Editorial, July 12, 2004.

8

India and the US: Issues of Convergence and Divergence

Indu Singh

"The history of Indo-US relations beings on the eve of America's entry into World War II. Before then, the United States had scant contact with India... In the late 1930s for example, US investment in India amounted to less than $50 million, with half in missionary school, hospitals or other non-business activities."[1]

Opposition to US Sponsored Alliance System

The end of the Second World War and India becoming an independent entity did not automatically intensify the Indo-American connections, as there were few areas of overlapping national interests and scarcely any business, intellectual or cultural contacts between the two countries. However, at the time when India and Pakistan were emerging as independent nations, the United States was giving shape to the policy of containment of communism, which became the driving force of its foreign policy for the next four decades. With both, India and the United States being vast democratic nations, there was never any lack of will or effort on both sides to put their relations on an even keel, but their postures on many bilateral and international issues, were often divergent and conflicting. Given India's size, population, location and the greatness of its culture and civilization Nehru wanted India to play a major and influential role in world politics especially in Asia. Consequently, when the US, in pursuit of its policy of containment of communism, was looking for allies to be part of its alliances, India adopted the policy of non-alignment. Not only this, Nehru even castigated the cold war alliance system as antithetical to a healthy, stable world order. The US even found irritating Nehru's style of sermonizing from the pulpit and teaching the world.

The Kashmir Imbroglio

In the following months the Kashmir issue further strained their relations. Initially, the United States was reluctant to become uninvolved in the Kashmir problem and so on April 21, 1948, together with Britain adopted a resolution in the Security Council for the setting up of the UN commission for India and Pakistan (UNCIP). But Nehru was angry and hurt, as the UN had failed to condemn Pakistan as the aggressor and was treating both with parity. He was of the opinion that the US had not judged the issue on its merits and so speaking to Gordon Walker, the British Commonwealth Office Under Secretary said "the motives of the United States were to get military and economic concessions in Pakistan."[2] And when in the days to follow, the US and Pakistan drew closer and Pakistan agreed to be part of the US alliance system, the US stood solidly behind Pakistan on the Kashmir issue. To India's chagrin, it now threw its weight behind Pakistan's incessant demand for plebiscite in Kashmir at all international forums. In fact, the Pakistan factor has all along been a crucial determinant in shaping Indo-US relations.

Military Aid to Pakistan

Once Pakistan was inducted into the SEATO in 1954 and CENTO in 1955, the US followed a policy of "parity between India and Pakistan, and armed the later to teeth in order to make such a policy meaningful. This, in addition to huge and regular economic assistance to Pakistan, made it bold enough to think in terms of "parity". This and the course of relations that unfolded between the two South Asian neighbours made Pakistan an idée fixe in India's foreign policy thinking and vice versa.[3] Pakistan's armed adventures against India, starting from Kashmir in 1948 to Kargil in 1999, were possible because of US arms supply to Pakistan. And when in 1962 the Chinese attacked India though the US did respond to India's request for

possible methodologies for dealing with catastrophic terrorism... They identified five states as particularly worrisome (from which acts of catastrophic terrorism could emanate) - Iran, Syria, Afghanistan, Pakistan and Greece."[6] In June 2000, a bipartisan commission of the US on terrorism called the National Commission on terrorism, headed by Paul Bremer, former Head of the Counter terrorism Division of the State Department, submitted a report to the Congress in which it had, *inter alia*, identified the above mentioned five countries as worrisome from the point of view of catastrophic terrorism...Unfortunately the report was not acted upon by the US Administration. After September 11, there has been a complete reversal, and one finds the US viewing Pakistan not as a worrisome state, from the point of view of catastrophic terrorism, but as a frontline ally against it.[7]

The September 11, 2001 attacks against the US revealed the ghastly face of international terrorism before the entire world. It brought into focus what countries like India have been repeatedly saying that international terrorism poses a serious threat to global peace and security in general and the integrity and unity of pluralistic democracies. However, the negative aspect of post September 11 developments from India's viewpoint was that Pakistan was relegated from the position of a 'suspected state-sponsor of terrorism of yesterday' to 'a privileged ally of the Western countries today in the war against terrorism'. India believes that Pakistan's sincerity, which was instrumental in the creation of Taliban outfit, cannot be trusted in this regard. While the end of the cold war did remove a bottleneck in Indo-US relations; a Soviet tilt in India's foreign policy but the US policy vis-à-vis India with regard to Pakistan has kept the ground open for suspicion in India about Washington's sincerity in improving relations with New Delhi.

Thus, on the one hand, the United States seeks to develop relations with India and has also entered into a strategic partnership with it; however, it is also careful about developing these relations not at the expense of US-Pak relations. One may even argue that US is trying to empower Pakistan in order to position it at par with India–an attempt to prevent the rise of India as a power to reckon with and continues to help Pakistan with up gradation of its military forces.[8] The latest decision of the US to supply F-16 fighter planes to Pakistan much against the wishes of India can also be cited as an example. Though the US has claimed that it wants to see India as a major power of the region and has offered F-18 planes to India also but India is fearful that such supplies would once again increase the arms race in the sub-continent. The US has always pressurized India but not to Pakistan particularly in the field of nuclear technology. There are evidences, which give weight to the above argument. US pressures upon former Soviet Union preventing the later to assist India in acquiring nuclear technology is well-known. However the Soviet Union ignoring US pressures concluded a deal with India for transfer of cryogenic engine technology. But the Soviet disintegration and emergence of crisis-ridden Russia helped the US to get the cryo-engine deal cancelled. The US pressure was so intense that Russia succumbed to it even though Boris Yeltsin, during his India visit in January 1993 had assured New Delhi that Russia would meet its treaty obligations.

India has taken note of the double standards in US foreign policy, be it on the issue of nuclear proliferation, international terrorism, human rights, trade, environment, etc. Washington speaks about protecting human rights only till its interests are not really threatened by doing so. China is a good example of this. China has successfully frustrated US attempts to censure Beijing on the issue of human rights violations.[9] Given its interests America has been constantly under pressure not to adopt anti-China stance. It has even been ignoring the facts, including those revealed by CIA about China's active involvement as the 'supplier of weapons of mass destruction-related goods and technology to foreign countries'.[10] Due to heavy lobbying from the American nuclear power industry, Washington goes back on taking strict action against China. The same is being done with Pakistan. It can be ascertained from the fact that despite of evidences that Pakistan had supplied the nuclear technology to North Korea, it has been given the status of the Major Non NATO Ally (MNNA). Such policies of the US make India apprehensive about the US intentions.

The US dominates the international system through what has been called, "the new institutionalism."[11] The UN has been completely marginalized by the US and its allies. The US puts in inexorable pressure on the developing countries through the UN, the World Bank and the IMF. A variety of US—brokered and US-led regimes are affecting the foreign policy autonomy.[12] India has been in the forefront of the peacekeeping operations of the United Nations. As one of the founder members and a country believing in the policy of peaceful co-existence, India's contribution in strengthening the hands of the United Nations has been unquestionable. Her faith and trust in the credentials of the world body as an arbiter of conflicts led her to take the matter of Pakistani aggression into her territory way back in 1948. But India's initial enthusiasm for the United Nations waned, like that of many other nations'; in the wake of the raw treatment it received on the Kashmir question. Even so, India continued to espouse various global and third world causes at the United Nations'.[13] Presently in view of the growing unilateralism of the US in the international affairs, the UN has been unable to do much which is evident in the case of Iraq. But India's decision of not sending its troops to Iraq as suggested by the US reflects the independence and maturity of Indian foreign policy. Her refusal was not without a reason as India has sent its troops to foreign countries for peace-keeping operations, but always under the auspices of the United Nations or on the basis of bilateral agreements with the countries concerned, albeit exceptionally. And as J.N. Dixit had observed, "India's decision to not to send its security forces to Iraq hints that the US is not functioning under any mandate of the UN, rather it is operating as an occupation authority. India cannot ignore the sentiments of the Islamic and Arab countries, which are resentful and concerned about the US military and political presence in Iraq. Given the growing opposition and resentment among the Iraqi people against the manner in which US is managing Iraqi affairs after the end of Second Gulf War, India should not do anything as it would diminish its credibility with the Iraqi people",[14] In view of this situation the opinion that India to be accommodated as a permanent member of the security council is gaining ground so that India might play a more effective role in the United Nations in transforming the existing iniquitous international order into a just world order, both politically and economically.

The terrorist attacks on US, it is argued, were the after effects of US policy of hagemonism. Its action in the Gulf War of 1991, the NATO strikes against Yugoslavia, Washington's role in the Middle East crisis, particularly its silence over Israeli use of force against Palestinians etc. The absence of Soviet Union as a countervailing power did not augur well for world peace and stability. Analysts believe that the US engagement in the regions it considered 'trouble spots' has been 'deeper and its failure more spectacular'.[15] And now by striking against Iraq, the US has opened a Pandora's box. Having opened a second front in Iraq, which is running disastrously badly, Washington faces the prospect of a long-term armed conflict with forces it neither understands nor seems willing to dialogue with. From a sociological point of view, the implanting of regimes friendly to Washington but alien to the geographical area in which they have been set up like Afghanistan and Iraq, it would make as much sense to open a kindergarten on Mars.[16] This situation demands that India has to play a significant role in the emerging international order. As an American scholar observes, "India is going to become increasingly engaged in the world and will make stronger claim to be one of the great states of the world..."[17]

Conclusion

How well the US receives the rise of world's largest democracy, will become clear as the events unfold themselves. At present, India is placed rather low in the global power structure. In terms of her military capability, India is more a regional power than a global one. However, given her size, potential, past track record a responsible member of the international community, India is destined to play a crucial role in world politics. India has great stakes in the new issues on international agenda, such as, terrorism and drug trafficking, environment, freedom of trade, technology, human rights, etc. Already it has been cooperating with Russia to bring the issue of international terrorism on the centre stage of the agenda of United Nations, so that the menace is dealt with in a unified and not a 'selective' way. Given the nature of US actions so far against the evil including the confidence and trust posed by Washington on Pakistan as an ally against terrorism, India can not but doubt the effectiveness of American actions. Such moves by the US only confirm the apprehensions in some circles that it is primarily interested only in securing itself from further acts of terror and is unlikely to act on behalf of other countries – like India, Russia, China, etc. who are also victims of terrorism– once its objective is achieved.

India has to wake up and raise its position to such a level as to play a decisive role in world affairs. Keeping in mind that national interests dominate over all other considerations, India can understand why the US is unable to keep its love for democracy and human rights while dealing either with China, or Israel or even Pakistan. She should, therefore, realize that depending upon support from either US or UK or any other country for its fight against terrorism would not help. Therefore, the right policy would be to stand on her guards while dealing with her security and territorial integrity and stepping up efforts at the global level to raise a consensus in favour of her stand. We must keep reminding ourselves that the US has an eye over the large untapped Indian market – a reason why it seeks cordial relations with India. How effectively India can play its card will determine the course of its position as a power to reckon with.

Notes and References

1. B. Raman: Terrorism: The New Context, *Strategic Analysis*, Vol. XXV, No. 9, December 2001, p. 996.
2. *Ibid.*, p. 996.
3. *Ibid.*, pp. 996-97
4. *Ibid.*, p. 997.
5. *Ibid.*
6. *Ibid.*
7. *Ibid.*
8. Jasjit Singh: India's Defence: The Challenges of 1990s, in M.S. Rasgotra, V.D. Chopra, K.P. Mishra (ed.) *India's Foreign Policy in the 1990s*, New Delhi, Patriot Publishers, 1990, pp. 74-75.

9. The United States and Asia in 1997, *Asian Survey*, Vol. XXXVIII, No.1, January 1998, p.103.
10. *Ibid.*, p.104.
11. Kanti Bajpai: *War, Peace, and International Order: India's View of World Politics,* in a project On Conflict or Convergence: Global Perspectives on war, Peace and International Order for Harvard Academy For International and Area Studies, Nov. 13-15, 1997 (Cambridge, Massachusetts, p. 9.
12. J.N. Dixit: Changing International Environment and India's Security, *Strategic Analysis,* New Delhi, Vol. 17, No. 8, November 1994, pp. 932-32.
13. Satish Kumar: *India and the Changing International System*, in M.S. Rasgotra et.al. edt. *op.cit*, p. 31.
14. *Ibid.*, p. 31.
15. For a critical appraisal of US policy, see, Immanuel Wallerstein, The Eagle Has Crash Landed, *Foreign Policy,* July-August 2002, pp. 60-68.
16. Washington's Two Achilles Tendons. *Pravda* (on line), January 12, 2004.
17. Stephen Philip Cohen: Indian Perspective on War, Peace and International Order, in a Project See Ref. No.11, pp. 29-30, quoted in Rajan Kumar: Indo-Russian Relations and The Emerging International Power Structure, *Journal of Peace Studies*, Vol. 9, Issue 6, Nov-Dec. 2001, p. 40.

10

Transiting from SAPTA to SAFTA: Challenges and Opportunities for India

Indra Nath Mukherji

The Islamabad declaration issued at the end of the Twelfth SAARC Summit on 6 January 2004 was in some respect a break from the past. Over the past few years SAARC Summits were being held as mere rituals. Quite often cooperation was hindered by the vicissitudes of political climate. The nuclear weapons tests carried out by India and Pakistan in 1998 and the subsequent military takeover in Pakistan in October 1999 truly reflect the factors underlying tardy progress. This is amply reflected in the recurring postponements of SAARC Summits. To illustrate, after the Tenth Summit held in Colombo in July 1998, so far only two summits could be convened in Kathmandu (January 2002) and in Islamabad (January 2004). In recent years adverse confrontation between the two major regional members, India and Pakistan has been the root cause of tardy progress.

The Twelfth SAARC Summit convened in Islamabad from January 4-6, 2004 held two years after the Eleventh Summit in Kathmandu, and was in some respect a Landmark in the evolution of SAARC. Given the thaw in Indo-Pak relations as reflected in the Joint Statement by the leaders of the two countries in the sidelines of the Summit, a number of notable achievements were recorded. The singing of the Framework Agreement of South Asian Free Trade Area (SAFTA) is a major milestone. Further, the commitment made at the Eleventh SAARC Summit in January 2002 for creation of a South Asian Economic Union was reiterated. The Agreement of SAFTA draws up a blueprint for trade liberalization programme. The agreement stipulates the following measures for trade liberalization:

Entry into force of the Agreement on January 1, 2006 upon the completion of formalities including ratification by all Contracting States (CS) and issuance of a notification thereof by the SAARC Secretariat. The Agreement supercedes SAPTA even though the frame works of concessions under the former remains in place.

Under the programme the non-LDCs are required to bring down their tariffs to 0-5 per cent in seven years (2013), except Sri Lanka which is required to do so in eight years (2014).

The LDCS are required to bring down their tariffs to 0-5 per cent in ten years (2016).

However, non-LDCs are required to bring down their tariffs to 0-5 per cent for the products of LDCs in the three years (2009).

The CS is required to announce a Sensitive List in respect of which trade liberalization will not apply. This list would be reviewed every four years or earlier.

The CS is required to notify the SAARC secretariat all non-tariff barriers (NTBs) to their trade on an annual basis, which is to be reviewed by a Committee of Experts to examine their compatibility with the WTO provisions.

Apart from the greater flexibility and special regard for the LDCs by non-LDCs in respect of various trade restrictive measures adopted by them, the CS agreed to establish appropriate mechanisms to compensate LDCs for their loss of customs revenue following trade liberalization.

Rules of Origin (ROO) have to be negotiated by the CS and incorporated in the Agreement as an integral part.[1] The above elements of the Agreement thus stipulates a number of preparatory measures before agreement the can be operationalised. These are:

(i) The preparation and announcement of a Sensitive List in respect of which trade liberalization would apply.

(ii) The determination of appropriate ROO that is expected to be more flexible than those accepted under SAPTA.

(iii) The announcement of NTBs on their trade by each CS to the SAARC Secretariat, and

(iv) A mechanism to provide for revenue compensation to LDCs by non-LDCs.

This paper examines the approach India could adopt in the fulfillment of the enabling conditions that would permit the SAFTA agreement to be implemented by January 2006.

Sensitive List

This list will be very important since it will set the extent to which the countries of this region would be willing to move towards trade liberalization. India has already prepared a list of sensitive products for imports from South Asian countries which has been put on the Ministry of Commerce website. It will be seen that most of the products in India's Sensitive List are mainly primary products drawn from live animals and animal products, vegetable products, prepared foodstuffs, fats and oils, rubber products, textiles, marble and ceramics, second hand motor cars, etc. a total of 96 products at 8 digit HS classification were valued at Rs. 279 corers in 2001-02 and 276 crore in 2002-03.[2] The five most important products were, in order of importance, cloves extracted, black pepper, cardamoms, almonds, pistachios, which together accounted for 55 per cent of total imports of all sensitive items. In order to permit meaningful regional trade liberalization, all SAARC Cs must endeavor to keep their lists of sensitive items to the minimum. Being a marginal importer from the region, India should ensure that not more than 5 per cent of its tariff lines accounting for no more than 5 per cent of its imports from partner countries in the region are put in the Sensitive List for imports from non-LDCs. As far as imports from LDCs are concerned, India could do away with the Sensitive List altogether.

Rules of Origin

As the SAFTA CS have to move from PTA to FTA, the application of appropriate Rules of Origin (ROO) becomes of prime importance since SAFTA does not anticipate any movement towards a customs union. Thus appropriate designing of ROO becomes crucial to the satisfactory functioning of a PTA/FTA.

The ROO should be so designed as not to become as protective as to act as a non-tariff barrier. At the same time it should ensure that it does not lead to trade deflection from non-member states and facilitates adequate value addition in originating states that contributes to an expansion of intraregional trade. Besides, the ROO must address the different levels of development of the CS. The LDCs are urging upon non-LDCs, particularly India to accept less restrictive ROO from the former. The rationale for this is that LDCs are resource-scarce economies and hence they have to depend on external sourcing to a large extent to manufacture exportable goods. However India's concern is that diluted ROO could lead to deflection of trade from third countries and thereby injure domestic industries. In such a case preferential trading could serve as a conduit for third country goods to enter the Indian market. The current ROO as applicable under SAPTA has been shown in the following Table:

Table 1: SAPTA Rules of Origin

	Before Amendment		*After Amendment*	
	For Non-LDCs	*For LDCs*	*For Non-LDCs*	*For LDCs*
Rule 3(a): Not wholly produced or obtained				
Domestic value Addition in an Exporting Country	**50%**	**40%**	**40%**	**30%**
Maximum Input permitted from Non-contracting States (i.e. from Outside the SAARC region)	**50%**	**60%**	**60%**	**70%**
Rule 4 (a): Cumulative Rules of Origin				
Aggregate Domestic Value addition in an Exporting Country including inputs source from with in SAARC region	**60%**	**50%**	**50%**	**40%**
Maximum Input permitted from outside the SAARC Region	**40%**	**50%**	**50%**	**60%**

Source: **SAARC Secretariat Homepage.**

It will be observed that the existing ROO is one-dimensional, relying only on the percentage test criterion. This could encourage the substitution of more costly domestic inputs for cheaper foreign inputs. It has thus been suggested that change in tariff heading as also specific process test criterion could be supplemented in identified sectors. In the latter case the percentage test criterion could be relaxed. There is further scope for relaxation of ROO without encouraging trade deflection. This could be done by:

- Encouraging greater regional input sourcing by providing more favourable regional accumulation.
- Even if tariff heading change criterion is accepted, this could be dispensed with when the concession receiving country is using say, less than 10 per cent of inputs from non-member states or say when it is sourcing more than 80 per cent of its inputs from other CS.
- Products of regional joint ventures could be permitted more favourable ROO.[3]

India thus should endeavour to accept ROO that does not lead to trade diversion while being flexible enough to permit LDCs to diversify their exports.

Revenue Implications

While undergoing trade liberalization, the LDC CS of SAFTA concerned that they may have to undergo considerable loss in customs revenue and hence a mechanism to compensate them for the revenue for - gone has been embodied in the text of the Agreement. The CS is presently examining this matter. In this context it may be worthwhile to make some estimates of the likely loss in customs revenue the CS are likely to sustain following trade liberalization.

This can be taken note of by estimating the loss in revenue for-gone by concession offering states under trade liberalization undertaken so far under SAPTA negotiations. In this context the difference in the MFN rates and the preferential rates have to be applied to the import values with respect to each product imported by the CS. The sum of revenue for-gone on each product has to be aggregated over all such products being imported to arrive at the total revenue of loss of each CS. It is further possible to identify the revenue loss sustained by each CS vis-à-vis it's trading partners receiving the concessions. Such an exercise would enable us to ascertain how much revenue loss each CS has sustained in favour of other partner CS. The loss of customs revenue of each contracting state vis-à-vis other partner CS on the basis of trade flows between 1997-98 has been presented in the Table 2:

Table 2: Revenue Loss Incurred on Account of Concessions Offered to Imports From Other SAARC Countries

Importing Country	*Revenue loss Vis-a-vis (100 US$)*							
	SAARC	Bangla-desh	Bhutan	India	Maldives	Nepal	Paki-stan	Sri Lanka
Bangla-desh	385.57	-	84.81	215.52	0.00	0.00	2.97	82.27
Bhutan	20.36	6.15	-	0.00	0.00	14.21	0.00	0.00
India	4749.18	2453.53	0.00	-	6.63	0.00	1638.90	650.11
Maldives	18.11	0.00	0.00	3.49	-	0.00	3.30	11.32
Nepal	46.32	2.77	11.03	NA	0.00	-	5.33	27.19
Pakistan	2993.96	1654.36	0.00	844.61	0.75	0.00	-	494.23
Sri Lanka	960.69	8.17	0.00	714.92	69.35	0.00	168.26	-
Total	**9174.19**	**4124.98**	**95.84**	**1778.54**	**76.73**	**14.21**	**1818.76**	**1265.12**

Note : Based on import data for 1997-98 in the case of Bngladesh, India, Nepal, Pakistan and 1998 for Bhutan, Maldives and Sri Lanka. Data for Pakistan has been derived from the partner country exports to Pakistan for the above-mentioned years. 15 per cent of the export value has been added to account for cost, insurance and freight charges.

Sources: Computed from National Publications of Contracting States, Bangladesh: Foreign Trade Statistics of Bangladesh, 1998, India: Monthly Statistics of Foreign Trade of India, DGCI & S Calcutta, 1997-98, Maldives: Database, Maldives Customs, Nepal: Nepal Overseas Trade Statistics, 1997-98, Trade Promotion Center, Kathmandu, Pakistan: Data obtained from Partner Countries.

Sri Lanka: External Trade Statistics, 1998, Statistics Division, Department of Sri Lanka.

The loss in customs revenue being shared by each CS vis-à-vis the rest has been shown in the following :

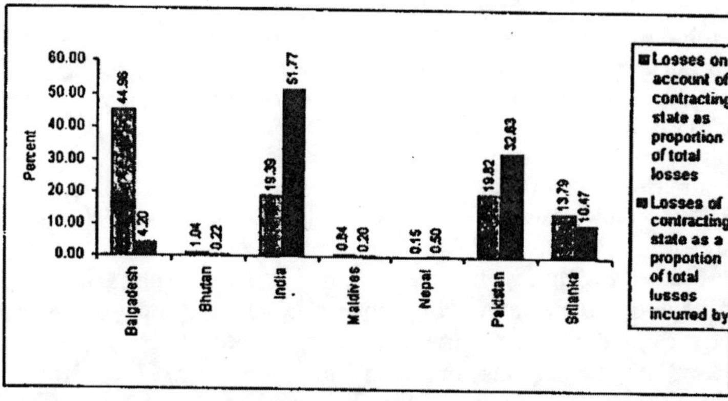

Figure 1. Share of revenue losses shared by the contracting states.

It will be observed that as a result of trade liberalization under the three rounds of SAPTA negotiations total revenue loss amounted to US$9.17 m. The largest revenue loss was sustained by India (US$4.75 m), equivalent to nearly 52 per cent of the total revenue loss sustained by all CS in the region. Next to India, Pakistan sustained a loss of nearly US$3 m equivalent to nearly 33 per cent of total revenue loss by all CS in the region. Sri Lanka's revenue loss was a little less than US$1 m. The remaining least developed countries namely; Bangladesh, Bhutan, Maldives and Nepal sustained fairly modest revenue losses. India's revenue losses were primarily in favour of Bangladesh and Pakistan. The loss sustained by Bangladesh and Pakistan in favour of India was relatively modest. Pakistan's revenue loss was mainly in favour of Bangladesh, India and Sri Lanka. The revenue losses incurred by Bangladesh and Sri Lanka in favour of Pakistan were relatively modest. Sri Lanka's revenue losses were primarily in favour of India and Pakistan and to some extent in favour of Maldives. India's revenue loss with respect to Sri Lanka was marginally lower. Pakistan's revenue loss in favour of Sri Lanka was relatively higher.

Under revenue compensation framework under negotiation, India, Pakistan and Sri Lanka would be required to compensate Bangladesh, Bhutan Maldives and Nepal for the revenue losses they sustain on account of tariff reductions. A look at Table 2 reveals that Bangladesh would be the country India would be called upon to compensate the most. On the basis of Bangladesh import data for 1998, Bangladesh would sustain revenue loss of US$0.22 million on account of import liberalization with India. This is based on preferential tariff of 10 per cent and import share of 3.5 per cent. On a pro rata basis if 95 per cent tariff reduction was effected, the revenue loss would be (0.22/10) 95 or US$2.05 million. Again when the import coverage is extended in full, the revenue loss would amount to (2.05/3.5) 100 or US$58 million. But this would be not until 2016, the phase-out time given to Bangladesh. The above analysis is however entirely static since in the meanwhile not only would India's exports to Bangladesh increase, but also Bangladesh's MFN tariff rates would also have declined. Hence revenue compensation would have to be worked out for each year separately. The above analysis suggests that India would not be burdened intolerably in case it agreed to compensate Bangladesh for its loss in revenue. However while agreeing to compensate Bangladesh and also other LDCs, India must ensure that this would be available only up to 2016, the duty–phase out period for LDCs and during this period the latter should undertake adequate fiscal reforms so as to have diversified their revenue base substantially so as not to be excessively dependent on customs revenue for resource mobilization.

Phasing out Non-tariff barriers

The World Bank has identified some of the NTBs in an overview of Trade Policies in South Asia to include:

- Bangladesh's list of banned and restricted products, and the institutional holdovers from its old general import licensing system.
- Other QRs e.g. Sri Lanka bans on imports of tea and spices, Nepal's ban on imports of machine made woolen yarns.
- TRIMS regulations, especially Pakistan's TRIMS applied to its auto industry.
- Pakistan's positive list for imports from India. This should be revisited, and when politically feasible, expanded or abolished, preferably in conjunction with the relaxation of

travel, communication and other barriers to business relations by both countries.

- Regulations, which prevent or restrict imports of second hand goods, especially in India and Pakistan.
- India's import monopolies of rice, wheat and other agricultural commodities, and its agricultural tariff rate quotas (TROs). These are linked, however, to a broader set of agricultural/food security policies, and removing or phasing out the import barriers would need to be part of broader reforms of these policies.
- State trading import monopolies of petroleum products, fertilizers and others.
- The use of sanitary and phytosanitary (SPS) rules and technical regulations to limit imports and protect domestic producers. Under the WTO SPS and TBT agreements, these rules are supposed to not to discriminate between imports and domestic products. It would be in the economic interests of South Asian countries to modify rules that are in fact discriminating (e.g. the Indian BIS rules for imported steel) and to ensure that new rules are framed and actually applied in a neutral manner. Pro active domestic initiatives to do this would be far preferable to allowing protective SPS and TBT rules to function in the expectation that an exporting country will perhaps eventually object at the WTO.[4]

Given the nature of non-tariff barriers mentioned above, the CS needs to identify these at the earliest with a view to relaxing them or at least ensuring that these do not unnecessarily act as hindrance to trade flows between the member states. It is unfortunate that the SAFTA agreement does not set any time limit to the phasing out of these barriers. India has a special responsibility to ensure that while applying NTBs from other CS, the measure is in conformity with WTO principles. A number of CS have been complaining that a number of anti dumping measures have not been in conformity with WTO principles. The complaint made by Bangladesh on its lead acid battery case is one that is most often cited. Since such exports to India are miniscule of the latter's total imports, the imposition of such duty has not been found to be untenable and according to the information received by the author, such duties have now been withdrawn. Other NTBs to which Bangladesh has drawn India's attention relates to customs valuation, testing requirements, inadequate physical facilities at land customs in India, labeling and marking requirements, especially for jute bags, mandatory standards requirements, measures, etc. constraining Bangladesh's exports to India. In this context India should do as much as it can to provide necessary technical assistance to Bangladesh and other LDCs (already provided for in the SAFTA Agreement) to help the latter in its capacity building, which could facilitate the country's exports to India.

India's Bilateral Initiatives

In recent years India has been proactive in its bilateral initiatives forging bilateral free trade agreements with not only countries with in the region, but even beyond. While such agreements traditionally with the Himalayan Kingdoms of Nepal and Bhutan, new arrangements have been established with Sri Lanka and discussions are on with Bangladesh. In case a bilateral free trade agreement is forged with Bangladesh, SAFTA would become even less relevant. This is to demonstrate that in case SAFTA does not work, India has other options. However there is much that India could do to make SAFTA work.

Notes and References

1. SAARC Secretariat, Agreement on South Asian Free Trade Area.
2. www.commin.nic.in
3. For an exhaustive discussion on the rationale of different criteria on rules of origin see V.R. Panchamukhi and Ram Upendra Das, "Conceptual and Policy Issues in Rules of Origin: Implications for SAPTA and SAFTA", *South Asia Journal*. Vol. 2, 2001.
4. World Bank. Workshop on Regional Trade Policies in South Asia, Colombo, October 2-3-2003.

11

Economic Co-operation in the SAARC Region: Potential, Constraints and Policies

S.D. Chamola

Strategic Location and Emerging Trends

The socio-economic profile, which includes the study of geographical location, population, recent history, economic problems regarding agriculture, trade, industry, transport, money and booking, etc., greatly influences the economic development of a country and a region. This is equality true to the SAARC countries comprising Bangladesh, Bhutan, India, Maldives, Nepal, Pakistan and Sri Lanka. This region is of strategic importance between the east and west with respect to defence, trade, transport population growth and economic development. The Indian Ocean, which plays an important role in defence, trade and water transport is in the proximity of the majority of these countries. The region has a geographical boundary of the Himalayan ranges in the north and the Indian Ocean in the south.

The total landmass of SAARC region is 3.3 per cent of the world and has one-fifth of the population. All the Seven countries can be grouped into different categories. First, there are two land-locked countries namely Bhutan and Nepal. Second, there are two island countries, i.e. Sri Lanka and Maldives and third, three countries, India, Pakistan and Bangladesh which have the Indian ocean in the South and South West and the Indo-Gangatic plains stretching along these countries. Four countries namely Pakistan, India, Bhutan and Nepal share the Himalayan ranges. Historically, Bhutan and Nepal have monarchical system of Govt. and were never under colonial rule whereas the other five countries had colonial legacy. The SAARC countries have many similarities and common problems in the process of economic development. These countries have the basic features of developing countries, i.e. they are agricultural which contributes a sizeable proportion to GDP, over populated, possess low level of technology, share in world trade is negligible and heavily dependent on developed countries for aid and trade. Recently, these economics have been liberalizing, privatizing, globalising and undergoing structural changes. These new economic reforms have started paying dividends as they have performed a faster economic growth in the last decade. Overall, the region grew by 4.5 per cent in 1990s in comparison with the world growth rate of 3 per cent. The emerging trend is that the contribution of agricultural sector to the GDP is declining and shares of service sector and secondary and tertiary sectors are increasing.

Although, the importance of regional corporation aid, trade and transfer of technology is known to these countries but the growth of Regional Corporation has been slow because the seven South Asian countries formed the South Asian Association of Regional Cooperation (SAARC) in 1985 as a first step towards regional cooperation. After a decade's existence, the South Asian Preferential Trading Agreement (SAPTA) was lunched by the SAARC in 1995 as the second step and the end of year 2001 was declared as the deadline to finalize a treaty for the South Asian Free Trade Association (SAFTA). Further, these seven SAARC countries signed a treaty that would lead to free trade and movement of goods paving the way for South Asian Economic Union along the lines of EU in future. The South Asian Free Trade Area (SAFTA) treaty seeks to remove trade barriers, phased elimination of tariffs and establishment of a ministerial level mechanism for administering the treaty and dispute settlement among members. The treaty will come into operation by January 1, 2006. The exchange of mutual experience among the countries is more relevant, cheap and cost effective and provides a vast scope for mutual cooperation in various areas. But mainly agriculture will continue to dominate these economies for many years to come because SAARC countries are predominantly agricultural which contributes a sizeable portion to the GDP, therefore this would provide a base for the development of the economy such as food for growing population, fodder for livestock, raw material and market for industries. It will continue to dominate the external trade and transport system.

Potential Areas for Cooperation

Areas of future co-operation among the SAARC countries have been discussed from time to time at different forums since 1985 when SAARC came into existence. Finally, twelve areas of cooperation have been identified. They are: (1) agriculture; (2) health and rural development; (3) meteorology; (4) telecommunication; (5) postal services; (6) transport; (7) scientific and technological development; (8) sports; (9) art and culture; (10) prevention of drug trafficking and abuse; (11) women and development and (12) education. All the SAARC countries are suffering from the common problems of poverty, unemployment, inflationary pressure, unfavourable trade balance, high budget deficits and low growth rates. In spite of these common problems, they have been adopting the policies contradictory to one another. These policy issues were more of competitive nature and less of complementary and cooperative nature. These divergences in solving their problems through competition among themselves originate from the historical facts. The colonial legacies of these countries linked themselves in the matter of aid and trade with developed economies of the world. The quest for foreign exchange, advance technology, foreign aid etc. dragged these countries to the western industrialized countries. This was imperative in the early stages of economic development also when there was shortage of capital investment and technology.

One of the most interesting developments of the last few decades is the regional regrouping of neighbouring sovereign states. Regionalism has become an important component of the New International Economic Order. Developments at the world level have forced these countries to come together and increase their bargaining power with industrially advanced nations of the world in different forums such as WTO, World Bank, IMF, etc., where more concessions can be obtained by the regional blocks rather than individual countries. These economic, social and political compulsions have compelled the countries of South Asia to form SAARC. It has now been realized that these countries can better solve their problems of poverty, unemployment, inflation and low rate of growth, by cooperating among themselves. The sooner the mutual fear and apprehensions disappear, the better for these economies. If we go in depth of the solution of the problems of these countries, it becomes apparent that there are more areas of cooperation than the areas of conflict.

The intra-regional trade can be increased among the SAARC countries by providing facilities to each other. For example, India and Bangladesh can consider signing a bilateral agreement for free movement of commercial vehicles, and use of southern Chittagong port as transit for ferrying goods to north eastern India to help reduce the Indo-Bangladesh trade imbalance. Similarly, private entrepreneurs can start joint venture into jute and composite textiles. In the same way, Indo-Sri Lankan trade can also be increased in various commodities like tea and rubber. The cooperation in infrastructural development has already been mentioned. Telecommunication, roads, transport, energy and other infrastructural facilities can easily be developed through mutual cooperation. For example Pakistan, India and Bangladesh, Nepal and Bhutan can easily be linked through rail and road transport. Bhutan and Nepal have hydro electric power potentials which can easily be exploited by India. The river valley projects on the river water flowing between India and Bangladesh, India and Pakistan, India and Nepal, Bhutan and India, Bhutan and Nepal can be developed in mutual interest and benefit. Besides this, by proper management of water resources, floods and droughts can be minimized for the benefit of their agriculture. The development of common telecommunication services can help in monitoring weather reports, international market fluctuations in prices and products, exchange of scientific information and also regarding the spread of pests and diseases.

Policy Measures to Promote Cooperation

In order to promote cooperation among SAARC countries a number of measures have already been suggested. They include:

1. Developing the information system by the SAARC countries among themselves rather than depending on the information provided by developed countries should reduce the information gap. Such a development will help the exports and the importers to locate demand and supply position of various commodities in SAARC region. This is the first pre-requisite for any cooperation in future.

2. As stated above, the external trade of SAARC countries has a historical colonial legacy and their economies are linked to the industrialized countries. This has led to the competition among themselves in the areas of exports and imports. There is a need of complementarities rather than competition now. Therefore, conscious efforts are needed to develop the economic complementarities by reorienting the economies of the region towards each other. Expansion of market for each other's commodities, reduction in transportation cost and other trade concessions can go a long way in this regard.

3. Expansion of trade is not possible unless there is cooperation in payments and financial transactions. There is an urgent need of establishing a good network of banks and other financial institutions for liberal credit facilities. The Asia Clearing Union (ACU) is inadequate and not geared to the task of SAARC countries. Only India, Pakistan and Nepal are the members of ACU. These countries will have to mobilize more resources to finance trade and solve exchange problems. The SAARC monetary Union on the pattern of European Union is still to go a long way but ultimately, if the SAARC is to take concrete shape efforts will have to be made for such a monetary union and common currency system.

4. Lowering of both tariff and non-tariff barriers would be helpful in promoting trade relations. These countries can enter into bilateral and multilateral arrangements for such concessions. They can give the most favoured nation treatment to each other for this the commodity-wise and service-wise identification approach for concessions should be adopted.

5. The political relations and regional conflicts, which are bilateral in nature, should not come in the way of trade. For example, there is a great demand of Indian goods in Pakistan and Bangladesh and due to the strained political relations; a lot of smuggling and unreported trade is going on in these commodities across the border. Legalizing these transactions and amending the trade legislations accordingly will not only help in trade expansion but also in improving political relations. Bilateral and non-economic issues should not be raised at the forums meant to deal purely with economic relations.

6. The fear of economic domination by India should be allayed. India shares 77 per cent of population, 72 per cent of area, 78 per cent of GDP, 88 per cent of exports and 81 per cent of imports in SAARC region. She will have to be very careful in her dealings with the other partners. India through its actions should demonstrate that it is a friend and not the policeman and dispel the apprehensions in the minds of the smaller countries of this region.

Agricultural Sector to be the Major Focus

The major focus of cooperation in the SAARC should be the agricultural sector because in all the SAARC economies agriculture contributes the substantial share to their GDP. There exist a vast potential of cooperation in the field of agriculture despite hostile and highly unfavourable world environment. This potential lies in the areas of production, marketing, finance, infrastructure and science and technology relating to agriculture. Fortunately, there is much to learn from one another in these countries. If we take the case of production technology we find that India and Pakistan have experienced green revolution therefore the other countries can learn from the experience of India in wheat and rice. Likewise the other commodities produced in other countries like cotton in Pakistan, rice in Bangladesh, fisheries in Maldives, tea and coconut in Sri Lanka, maize in Nepal and Bhutan etc. can be used for the benefit of others. The list can be prolonged by further investigations. There is much to learn in inputs management especially in fertilizers, soil and water management, farm mechanization, crop rotations etc.

There is a scope for cooperation also in the areas of marketing of produce both inside and outside the country. For both internal and external marketing, the first requisite is information system and transport cost. The setting up of SAARC Agriculture, Information Centre at Dhaka is a step in the right direction as it is fulfilling the information needs of member countries. It is required to a keep a contact with agricultural organizations of member countries and work as a common platform for exchanging information regarding the pests and diseases of various crops and technical know- how for their control. The SAIC provides the possibility of cooperation in the field of crop production, animal husbandry, fisheries, forestry, wild life preservation and marketing intelligence.

The scope in external marketing i.e. exports and imports are the most important area of cooperation and coordination. In this regard a number of steps are required. First a common approach to deal with the developed countries is required to be evolved. Many of SAARC countries have monopoly in tea, jute, spices, coconut and some fruits and vegetables. If these countries could agree to cooperate and formulate a common front, they can gain superior bargaining power in their exports. They have vast bio-diversity in the forms of plants and animals, which are not found in the industrially advanced countries. They can use this potential in their favour by combining themselves in a common pool. Many other items can be explored by conducting intensive research. There is highly unfavourable environment in the world for the growth and sustenance of agricultural sector of these developing countries of SAARC as the WTO accord's provisions for Plant Breeders Rights, Seeds, Subsidies, opening of market for the import from developed countries, patenting etc., are highly damaging for the smooth growth of agricultural sector in these countries. Apprehensions about the WTO accord have already been articulated in farmers' agitations and political opposition.

The external gains could be consolidated only when conscious efforts are made to develop economic compatibility and avoiding of competition. This is possible only when they reorient their economics towards each other. They should try to expand the size of markets for intra-SAARC trade and also to reduce the cost of transport. The least developed SAARC countries could supply timber and timber products, natural gas, raw jute, raw cotton etc. to other member of SAARC. There is enough scope for joint marketing in the agricultural value-added products. Developed countries in SAARC region such as India and Pakistan produce sufficient quality agricultural based products, which can be substituted in imports from industrially developed countries to the SAARC countries. For example, Pakistan can meet Sri Lanka's requirement of cotton yarn and in turn, get tea, rubber and some consumer goods. Sri Lanka's copra and coconut can find a large market in India were there is a shortage of vegetable oil. Pakistan can export surplus rice, cotton and textiles to Bangladesh where these products fetch a good market and in turn Bangladesh can get good markets for jute and newsprint in Pakistan. Indian products can find good markets in Pakistan especially in intermediate and capital goods. Likewise India can also supply fruits and vegetables to Sri Lanka and Maldives. Many other commodities can be identified by mutual discussion. Agricultural research and education is the most potent area for cooperation. India and Pakistan have developed fairly advanced agricultural technology, which is more relevant and less expensive for the other SAARC countries. India has one of the widest and best networks of agricultural education and research in the world. All SAARC countries can benefit from it by getting their students and scientists trained in Indian agricultural universities and research institutes. Specific research centers can be developed for each SAARC country according to their commodity specialization. There is also urgent need to develop a common syllabus and course catalogue in agricultural education, research and extension management.

Specialized financial institutions can be developed for the development of agriculture in these countries on the pattern of Asian Development Bank, FAO, UNDP and World Bank. The successful experiment of Gramin Banks in Bangladesh can be replicated in other SAARC countries also. The Indian experience of rural development, public distribution system and government intervention in financial sector reform can greatly enhance the experience of other member countries. The international trade theory of comparative cost can also be applied in these countries. In place of producing each and every produce, they should concentrate on products, which can give them comparative cost advantage. A mention has already been made of the various commodities in which each SAARC countries can specialise.

Major Irritants in Mutual Relationships

Apart from the historical reasons, there are many other factors for non-cooperation among the SAARC countries. The political differences and mutual suspicion and lack of trust are the greatest enemies of cooperation among these. The Kashmir problem between India and Pakistan, water and refugee disputes between India and Bangladesh, the Indian military intervention in Sri Lanka, the trade and transit treaty between India and Nepal, the ethnic problem between Bhutan and Nepal etc. are some of the troubled spots in the SAARC region which restrict these countries to come in open and cooperate whole heartedly. Political factors supersede the economic factors and the economic factors also compel these countries to compete with each other. For example, there is competition between India and Sri Lanka for export of tea, between India and Bangladesh for jute, India and Pakistan for rice, Pakistan and Sri Lanka for cotton textiles etc. in the world market. The fear of India, which dominates in terms of area, population, technological advancement and military might in this region is another important factor for continuous and slow growth of cooperation among SAARC countries. Religious and cultural factors, which dominate the course of growth, also put hindrances. For example, Pakistan prefers economic and cultural cooperation with Islamic countries; Nepal and Bhutan are religiously and culturally closer to India as these countries are dominated by the Hindu and Buddhist religions. The different levels of economic development also create apprehensions. India and Pakistan are most advanced whereas Bhutan, Nepal and Maldives are not so developed. These economic disparities create the apprehensions in the minds of the less developed countries that the relatively developed partners will exploit them.

Conclusion

Despite the lack of trust and irritants there is vast scope for cooperation among the SAARC countries. Agriculture should be the main focus of cooperation because these countries have core competence in this sector and their economies are dominated by agriculture sector. However constant attempts should be made to remove the major irritants of mutual apprehension in the form of political and economic domination by India. The need of the hour is the sincerity of purpose and honesty in efforts. These countries must learn the lesson that in cooperation we swim across the turbulent river while individually we are drowned even in the still waters.

Acknowledgement

The author is thankful to Dr. V.R. Panchamukhi particularly and also to the Research and Information System for the Non-aligned and other Developing Countries, New Delhi for providing financial support.

Notes and References

Research and Information System for Non-Aligned and Other Developing Countries Economic Cooperation in the SAARC Region: *Potential, Constraints and Policies*, Interest Publications, New Delhi. 1990.

J.N. Mukherji: *Transition of SAPTA to SAFTA: Emerging Opportunities to Trade and Investment in SAARC Region.* Background Paper of National Seminar Organized by FICCI, New Delhi 15 November 1995.

SAARC Chamber of Commerce SAARC Preferential Trading Arrangement. 1993.

Research and Information System for the Non-Aligned and other Developing Countries SAARC Survey of Development and Cooperation, New Delhi, 1995.

Poonam Sethi: *Towards a Free Trade Arrangement in South Asia*, Indian Institute of Foreign Trade New Delhi. 1995.

P.A. Joy: *Towards a Free Trade Arrangement in South Asia*, Indian Institute of Foreign Trade, New Delhi, 1995.

SAARC Agreement on SAARC Preferential Trading Arrangement (SAPTA), Kathmandu, SAARC Secretariat.

SAARC Meeting of the Committee on Economic Cooperation (4th) Dhaka (21-21 Nov. 1993), Report Kathmandu SAARC Secretariat.

TRADE STATISTICS WITH PAKISTAN

Dated : 30/3/2004

Values in US$ Million

Country : Pakistan

S.No.	Year	1998-99	1999-00	2000-01	2001-02
1.	EXPORT	106.10	92.95	186.83	144.01
2.	% Growth		-12.40	101.01	-22.92
3.	India's Total Export	33,218.49	36,822.49	44,560.29	43,826.73
4.	% Growth		10.85	21.01	-1.65
5.	% Share	0.32	0.25	0.42	0.33
6.	IMPORT	214.45	68.21	64.03	64.76
7.	% Growth		17.34	1.61	1.74
8.	India's Total Import	42,388.71	49,738.06	50,536.46	51,413.29
9.	% Growth		17.34	1.61	1.74
10.	% Share	0.51	0.14	0.13	0.13
11.	TOTAL TRADE	320.55	61.16	250.86	208.76
12.	% Growth		-49.72	55.66	-16.78
13.	India's Total Trade	75,607.44	86,560.55	95,096.75	95,240.01
14.	% Growth		14.49	9.86	0.15
15.	% Share	0.42	0.19	0.26	0.22
16.	TRADE BALANCE		24.73	122.81	79.25
17.	India's Trade Balance	-9,169.99	-12,915.57	-5,976.16	-7,586.56
	Exchange rate: (1 US$)=Rs.)	42.0706	43.3327	45.6844	47.6919

TRADE STATISTICS WITH BANGLADESH

Dated : 30/3/2004

Values in US$ Million

Country : Bangladesh

S.No.	*Year*	*1 9 -99*	*1999-00*	*2000-01*	*2001-02*	*2002-03*
1.	EXPORT	995.64	636.31	935.04	1,002.18	1,176.00
2.	% Growth		-36.09	46.95	7.18	17.34
3.	India's Total Export	35,218.72	36,822.49	44,560.29	43,826.73	52,719.43
4.	% Growth		10.85	21.01	-1.65	20.29
5.	% Share	3.00	1.73	2.10	2.29	2.23
6.	IMPORT	62.40	78.15	80.51	59.12	62.05
7.	% Growth		25.24	3.01	-26.57	4.90
8.	India's Total Import	42,388.71	49,738.06	50,536.46	51,413.29	61,412.13
9.	% Growth	17.34	1.61	1.74	19.45	
10.	% Share 0.10	0.15	0.16		0.16	0.11
11.	TOTAL TRADE	1,058.04	714.46	1,015.55	1,061.30	1,238.05
12.	% Growth	-32.47	42.14	4.50	16.65	
13.	India's Total Trade	75,607.44	86,560.55	95,096.75	95,240.01	114,131.50
14.	% Growth		14.49	9.86	0.15	19.84
15.	% Share	1.40	0.83	1.07	1.11	1.08
16.	TRADE BALANCE	933.24	558.15	854.54	943.06	1,113.95
17.	India's Trade Balance	-9,169.99	-12,915.57	-5,976.16	-7,586.56	-8,692.70
	Exchange rate: (1 US$)=Rs.)	42.0706	43.3327	45.6844	47.6919	48.395

TRADE STATISTICS WITH BHUTAN

Dated : 30/3/2004

Values in US$ Million

Country : Bhutan

S.No.	*Year*	*1998-99*	*1999-00*	*2000-01*	*2001-02*
1.	EXPORT	9.56	7.57	1.08	7.60
2.	% Growth		-20.78	-85.78	605.38
3.	India's Total Export	33,218.72	36,822.49	44,560.29	43,826.73
4.	% Growth		10.85	21.01	-1.65
5.	% Share	0.03	0.02	0.00	0.02
6.	IMPORT	6.13	18.01	21.09	23.92
7.	% Growth		194.00	17.08	13.42
8.	India's Total Import	42,388.71	49,738.06	50,536.46	51,413.29
9.	% Growth		17.34	1.61	1.74
10.	% Share	0.01	0.04	0.04	0.05
11.	TOTAL TRADE	15.69	25.59	22.17	31.52
12.	% Growth		63.11	-13.37	42.19
13.	India's Total Trade	75,607.44	86,560.55	95,096.75	95,240.01
14.	% Growth		14.49	9.86	0.15
15.	% Share	0.02	0.03	0.02	0.03
16.	TRADE BALANCE		3.43		
17.	India's Trade Balance	-9,169.99	-12,915.57	-5,976.16	-7,586.56
	Exchange rate: (1 US$)=Rs.)	42.0706	43.3327	45.6844	47.6919

TRADE STATISTICS WITH MALDIVES

Dated : 30/3/2004

Values in US$ Million

Country : Maldives

S.No.	*Year*	*1998-99*	*1999-00*	*2000-01*	*2001-02*	*2002-03*
1.	EXPORT	8.38	7.30	24.61	26.88	
2.	% Growth		-12.84	237.10	9.20	
3.	India's Total Export	35,218.72	36,822.49	44,560.29	43,826.73	52,719.43
4.	% Growth		10.85	21.01	-1.65	20.29
5.	% Share	0.03	0.02	0.06	0.06	
6.	IMPORT	0.05	0.40	0.19	0.40	
7.	% Growth		671.34	-52.63	108.73	
8.	India's Total Import	42,388.71	49,738.06	50,536.46	51,413.29	61,412.13
9.	% Growth		17.34	1.61	1.74	19.45
10.	% Share	0.00	0.00	0.00	0.00	
11.	TOTAL TRADE	8.43	7.70	24.80	27.27	
12.	% Growth		-8.63	222.03	9.96	
13.	India's Total Trade	75,607.44	86,560.55	95,096.75	95,240.01	114,131.50
14.	% Growth		14.49	9.86	0.15	19.84
15.	% Share	0.01	0.01	0.03	0.03	
16.	TRADE BALANCE	8.32	6.90	24.42	26.48	
17.	India's Trade Balance	-9,169.99	-12,915.57	-5,976.16	-7,586.56	-8,692.70
	Exchange rate: (1 US$)=Rs.)	42.0706	43.3327	45.6844	47.6919	48.395

TRADE STATISTICS WITH NEPAL

Dated : 30/3/2004

Values in US$ Million

Country : Nepal

S.No.	*Year*	*1998-99*	*1999-00*	*2000-01*	*2001-02*
1.	EXPORT	122.41	151.23	140.84	214.46
2.	% Growth		23.54	6.87	52.28
3.	India's Total Export	33,218.72	36,822.49	44,560.29	43,826.73
4.	% Growth		10.85	21.01	1.65
5.	% Share	0.37	0.41	0.32	0.49
6.	IMPORT	144.85	188.63	255.08	355.94
7.	% Growth		30.23	35.23	39.54
8.	India's Total Import	42,388.71	49,738.06	50,536.46	51,413.29
9.	% Growth		17.34	1.61	1.74
10.	% Share	0.34	0.38	0.50	0.69
11.	TOTAL TRADE	267.26	339.86	395.92	570.40
12.	% Growth		27.16	16.49	44.07
13.	India's Total Trade	75,607.44	86,560.55	95,096.75	95,240.01
14.	% Growth		14.49	9.86	0.15
15.	% Share	0.35	0.39	0.42	0.60
16.	TRADE BALANCE				
17.	India's Trade Balance	-9,169.99	-12,915.57	-5,976.16	-7,586.56
	Exchange rate: (1 US$)=Rs.)	42.0706	43.3327	45.6844	47.6919

TRADE STATISTICS WITH SRI LANKA

Dated : 30/3/2004

Values in US$ Million

Country : Sri Lanka

S.No.	*Year*	*1998-99*	*1999-00*	*2000-01*	*2001-02*
1.	EXPORT	437.13	499.27	640.14	630.89
2.	% Growth		14.22	28.22	-1.45
3.	India's Total Export	33,218.72	36,822.49	44,560.29	43,826.73
4.	% Growth		10.85	21.01	-1.65
5.	% Share	1.32	1.36	1.44	1.44
6.	IMPORT	37.68	44.23	45.01	67.38
7.	% Growth		17.40	1.75	49.71
8.	India's Total Import	42,388.71	49,738.06	50,536.46	51,413.29
9.	% Growth		17.34	1.61	1.74
10.	% Share	0.09	0.09	0.09	0.13
11.	TOTAL TRADE	474.80	543.50	685.15	698.27
12.	% Growth		14.27	26.06	1.92
13.	India's Total Trade	75,607.44	86,560.55	95,096.75	95,240.01
14.	% Growth		14.49	9.86	0.15
15.	% Share	0.63	0.63	0.72	0.73
16.	TRADE BALANCE	399.45	455.04	595.14	563.51
17.	India's Trade Balance	-9,169.99	-12,915.57	-5,976.16	-7,586.56
	Exchange rate: (1 US$)=Rs.)	42.0706	43.3327	45.6844	47.6919

12

India and SAARC: Challenges and Opportunities

Saroj Pathak

Regionalism and regional cooperation constitutes the most perceptible trend of the post-Second World War international relations. World has witnessed emergence of a score of regional organizations in various parts of the globe for promoting cooperation among nations for achieving common national and international goals of their respective foreign policies in the social, economic, political and strategic spheres. All these organizations have been formed under Article 52 of the United Nation's Charter, which provides for existence of regional arrangements or agencies for dealing with such matters, which relate to the maintenance of international peace and security as appropriate for regional action and are consistent with the purpose and principles of UN charter. However, it should be noted here that though this trend became more evident in the modern era, historical facts point out that states within limited geographical areas have tended to make collective efforts to attain certain common objectives since ancient times.

The term region means geographical closeness, common historical experiences, and affinities in respect of culture, religion as well as similarities in world outlooks, development strategies and political system to some extent. Logically, the common factors binding the nations, which form part of a region, are likely to have common problems and goals in national and international fields. This commonality necessitates common solutions through cooperative actions. In this sense, "cooperation connotes an acting together, in agreement, for the sake of common ends. Cooperation may be eager or reluctant, extensive or limited but it is something more than indifference or non-action."[1] This desire for co-operation needs some machinery or instrument. Thus, according to Padelford "a regional arrangement in the sphere of international politics may be described as an association of states, based upon location in a given geographical area, for safeguarding or promotion of the participants' common interests. The terms of this association are fixed by a treaty or other agreement"[2] Now coming to the subject of this paper i.e. India and SAARC—the challenges and opportunities, one finds a large number of studies dissecting, analyzing, drawing conclusions and bombarding with suggestions for the improvement so far as the performance of SAARC in promoting regional cooperation is concerned. They all point out without any difference of opinion firstly, that SAARC as a regional organization on the whole has not been able to make a mark as a viable means to promote regional cooperation in the region. Secondly, they also put a question mark upon the ability of India to steer the organization ahead towards progress. It is felt that India being the largest, economically the most developed and potentially the most powerful nation in the region has special responsibility and role to play in the SAARC affairs. SAARC is also compared with other regional organizations existing side by side in the neighbourhood and other parts of the world, which have become an object of envy due to their remarkable achievements and suggestions have been made that it should learn lesson from their experiences. Thus, in this paper an attempt has been made to take a holistic view of the problems and challenges confronting South Asia, SAARC and India in order to explore what India could and should do to strengthen and smoothen the working of SAARC in future to make it a viable instrument of regional co-operation in an area of globe where it is most urgently needed.

Evolution of the Idea of Regional Co-operation in South Asia and India

India from the time it obtained independence from foreign rule has always been keenly interested and deeply committed to the idea of regional cooperation for the solution of common problems in various fields viz. the cultural, economic political ones. Jawaharlal Nehru stressed the unity and solidarity of Asia repeatedly in his speeches and writings. He was also quite eloquent about India's responsibility rather India's "destiny" to play an active role in this respect because of the geographical and historical compulsions. In the very first broadcast to the nation on September 7, 1946, he said, "We are of Asia and the people of Asia are nearer and closer to us than other. India is so situated that she is pivot of Western, Southern and South-East Asia". Likewise, on another occasion he reiterated the same by observing that "When we talk of Asia, remember that India, not because of any ambition of hers, but because of the force of circumstances, because of geography, because of history and because of many other things, inevitably has to play a very important part in Asia... Even if you think in terms of regional organizations in Asia..you have to keep in touch with the other regions. And whatever regions you may in mind, the importance of India cannot be ignored."[3]

Hence, in order to create an atmosphere of cordiality and cooperation, he called Asian relations conference in New Delhi were he emphasized the fact that countries of Asia have to meet together on an equal basis in a common task and endeavour and observed that "It is fitting that India should play her part in this new phase of Asian Development". Not only this, he also specifically hoped that some permanent Asian Institute for the study of common problems and to bring about closer relations will emerge also perhaps a school of Asian studies. Much more could be done in his view but it was left to the conference as he said "I shall not venture to enumerate all the subjects; for it is for you to discuss them and arrive at decisions."[4]

The Asian relations conference, as the results show, did not produce anything concrete in this respect. Rather, as is well known, the delegates from some countries expressed their apprehensions of brown domination. Nehru made some more attempts for forging unity among Asian countries without any worthwhile achievement. However, it may be noted that although he very clearly realized the need and importance of Asian unity he hardly made any specific mention of South Asia as such.

Obviously, South Asia was only a part of his wider perspective of Asian affairs sharing more or less similar problems but distinct from the regions of the world. Therefore, his vision was for the whole of Asia not only for South Asia. Besides, though he focused on Asia's immediate problems such as food, clothing, education and health, he seemed to be more concerned with the problems of war and peace because in his view peace was an essential condition in the wider context to move towards the solution of other problems. Thus, there was more emphasis on eradication of colonialism, racialism etc. which were perceived as threat to peace and stability. More over, during Nehruvian era India was not materially in a position to take initiative for regional cooperation in a big way because of its own domestic problems.

Ultimately when the initiative for the formation of SAARC came from Bangladesh towards the end of 1970s, India neither took it seriously nor contributed much for transforming it into reality. SAARC was at last established in 1985 at Dhaka where all the seven countries of South Asia; India, Pakistan Bangladesh, Bhutan, Nepal and Sri Lanka signed the charter. Incidentally, SAARC, which is only 20 years old, happens to be the youngest regional organization. It has held 12 submit meetings during this period attended by the heads of state and Governments of the member states. The last one was held in Islamabad in January 2004 and the 13 meeting scheduled to be held in January 2005 in Bangladesh the country of its worth was postponed due to the Tsunami disaster and later on also due to the political upheaval in Nepal. Besides, the submit meetings which constitute the apex of the institutional framework, there is a council of Foreign Ministers, a standing committee comprising of the Foreign Secretaries and also a number of technical committees. Despite the facts that SAARC's movement towards its goal has not been very smooth and fast but all the committees and summits have been working fairly regularly. Two out of 12 summits (second in 1986 and eight 1995) had been held in India at Bangalore and New Delhi respectively. Through the span of 20 years for an organization's life is not long enough to judge its success but still one can draw some conclusions from the trends and actual performance which indicate a degree of pessimism and skepticism. Before going into the detailed discussion of SAARC as regional organization, it becomes worthwhile to examine briefly the growth of regionalism in South Asia.

The main factors, which have obstructed the growth of regional co-operations in South Asia, can be summarized as colonial legacies, problems of national integration, disparities in the level of economic growth, geographical diversities with regard to size, population and power potential and the role of external powers. The most important factor in this respect has been the Indo-centric nature of the region. It means that India is the center of the region, which shares common borders with all of the six countries while none of them share border with each other. This has implications in terms of cultural identities, economic patterns and historical experiences. Conversely there is a bit of India in every other country of South Asia. As against this, there is hardly any thing of significance which is common between them.[5] The second characteristic of South Asia is its unbalanced and asymmetrical power structure.[6] As a result of this South Asia has become "India centered" and India has often been seen as a big brother or bully by her smaller neighbours. It is also believed by some that history of South Asia does not provide a model of regional cooperation. But this point of view is belied by the European example. If Germany and France, which were known to be the traditional enemies of yesteryears, can come together for fruitful regional cooperation why South Asian countries can not forget their differences and engage themselves in cooperative endeavour for mutual benefit?

Undoubtedly, the root cause of tension and conflict in South Asia has been the colonial policy. The partition of India on religious basis into two independent nations has created a series of problems in the sub-continent. Colonial rule left the boundaries undemarcated and ambiguous which, created several territorial disputes between the countries of the region. Further, as a result of British colonial policy in almost every country of the region, there are ethnic minorities, which have their origin in another country of the region. Thus, because of this in South Asia's "domestic ethno political troubles and conflicts tend to spill over to inter state relations...The domestic ethno political configurations hold the key to inter-state tensions and conflicts. These configurations are tissues made of linguistic, cultural and religious fibers, inseparable from one another."[7] These inter-state disputes have had adverse impact on regional cooperation in South Asia. Sadly, the position of SAARC has been that of a hostage of political troubles among its member countries."[8] It is generally being observed that SAARC tends to become victim of intra-regional tensions at times.

The first such situation occurred when Sri Lankan President Premadasa threatened to boycott the summit scheduled to be held in December 1990 in Maldives unless the Indian Peace Keeping Forces (IPKF) withdrew from Sri Lanka in 1989. Premadasa did not attend the meet even when Indian Peace Keeping Forces withdrew from Sri Lanka. Thus, the SAARC process had a severe jolt as a result of Indo-Sri Lankan relations. The second crisis followed as a result of India's reaction and refusal to attend next summit meeting in 1991 because India was upset at Premadasa's attempt to isolate her and raise bilateral issues in SAARC forum. Indo-Bangladesh relations too had their share. The summit had to be postponed in the aftermath of the Babri Masjid episode of 1992 because India made it clear that "the atmosphere was not right for such conference". Indo-Pak relations perhaps have posed most serious challenge for SAARC unity and have "constituted the Achilles heal" of regional co-operation in South Asia. Pakistan has lobbied at the summits and at ministerial meetings that SAARC should take up bilateral issues too. It has also suggested amendment in the charter for this purpose. Pakistan has been consistently harping on its stand that no worthwhile progress could be expected unless India resolved the 'Core problem" of Kashmir to her satisfaction[9] India too has strongly opposed these attempts.

Indo-Pak tensions have cast a permanent shadow over the full utilization of SAARC potential for regional cooperation as is evident from the fact that two recent Summits XI and XII became victim of this syndrome in the wake of Kargil conflict and Pakistan's continued support to cross- border terrorism. On the postponement of the XII summit, *The Hindu* was quite critical of both India and Pakistan's attitude in its editorial of December

11, 2003, which said "In normal circumstances, summit meetings that produce little can be subject of ridicule, but not so in South Asian context where relations inter se are usually so poisonous that even gestures of friendliness are of inestimable value...The postponement has once again demonstrated that the leaders of the region are unable or unwilling to conceptualize and work for a future in which a wholesome co-existence would replace unhealthy confrontation of the present. While Islamabad did contribute to the unfortunate development through its tardiness in implementing key-economy and trade measures, New Delhi must take most of the blame for failing to preserve the principle that summit level meetings of SAARC must be held on a regular basis-irrespective of progress on specific matters, so that institution's life is sustained". Despite these stumbling blocks the process continues. Truly it is better late than never. Although, the current uncertain phase of Indo-Bangladesh ties threatens to take the shine off the 13th SAARC summit[10] which was to take place in Dhaka in January 2005. But despite some hiccups and road blocks SAARC has travelled a long way and has to some extent "belied the skepticism of its critics and has succeeded in evolving its own rhythm in forging a distinct regional identity."[11] It has definitely shown a new dynamism and direction in the post cold war period. There has been a steady increase in the activities, which indicate an overall progress in regional cooperation. The SAARC secretariat at Kathmandu is playing an active role in coordinating its activities. The Integrated Programme of Action, which enumerates 12 areas of cooperation ranging from agriculture, environment to women's development is fully in place.[12] A wide range of activities has been taken in almost all areas of cooperation.

Establishment of a three window South Asian Development Fund in June 1996 is a remarkable achievement of SAARC for accelerating the implementation of approved projects and programmes of IPA. SAARC Audio-Visual programme is also fully operational and SAARC exchange of fellowship is also working well. SAARC has focused its attention on various socio-economic areas of common concern like eradication of poverty, girl child, youth, literacy, shelter etc. It has also evolved common stands in international forums like UN Conference on Environment and Development in 1992, Fourth World Conference on Women in 1995 and World Food Summit in 1996.[13] Landmark achievements of SAARC have been signing of SAPTA (South Asian Preferential Trade Arrangements), establishment of SAARC Food Security Reserve, Convention on Narcotic Drugs and Psychotropic Substances and Convention on Suppression of Terrorism and Convention on Preventing and Combating Trafficking in Women and Children for prostitution in member states.

SAPTA, the most important achievement of SAARC which became operational in 1995 aims to step by step liberalization of trade in the region through negotiations for exchange of trade concessions on tariff and para tariff leading to the establishment of Free Trade Area (SAFTA). But the progress in this direction is modest.

India's Contribution and the Challenges

India has been taking active interest in the activities of SAARC since its inception. It was at Banglaore summit in 1986 that the establishment of a Secretariat at Kathmandu with Secretary General completed the formal organization of SAARC. The expenses of the secretariat are borne by the members. India's contribution in terms of percentage was the highest i.e. 32 per cent of the total – the rest shared by other six: 23 per cent by Pakistan and Bangladesh, Nepal shared 11 per cent and Bhutan and Maldives 5 per cent each.[14] Till 1988 India's contribution amounted to US$ 118873.80. India has also contributed maximum amount i.e. 1532,200 metric tons of food grains to SAARC food reserve.[15] India's exports and imports from SAARC has also increased significantly during the first decade of its existence. Percentage of share of SAARC in India's total exports showed an increase while imports remained low. This gap between export and import has to be removed.

In order to promote economic cooperation, India has taken a number of initiatives. It has doubled the ceiling for overseas Indian investment in SAARC to US$30 millions for promotion of business opportunities. India had made efforts on its part to speed up momentum towards SAFTA. It had proposed a separate SAFTA Treaty which was signed in Islamabad at 12th Summit in

January 2004. The agreement would "enter into force" on January 1, 2006.[16] There is no doubt that India's role in transition of South Asia from SAPTA to SAFTA has to be significant. Under the first two rounds of SAPTA negotiations India offered maximum concessions covering 1000 tariff lines. It also offered the maximum number of tariff cuts with special concessions to the least developed countries.[17] In the third round of SAPTA negotiations held in 1998, the number of concessions increased to a total of 3456 tariff lines. More than half concessions were given by India. India already has free trade agreements with Nepal, Bhutan and Sri Lanka. These c ountries also had preferential trade agreement with India.[18]

Thus, on the basis of the foregoing one can conclude that SAARC, despite all the problems, is moving slowly towards regional cooperation in socio-economic fields. The slow progress is, as discussed earlier, due to the asymmetrical nature of geographical, historical and economic profiles of South Asian countries, which in turn gives, rise to a kind of apprehension about Indian domination among smaller countries of the region. Therefore although regional cooperation has been set in motion, the obstacles still exist and pose a challenge before SAARC and India both. The conflictual relationship between India and Pakistan poses another challenge. When these challenges are met successfully with strong political will, an atmosphere will automatically be created for cooperation and also collectively working towards the goal of making the region self-reliant in economic field, progressive in social field and confident in the international field.

Notes and References

1. Surendra Chopra (ed.) *Studies in India's Foreign Policy*, Amritsar, 1983. See chapter by Surjit Mansingh "Cooperation in South Asia: Imperatives and Obstacles". pp. 395-96.
2. Norman J. Padelford and George A. Zinedin: *Dynamics of International Politics*, New York, 1967, p. 451.
3. Jawaharlal Nehru: *India's Foreign Policy*. Govt. of India, New Delhi, 1961 p. 22.
4. *Ibid.*, p. 252.

5. Bimal Prasad: (ed.) *India's Foreign Policy: Studies in Continuity and Changes,* New Delhi, 1979. See chapter by S.D. Muni, p. 106.
6. *Ibid.*, p. 108.
7. Bhabani Sen Gupta: *South Asian Perspectives: Seven Nations in Conflict and Cooperation*, Delhi, 1988, pp. 14-15.
8. V.P. Dutt: *India's Foreign Policy in Changing World,* New Delhi, 1999, p. 193.
9. *Ibid.*, p. 195.
10. *The Hindu:* July 25, 2004, see Article by C. Raja Mohan on Indo-Bangladesh relations.
11. L. Mansingh. M. Venkatraman, J.N. Dixit, Bhabani Sengupta (ed.) *Indian Foreign Policy: An Agenda for 21st Century.* Vol. 2 New Delhi, 1998. See Nancy Jetly's article, p. 3.
12. *Ibid.*, p. 4.
13. *Ibid.*, p. 6.
14. P.K. Misra: "Dhaka to New Delhi: One Decade of SAARC", *India Quarterly,* Jan-June 1996 p. 76.
15. Debendra K. Das (ed.) *SAARC: Regional Co-operation and Development Perspectives. Problems and Politics,* New Delhi, 1996, p. 70.
16. *The Hind:,* 11 July 2004.
17. I.K. Gujral: Continuity and Change : *India's Foreign Policy,* Delhi, 2003, p. 184.
18. B.C. Upreti, M.L. Sharma, S.N. Kaushik (eds.) *India's Foreign Policy Emerging Challenges and Paradigms*, Vol. II, Delhi, 2003, pp. 484-87.

13

Growing Nuclear Danger in South Asia: Prospects for Cooperative Denuclearisation?

Jyotirmoy Banerjee

Nuclear Dilemmas in Indo-Pakistani Relations: Level One

With the nuclear skeletons out of their cupboards way back in May 1998, India and Pakistan count as Nuclear-Weapons States (NWS). In 2001, the Indian armed forces even conducted a military exercise dubbed 'Operation Poorna Vijay' ('complete victory') in a simulated nuclear war environment. But the smug satisfaction in New Delhi and Islamabad at the possession of awesome nuclear weapons is only surface deep. Just beneath, there continue to lurk a large number of dilemmas and questions. These problems may be grouped together as those of level one, or conventional relations between states. Terrorism has introduced a fresh dimension to the nuclear question, which can be called as level two problems.

A large amount of scholarly literature speculating about the South Asian nuclear scene is available. But most of the South Asian scholarly outpourings on the subject have sure footing only in Western sources, largely emanating from the USA. The Indian and Pakistani governments have, not unexpectedly, apotheosized all data on their nukes and placed them on a sacred altar, which only the highest priests of government can reach. Gorbachev's 'transparency' or the US 'Sunshine Act' were never heard of in the Byzantine bureaucracies of our subcontinent. This near-total secrecy, which is also a convenient way to cover up bungling, turn the South Asian scholarly outpourings into relatively low-grade ore. However high the expertise, near-absence of hard data undercuts its intrinsic value. The bulk of South Asia's publications relates to what ought to be done. Understandably, there is little discussion of the details of ground realities. Moreover, focused discussion of specifically cooperative denuclearisation is few and far between. This paper is an attempt to fill that lacuna in the South Asian context, with due acknowledgement of the existing caveats the size of Californian speedways.

A look at the declared yields of the tests by both sides shows that the mode average yield is skewed towards lower-yield nukes.[1] The low-yield nukes carry the unmistakable stamp of being tactical, or counterforce, weapons. Of course, even low-yields can create massive collateral damage in the densely populated Kashmir-Punjab sector on both sides of the border. Whatever the opaque intentions behind these low-yields, they have a tendency to lower the nuclear threshold. The temptation to reach for them will be high when either side is losing heavily in a conventional war. This is likely to be truer of a military-dominated Pakistan with deep-rooted fundamentalism. Islamabad's declared policy is also to keep the nuclear option open. Hence it refused to pledge No-First-Use (NFU), unlike New Delhi.

The second dilemma relates to the reliability of the nuclear warheads and their delivery systems. Half-a-dozen hot tests by each side including Pokharan I of 1974 are grossly inadequate to ensure the reliability of the nukes at critical times. The nuclear veteran nations, on the other hand, tested theirs for over four decades (China since 1964) before halting hot tests. Even then they have retained the option of continuing with cold tests via computer simulation. So, weaponisation needs more tests. At a seminar in New Delhi a scientist pointed out that India's 45-Kt nuke weighed about 1,000 lbs. That weight, but not yield, ought to be reduced in order to weaponise it. This needs further field tests. But neither India nor Pakistan can afford to carry these in face of international disapproval and sanctions. So their weponisation leaves room for doubt.

The third dilemma relates to India's No-First-Use (NFU) declaration. Along with New Delhi's declared posture of 'second strike' only, NFU is politically facetious but in practice facile. Time and space are against the two South Asian neighbours. In the US-Soviet/Russian case, each side would have half-an-hour of early warning. But in South Asia, our geographical contiguity leaves either side 3-6 minutes to choose a reaction to an attack underway. If it receives warning that a hostile nuclear attack is underway would India wait till it is nuked because of its NFU? Further, to maintain a credible second strike capability our retaliatory assets must be hardened with mobile, easy-to-hide missiles, nuclear blast-proof, super-concrete and widely dispersed underground silos and command centres, secure communications, SLBM-submarines, etc. The sea-leg of nuclear deterrence, which is harder to detect, is yet to be developed by either side. Fourth, early warning sensors of both countries are sub-optimal. Both heavily depend on radars but how good these are is an open question. US-style hi-tech satellite early warning is hardly in place. Even the US and Russian early warning network have set off a number of false alarms in the past. In 1995, Russia mistook a civilian rocket flying in the vicinity of Norway as a US Trident Submarine-Launched Ballistic Missile (SLBM). So, if the sophisticated machines of the nuclear veterans sometimes err, what guarantee is there for South Asian machinery? The Purulia arms-drop case in India some years ago revealed a window of vulnerability as wide as the Indo-Gangetic plains in our air defence network.

Fifth, both sides have reportedly kept their nukes dispersed and in unassembled form. This is supposed to reassure each other and put up a good face to the 'international community'. This status has been called 'recessed deterrence' by Jasjit Singh and 'force-in-being' by Ashley Tellis of RAND. It is a state of relaxed deterrence in normal times. The question, however, is, can these components be assembled, deployed and launched in 3-6 minutes? The anxiety to launch will be all the more if there is no way of knowing whether the incoming first strike is counterforce meant to disarm one's retaliatory, or second strike, capability. The alternative postures are even more disastrous.[2] These are launch-on-warning and, the worst, pre-emption. The terms are self-explanatory. But these doctrines seem better suited in the South Asian context due to severe time constraints, which allow no deliberation. Despite an Indo-Pakistani agreement reached in December 1988 on sparing attacks on each other's nuclear facilities, desperation in crisis, unauthorised launch by hotheads, launch by miscalculation or by accident are real dangers, especially so in South Asia not known for efficiency.

A sixth question relates to the status of the chain of nuclear command. Media reports have suggested that Pakistan's National Command Authority is streamlined and ready to face a nuclear emergency decision- making better than India's less organised command chain. New Delhi seems to be belatedly waking up and trying to rise above inter-service rivalry to get a single-point nuclear decision making the post of Chief of Defence Staff (CDS), in place. Given the few minutes of reaction time, bureaucratic bungling and South Asia's famous red-tapism are the last things we need. In sum, the dubious capability of the nukes, their delivery systems and the early-warning apparatus is bad enough. The alarming rate at which the Indian Air Force's MiG-21s—mishaps have occurred even with the elite MIG-29s in spring 2002— have been reportedly crashing while on routine flights in the recent past points to a serious flaw at our maintenance culture. The Pakistani air force also has a matching record of crashes. It was incredible that Premier Vajpayee's Boeing 737-200 aircraft, flying a three-nation tour in late 2001, reportedly did not even have a telephone for the nation's leader to communicate with the ground, a basic amenity which commercial airliners routinely offer to their passengers![3]

Indeed, India's nuclear doctrine of 'minimum credible deterrence' says nothing. There is instead need for a clear cut doctrine that spells out various scenarios in which nukes may be used. And this doctrine must be conveyed to our adversaries and the world at large, just as the US and the USSR had done in the past, to avoid miscalculations and adventurism that would cost both adversaries dearly.

International Terrorism and the Nuclear Threat: Level Two

A brand new dilemma has burst upon the international scene with sudden urgency since 11 September 2001. In novelty and scale it has beaten the burgeoning literature of thrillers on terrorism. The Al Qaeda terrorist network easily conquered world headlines. A surprise terrorist seizure of nuclear materials in South Asia, especially in Pakistan immediately neighbouring troubled Afghanistan, has suddenly metamorphosed from a mere Tom Clancy thriller or RAND conjecture to a real, nightmarish possibility. Al Qaeda is known to have sympathisers and contacts among segments of nuclear scientists in several countries including Pakistan. Evidence has been found in Afghan caves and safe houses that it was seriously trying to produce Weapons of Mass Destruction (WMD), including the nuclear bomb. Even if the terrorists of various ilks do not have the infrastructure to build a bomb, they can always make a 'dirty' bomb. This device will use conventional explosives to spread radioactivity over a large populated area. Slow, painful cancer death is hardly more attractive than attaining instantaneous, violent and recalcitrant nirvana! It is also entirely possible that while terrorists provide smuggled nuclear hardware, impoverished ex-Soviet scientists may pass on their know-how in exchange for good money. Hence, the nuclear weapons problem in South Asia—and elsewhere—has now become a dual one. The conventional level is that of inter-state nuclear balance between India and Pakistan, our level one. But the second level, which needs the most urgent attention and even surpasses the threat posed by the first, is the one introduced by non-state actors, or terrorist organisations. No nation is well prepared to face this particular type of threat. It is unusually complicated by the fact that the terror phantoms are mostly anonymous and cannot be pinned down to a clear-cut domiciliary region. Nuclear deterrence is as useful against them as an eight-inch battleship artillery piece against Kolkata's mosquitos. In the following analysis, we shall first continue with our first level. It will research the Indo-Pakistani nuclear scenario, with China's nuclear arsenal also casting a long shadow over them. Next, we shall turn to the very real threat posed by the second level, that of terrorism, as related to nuclear weapons security in South Asia.

The Obstacles

Past nuclear agreements between the US and the USSR did not seek to control nuclear warheads directly but focused instead on delivery systems. But an effective way to nuclear weapons reduction can be direct control over the warheads and the materials needed to manufacture them. Besides 'national technical means'— euphemism for espionage— there is undoubtedly need for cooperative verification measures.[4] These would include: declarations of the location and status of all nuclear warheads and fissile material stockpiles, verification of these declarations via on-site inspections and exchanges of data on the design and operating history of the production facilities, verification of the dismantling of nukes and of the storage and disposition of the fissile materials contained in them, verification of a ban on the production of additional fissile materials for weapons, and improved IAEA safeguards on peaceful nuclear activities.

Verification procedures would include checking data on warheads, or canisters containing pits, with ground reality. Regular and short-notice inspections at declared facilities would combine with challenge or suspect-site inspections. The use of tags to identify a warhead on the list provided could be helpful in a random sampling. But whether the latter, though fissile materials, were authentic warheads could not be so easily determined without revealing sensitive design information. In such knotty cases, a combination of radiation and other distinctive signatures could be taken to 'fingerprint' types of nukes or pits. These could then be used as a template to ensure the authenticity of the contents in tagged canisters. A detailed signature would be extremely difficult to fake and, at the same time, should be so prepared that design information stays hidden. It would also be necessary to ensure that untagged objects do not contain nukes or pits. In 1989 the US and the USSR conducted reciprocal demonstrations of tagging techniques for ballistic missiles. Declared warheads would have their tags authenticated while other objects would be inspected at random for nuclear materials.

Inspecting fissile materials would pose greater difficulties than nukes. The latter can be counted but not fissile material. Also, it is near impossible even for the possessor state to come up with 100 percent accurate figures in its inventory. However miniscule, a small percentage of fissile materials will remain in pipes and glove boxes, spent fuel and metal scraps and so on. So error by the owning state could easily go up to a few percentage points, which would correspond to a number of weapons. Visiting inspectors with their own methods are expected to add to the error. Ways have to be found to overcome this problem with fissile materials.

Level One: The Nuclear Weapons Problem in South Asia

Having recognized the technicalities involved in a denuclearisation project, we now turn to the available information on the respective nuclear arsenals of the two South Asian rivals. The analysis here continues along level one.

The declared yields in Kt of TNT of the nuclear devices which India tested on 11 and 13 May 1998—Pokharan II were 43, 12, 0.3 on the first day, and 0.5 and 0.3 on the second. Pokharan I, way back on 18 May 1974, had 15 Kt yield. Pakistan's tests in Ras Koh in the Chagai Hills on 28 and 30 May 1998 yielded 12, 25, 3, sub-Kt on the first day, followed by 12 Kt on the second. While India insisted that it had successfully tested a thermonuclear device, controversy surrounded its claim.[5]

Indo-Pakistani CBMs and CSBMs

To be sure, the Indo-Pakistani scenario has not been all hostility. A certain amount of Track II 'diplomacy' has been going on between the two rival nations. Indian and Pakistani scholars have been visiting each other's countries on academic missions. Such exchanges provide an opportunity for people-to-people contact and to hear the other side's views, to open a dialogue as a first step towards building mutual confidence. Meets in other fields like sports have not been unusual.

In 1996 and 1997 interaction took place between the two sides along with Asia Society and the Japan Institute of International Affairs. The discussions included nuclear issues. At a conference in September 2001 sponsored by the Indian Council for Social Science Research experts from the two countries agreed on the need to develop contacts between civil society groups, easing of media reporting on each other, and of visa rules to boost exchanges and contacts. Pakistani delegates quite openly criticised their own legislators for their "scant regard for the democratic process." The conference stressed the need for the then approaching Indo-Pakistani Agra summit to agree on "specific" CBMs between the two nations. Besides, the Neemrana Group, named after a fort in Rajasthan and consisting of former Indian and Pakistani government officials as well as private individuals, has been meeting regularly since 1991. The Times of India reported on 27 April that even in the middle of the Indo-Pakistani border tension, an Indo-Pakistani non-governmental seminar was held in Islamabad in March 2002; the Indian delegation also talked to Musharraf.[6]

At the government level, certain steps towards CBMs and CSBMs have indeed been taken. We have already seen an agreement reached in December 1988 not to attack each other's nuclear facilities. It was ratified four years later. The Lahore Declaration of February 1999 added the holy intention of the two sides to avoid conflict, given the nuclear dimension to the security environment, which had been added the preceding year. Besides, India offered expert-level official talks on nuclear CSBMs on the sidelines of the Colombo SAARC meet in 2001. Islamabad reportedly had agreed to continue the dialogue.[7]

Pakistani leader General Musharraf matched the Indian offer with his own at the UN General Assembly in November that year. He said that his country was ready to discuss "nuclear and missile restraints as well as nuclear risk reduction measures with India in a structured, comprehensive and integrated dialogue". The last two adjectives suggest that he probably wanted to include the Kashmir question too. He further stated that he was ready to formalise a bilateral treaty" to create a regime of "mutual test ban", confidence-building measures and non-use of force.[8] It all sounded very nice except that Indian and Pakistani proposals and counter-proposals on strategic issues have been a dime a dozen. When Vajpayee had offered a no-first-use of nukes agreement to former Pakistani Premier Nawaz Sharif during the Colombo SAARC summit of 1998, the latter had countered the Indian offer by pulling out Islamabad's old offer of a wider non-aggression pact to which New Delhi would never agree. One reason why India found similar Pakistani offers unacceptable in the past was that these would define security strictly within the geographical confines of South Asia. But India could ill-afford to overlook the potential Chinese nuclear threat emanating from beyond. Often, these offers are played to various domestic and international galleries to gain political mileage. As veteran Pakistani commentator M.B. Naqvi aptly put it, each side knows that the other will reject the offer. "The aim is to score points. The two have gone round this mulberry bush many times since the 1980s while cynically proliferating atomic weaponry."[9] The Agra summit also suffered a shipwreck; no agreement was reached and no progress was made towards CBMs or CSBMs. However, the silver lining is not altogether absent. On 1 January 2002 India and Pakistan lived up to their mutual promise and exchanged lists of their nuclear installations and facilities under Article 2 of the agreement, which banned attacks on these. The article required the two sides to furnish their updated lists of nuclear installations on 1 January every year. The two governments also joined 84 others in an agreement to continue talks to develop an international instrument to govern ballistic missile proliferation. When India test fired its road-mobile, solid-fuel, short-range' Agni missile on 25 January, it put Pakistan on notice 48 hours before under a MoU signed in Lahore. The Conference on Interaction and Confidence Building Measures in Asia (CICA) represents another way of enhancing CBMs. In June 2004 officials of the newly elected Congress-led government in India and their Pakistani counterparts held nuclear risk-reduction talks, possibly focusing on the hotline and other measures to cut chances of accidentally nuking each other. Follow-on talks are expected later that year.

As of April 2002 Islamabad continued to refuse to hand over the twenty terrorists demanded by India. However, its Foreign Minister Abdul Sattar sweetened the pill by saying that while there was no extradition treaty between the two countries, the 1987 South Asian Association for Regional Cooperation (SAARC) document on extradition might serve as a framework for the purpose.[10]

Other steps already taken to enhance CBMs or CSBMs include hotlines set up between the Army Headquarters of the two neighbours and the sector commanders on either side of the Line of Control (LoC) in Kashmir. Way back in 1992 there came an agreement to provide the other side with prior notification if one side was going to conduct a military exercise involving over 10,000 troops. A military no-fly zone along the common border had also been established. However, there have been periodic allegations of violation by both sides. The 800,000-strong Indian army deployment which started since 19 December on the Pakistani border under 'Operation Parakram' has been dubbed a 'manoeuvre' rather than an 'exercise' to avoid requirements of the agreement.

The need for CBMs, CSBMs and Track II meets is felt among the educated in both countries. Pakistan's veteran journalists M.B. Naqvi, and former military officer Lodi, for example, have stressed these. Like the present author and like-minded Indian scholars, these Pakistani experts are also keen on lowering the enormous barrier of mistrust between the two countries. The US-Russian record could be of enormous help here. Lodi makes a substantial point when he says that besides the purely military related CSBMs, CBMs and Track II must receive high priority. This is because the position of the two governments have hardened over the decades, and there remains little room for either to manoeuver. People-to-people contact can initiate change grass roots-level attitudes and perceptions about the other side. This, in the long term, would encourage the respective governments to undertake serious effort to defreeze their hitherto immobile stances.

However, continued cross-border terrorism in Kashmir and Islamabad's crocodile tears over the alleged plight of the Kashmiris in India continues to mar any efforts at reconciliation. As of winter and spring 2002 all silver linings seem to have vanished along with the tenuous bus and train links connecting the two countries. An abundance of jingoistic rhetoric has emerged from both New Delhi and Islamabad. Compounding that threat is our level two, that posed by international terrorism.

South Asia: Need for Unambiguous Nuclear Doctrine and Strategy

There is a large measure of consensus among defence intellectuals that for India, the bomb is more a political instrument than a means of war. India's bomb is not Pakistan-specific but takes the growing Chinese nuclear potential into account, too. China in recent years has upgraded its ballistic missiles based in Tibet to the so-called CSS-5s. A significant percentage of its missiles are based there. This is of strategic concern to India's defence planners. As we noted, to Pakistan, where the military dominates the nuclear debate, the nuke is a tool of war to get even with the numerically superior conventional Indian military. In an interview with the German news magazine Der Spiegel in spring 2002 Musharraf reiterated that view openly. He reportedly observed that if India's pressure on Pakistan was stepped up, it might reach a point where Islamabad would press the nuclear button.[11] Islamabad seems to believe that its nukes will deter India from launching conventional strikes while Pakistan could go ahead with waging its proxy war in Kashmir. Kargil in mid-1999 epitomised this line of thinking. It took numerous terrorist attacks over the past decade but particularly the ones against the Kashmir Assembly in October and Parliament on 13 December 2001 to galvanise India into unabashed military mobilisation along the Pakistani border. Already there had been reports that India, having tested a second time its long-range missile Agni II on 17 January 2001, was going to weaponise it to make it "ready for battle status". New Delhi's militant mood upset Islamabad's applecart, as we noted. The USA, sensing that its own counter-terrorist military and other operations in Afghanistan might be jeopardised by an outbreak of war, arm-twisted Musharraf to stop bothering India and crack down against terrorists operating from Pakistan.[12] Musharraf had little choice but to go through the motions.

But India remained skeptical and spurned several Pakistani offer of 'talks'. New Delhi insisted upon effective Pakistani measures against the export of cross-border terrorism and handing over of twenty terrorists wanted for various atrocities committed against India before any meaningful talks could begin. For instance, the leader of Jamait-e-Mohammad (JeM), which had for long been on New Delhi's counter-terrorism crosshairs, Masood Azhar, had to be set free from captivity in India when an Indian civilian passenger aircraft was hijacked to Kandahar. He found refuge in Pakistan. Following Musharraf's ban on his JeM, he simply changed its nomenclature to Jamait-ul-Furkan and re-emerged in Kashmir.

Hence, the Indian armed forces remained poised on alert on the border. The army declared its resolve to take "relentless" measures against infiltration and terrorism in Kashmir by installing electronic detection devices on the border. On 4 April 2002 Defence Minister George Fernandes reiterated New Delhi's stand and ruled out any troop pullout from the border so long as Pakistan did not prove its sincerity. It should be noted here that Russia, which is the largest arms supplier to India, unreservedly supported India's stand on Kashmir in February when its former Foreign Minister Igor Ivanov came visiting. Chechnya after all is Moscow's Kashmir.

Continuing with our conventional, level one analysis: how does one assess the Indo-Pakistani nuclear relations in 2004? It is a matter of serious concern for the international community since for the first time in the Post-Cold War era, two rival nuclear powers, located in close proximity to each other, are poised dangerously on the brink. What are the chances that if a conventional war breaks out between India and Pakistan, it will cross the nuclear threshold? In March 2002 CIA boss George Tenet warned that the risk of an Indo-Pakistani war was high. Reports in fall 2003 suggested that Pakistan was aiding Saudi Arabia secretly with nukes and exchanging nuclear technology with North Korea in exchange for the latter's missiles, just as India supposedly had entered into a shady partnership on nukes with Iran. Both India and Pakistan continued their ballistic missile tests in fall that year.

The urgent need is that of clear-cut and well-publicised nuclear doctrines from either side so that miscalculations can be avoided in a situation as obtains in spring 2002. A large chunk of Pakistan's cities and towns are concentrated within a 30-mile wide corridor, a convenient target for India's more numerous nuclear arms. The bottom line in a nuclear exchange will likely be a damaged India but an exterminated Pakistan.

Hence, observes M.B. Naqvi, India is deliberately playing a kind of chicken strategy, defying Pakistan's threat to cross the nuclear threshold. The Indian warlike posture has also pushed the US to pressure Musharraf to act against terrorists and extremists in his country; otherwise Pakistan has to divert its resources to meet the Indian threat, resources the USA needs for its own campaign in the region. Naqvi reiterates what we noted earlier, that Islamabad's thinking was that it could go on pursuing its Kashmir policy of encouraging anti-Indian activities. Zia-ul-Haq had been instrumental in giving it an additional jihadi twist. India would be faced with the dilemma of whether to retaliate against a nuclear-armed Pakistan in what after all was a classic proxy war. The nuclear factor since 1998 may have even boosted Islamabad's conviction that the chances of India's retaliation had become even more remote.

But following 13 December 2001 India determinedly mobilised and deployed troops on the Pakistani border. The accompanying talk was of even 'hot pursuit' of the intruders in Kashmir back to their bases in Pakistan. The Indian posture and tough talk revealed that the Pakistani strategy of scaring New Delhi with the prospect of nuclear war had backfired. "Indians took some beating before realising that they too can play at the same game. Now they have "challenged" Pakistan "to a war and do its worst", observes Naqvi. Islamabad has realised the consequences of an all-out war for itself. It does not have the first strike capability to overwhelm India. Rather, it is an all-out Indian retaliation that could be overwhelming. So it has opted for "peace", "sanctity and common sense", concludes the astute Pakistani journalist.[13]

Level Two: Nuclear Terror in Russia and South Asia

The problem of Russia's ageing nuclear weapons and nuclear waste has bee bad enough. The sudden prospect of international terror networks grabbing these has only made things worse. Following the September 2001 terror attacks on the USA, President Bush stepped on the gas to surge fast on enhanced safeguarding of Russian nuclear materials. The November 2001 Bush-Putin summit spawned an agreement to create "a new strategic framework" to enhance security of their countries and the world community at large. As part of that framework there would be prevention of "illicit nuclear trafficking". The US-Russia Nuclear and Terrorism Threat Reduction Act of 2002 (NTTRA) reflects Bush's determination to devote more funds and resources to contain the compounded danger emerging from Russian—and other—nuclear arsenals. After 9/11 the danger of hostile states and especially terrorist outfits gaining access to loosely guarded nuclear arsenals, primarily in Russia but now also in South Asia, is real. Russian leader Putin has asserted that the terrorists carrying out attacks in the USA, India and Russia itself spring from the same source. The renewed endeavour to minimise and neutralise the Russian danger seems justified. Moscow lists 200 organisations as terrorist outfits. Many of these are keen to obtain nukes. The Russians broke up 601 attempted transactions since 1998. IAEA reported 376 such incidents since 1993 and Turkey 104. In August 1994 the German secret police arrested two Colombians arriving in Munich airport from Moscow with half kg. plutonium in their suitcase. The news created a sensation with headlines talking about 'loose nukes' and Russia's 'atomic mafia'. Recently, a UN nuclear watchdog agency sent a team to try to seize two portable nuclear devices, which found their way to Georgia's breakaway province of Abkhazia. While most cases of smuggling detected so far have been in Russia's western border, the country's less secure southern borders with Central Asian states are particularly worrisome. Traditional routes of trade between south Russia's mountainous regions and those states provide a readymade conduit to volatile Afghanistan and some of its neighbours which have a large concentration of various terrorist groups.[14] No wonder that Russian border guards have been deployed in some of these states. There are parallels in the Russian situation and the turmoil around, and potentially in, Pakistan as far as nuclear weapons and materials are concerned. The breakaway Chechno-Ingushetia autonomous republic in Russia hosts a Bear-H bomber base near Mozdoc. The base would normally have gravity bombs and cruise missiles. Their theft or seizure is a possibility, which worries Moscow. Russia is never far from the risk of suffering a breakdown in other regions of the vast country where tactical or strategic nukes such as mobile SS-25 ICBMs are located.[15]

The Afghan turmoil, already spilling over into Pakistan, may similarly lead to the erosion of central authority in Islamabad or even its breakdown altogether. This will increase the chances for radical elements to gain control of Pakistani nuclear materials that would be bad news for all and sundry. Many of the technical and political factors sketched above would seem to be highly relevant to South Asia. The danger seems to apply especially to Pakistan because of radical elements deeply embedded in the latter's military, intelligence (ISI) and fundamentalist groups, and given that it not only directly faces the uncertainties emanating from neighbouring Afghanistan but has long been deeply involved with the radicals and terrorists based there.[16]

Though the US won the first round of military campaign against the terrorists in Afghanistan, the latter are far from totally subdued. They proved their mettle by their reckless suicide bombings and last-ditch battles. Further, the 'shoe bomber' case, the brutal murder of the American newsman Daniel Pearl, and al Qaeda's leaflets circulating in April 2002 in eastern Afghanistan which promised lucrative rewards in US$ for dead or alive Western soldiers of the peacekeeping force again revealed the fanatical determination of the terrorists to wreak damage.

The possibility of terrorists gaining access to nuclear materials in South Asia, especially in Pakistan, has loomed large in US calculations. International terrorism since 9/11 immediately raised the question how secure the nuclear arsenals and stockpiles of India and Pakistan were and whether terrorists could seize them and use against the USA. As we already noted that little concrete information on security matters is given out by these two countries, unlike the USA. Nuclear weapons-related matters are kept under a double wrap. With that lacuna noted, the study on the Indian nuclear scene by scholars at the Institute of Strategic Studies in Islamabad observes that India's expansive nuclear programme, much of which is not IAEA-safeguarded, is highly vulnerable to illicit access by international terrorists. The big country has a thriving underworld, and over a dozen insurgencies are active there. Some of these elements would not hesitate to gain access to nukes. It says that India's nuclear programme grew "too quickly", without observing proper safeguards. It further alleges that lack of accountability and wide dispersal of unsafeguarded nuclear facilities pose a potential hazard. Of India's 14 nuclear plants, only four are safeguarded. Moreover, uranium mining remains potentially hazardous. There is lack of adequate safety measures for the population living around these mines, largely 'dalits' or some of the poorest strata of Indian society. Financial rewards from sale of illicit nuclear expertise, the study alleges, may have become a serious threat for India's scientific community, an observation reminiscent of the acute problem in Russia in this regard. Existing international conventions on nuclear safety do not deal much with questions of nuclear reactor design, safety features governing the mining of radioactive materials, nuclear theft and so on. Hence, India needs to tone up its nuclear administration, whether civilian or military.[17]

Pakistan's Nuclear Arsenal

Seymour M. Hersh in his high-profile article in the *New Yorker* magazine on 5 November 2001 raised questions about Pakistan's nuclear weapons security. Three days before the article appeared in print, Pakistani Foreign Minister Abdul Sattar had smoothly countered US press speculations by observing that Islamabad had already strengthened in February "plans for the security of the custodial safety and command and control" of the weapons. The *Washington Post* reported that Musharraf had quickly moved his nukes to six secret sites within 48 hours of the 11 September attacks. A few days later, on 19 September, Musharraf laid down his cards in a major speech to the nation that was startling in its anti-jehadi tone. The speech was tailored to justify his siding with US war preparations. Three months later he radiated an image of confidence by telling The Far Eastern Economic Review that his nukes were "absolutely secure."[18] Musharraf had his reasons. He had proceeded to restructure his nuclear command chain, which had been overhauled in 2000, once again in October as the US campaign in neighbouring Afghanistan began. He thereby wanted to weed out Taliban-sympathisers from his own security force as precautionary measures. However, the ongoing US sanctions following Pakistan's nuclear tests in 1998 probably impeded better nuclear safekeeping.[19] Notwithstanding Islamabad's smooth talk, the Hersh report revealed that US commando units were training with their Israeli Unit 262 for the event that Pakistani radicals toppled Musharraf and either they or the terrorists seized the nukes. The Israeli unit, according to an

Asia Times report of 7 October 2001, specialises in assassinations, theft and destruction of foreign nukes. The joint training reflected concern of the respective countries about the realities of Pakistan's nuclear security. Other reports in a similar vein followed. Dawn dated 23 October 2001 quoted that US military had conducted over twenty-five war games simulating the Indo-Pakistani scenario each one of them had resulted in a nuclear war. Interestingly though, the Hersh article focuses entirely on the security of Pakistani nukes though neighbouring India is an also a NWS state. News of the arrest of two former Pakistani nuclear scientists in Lahore on 23 October with alleged Al Qaeda links did hardly anything to modify Hersh's assertions. Dawn reported again on 30 October that the US had held intensive talks with Pakistan on the latter's are nuclear command and control system. Joseph R. Biden, Chairman of the powerful Senate Foreign Relations Committee, confirmed that Bush was consulting senior leaders on plans to neutralise Pakistan's nuclear capability should Musharraf fall from power and expected Pakistanis to enhance measures for safeguarding the nukes. Washington also urged upon Islamabad to step up greater CBMs with India. After all, the latter would be as much worried as the USA or Israel, should Pakistani nukes fall into the hands of forces viscerally hostile to New Delhi. It might even goad the latter on to consider a pre-emptive nuclear strike against Pakistan. Way back in 1981 Israel had made pre-emptive air strikes against Iraqi nuclear weapons centres. Low profile Indo-Israeli security contacts at the time had set off speculations about similar Indian strikes against the not so clandestine 'Islamic bomb' programme of Pakistan.[20] So, in this particular scenario, terrorism might act as a catalyst for an inter-state nuclear war! Here was the possibility of the two levels of nuclear danger fusing together.

Ways Out: A Beginning With Nunn-Lugar Initiative

Pakistan's nuclear scientist Mansoor Ijaz and former CIA Director R. James Woolsey had broached the possibility of applying the Nunn-Lugar initiative to South Asia's nuclear arsenals way back in November 2001.[21] Four months later, Senator Richard Lugar himself, who is a ranking member of the Senate Foreign Relations Committee, announced that the Bush Administration had strongly endorsed his proposal to extend the

Nunn-Lugar initiative to South Asia's nuclear security.[22] He expressed the hope that both India and Pakistan would cooperate with the US in this programme which would include safe storage, accountability and planned destruction of nuclear warheads and materials that might otherwise fall into terrorists' hands. After all, reports kept coming in that the terrorists in Afghanistan were far from finished and were regrouping in remote sanctuaries, including Pakistan. In March 2002 they put up a stiff fight against US-led Operation Anaconda in eastern Afghanistan. Next month they made several attacks against the newly installed interim government in Kabul and the international peacekeeping force.

Senator Lugar also mentioned that Islamabad had faced certain difficulties in dispersing its nukes to six different sites. He added that suggestions had been made in Islamabad to turn to China for help. That same month, March 2002, the CIA chief's warning of the danger of an Indo-Pakistani war was sounded. If Nunn-Lugar is extended to South Asia, the US Defense Threat Reduction Agency (DTRA), which oversees the nuclear threat reduction programme in Russia, will presumably come into operation in the subcontinent.[23] The Bush Administration's defence request in Section 8171 of FY 03 specifically required the Secretaries of Defence, State and Energy to submit a report to Congress describing steps that have been taken to develop cooperative threat reduction programs in India and Pakistan."[24] It has also added an additional requirement that the report recommend any changes in existing law which are "an impediment to the full establishment of such programs, a timetable for implementation of such programs, and an estimated five-year budget that will be required to fully fund such programs." The seriousness of the US attention to a possible Empty Quiver-type case (US Defence Department jargon for missing nukes) in South Asia was seen in that Washington suddenly revived its interest in the fate of the 100 gms. of plutonium it had given to India decades ago under its Atoms for Peace Programme.[25]

A Cooperative Denuclearisation Agenda for South Asia

P.R. Chari proposed a clear-cut denuclearisation agenda for NWS states several years ago that is applicable to the present

Indo-Pakistani scenario.[26] His agenda, partly adapted, is as follows:

1. De-targeting and de-alerting nuclear missiles,
2. Establishing a UN register of nuclear arms for greater transparency
3. Separating nukes from missiles (and other delivery vehicles like bombers),
4. Placing excess weapons-grade fissile materials from retired nukes and production facilities under international control,
5. Making a firm commitment in multinational fora to the goal of nuclear disarmament and ultimate elimination of nukes, and
6. Assuring non-NWS states of banning use of nukes against them.

In addition India and Pakistan might consider the following:

1. Declare an indefinite ban on nuclear testing, including computer simulation,
2. Ban fissile material production for nuclear weapons,
3. Declare their stockpiles of weapons-grade fissile materials,
4. A legal framework to ensure non-transfer of their nuclear technology; on this score both states have so far shown commendable behaviour,
5. Declare no-first-use; Pakistan has refused to follow India in this due to its own military calculations, as noted, but under appropriate international guarantees might take a fresh look at its position,
6. India could link its ban on testing and production of nukes and related materials to progress of other NWS states towards similar denuclearisation goals, notably China (which will in all probability bring in the USA and Russia because of Beijing's own nuclear calculus).

An Effective Verification Regime for South Asia

A comprehensive verification system needs at least three major components: measures to monitor restrictions placed upon the number of nukes and the quantum of fissile material production and stockpiles allowed, in addition to improving safeguards on peaceful nuclear activities, measures to monitor the warheads, delivery vehicles and launchers as per agreements reached, and measures to monitor restrictions on the deployment and alert status of nuclear forces. Some of these measures like monitoring may be undertaken by the IAEA. A verification authority set up bilaterally can accomplish other verification tasks. Given the many precedents between the USA and Russia, there should not be any particular difficulty in setting one up in South Asia.

Past nuclear agreements did not seek to control nuclear warheads directly but focused instead on delivery systems. But meaningful reductions in the nuclear arsenals of the two sides require direct control over the warheads and the materials needed to manufacture them. The Fissile Material Control Treaty is one of the methods that may be followed.

US interest in providing security to South Asia's nuclear arsenal is welcome. Washington under Bush seems determined to overcome the post-Pokharan sanctions hurdles for both India and especially Pakistan, the arsenals of which seems to be in greater danger. In fact the Bush Administration already started easing some of the Clinton-era sanctions when Islamabad pledged to help Washington in its anti-terrorist campaign. The US has hi-tech devices to render stolen nukes useless and should be willing to supply these to the two South Asian rivals. These devices include vaults, sensors, alarms, tamper-proof seals, closed-circuit TVs, and labels to identify, track and secure nuclear materials.[27] At the same time, however, Bush's plans for NMD might act as a disincentive for nuclear arms control and denuclearisation. China, along with Russia, considers NMD as destabilising the nuclear balance. This might goad it on to produce more missiles. India and, hence, Pakistan, will then follow suit. On the other hand, a US Theatre Missile Defence (TMD) meant to protect friendly nations may conceivably extend to South Asia and accelerate indigenous denuclearisation.

New Dimension of Research

India and Pakistan have taken a leaf from the US-Soviet nuclear arms race. They should now relate to various nuclear arms control agreements reached by the superpowers even in the heydays of the Cold War. To be sure, not all these agreements have been finalised or are fully operational. Yet there have also been remarkable successes like wiping out the intermediate-range missiles (INFs). These arms control and arms cut measures have been backed up by an array of confidence-building measures (CBMs).

Urgent Need of Research on South Asia's Denuclearisation

There is ample scope for Indian and Pakistani scholars and government experts to study the US-Soviet/Russian agreements and related arrangements thoroughly, other instruments of WMD and especially nuclear control provided by the UN, the IAEA and other agencies, and then focus on measures to adopt the relevant ones while inventing others — all with a view not only to keep the nuclear genie corked but get rid of the bottle altogether, and on a cooperative basis. Our two governments must also be more forthcoming with information on their respective nuclear arsenals, like the USA and West Europe. Greater openness would help build informed and responsible public opinion. Vajpayee's Evolution of India's Nuclear Policy, submitted to the Parliament on 27 May 1998 followed next year summer by the National Security Advisory Board's (NSAB) draft Indian Nuclear Doctrine are pretty low-grade ores. Indeed, NSAB Chairman K. Subrahmanyam himself later complained in this vein.[28] Islamabad, of course, offers even less. Peaceful coexistence is an achievable goal. Bitter enemies of yesteryears like France and Russia on the one hand and Germany on the other, and Japan and the USA, which had even nuked the former, have achieved it. So why cannot India and Pakistan bury the hatchet, even if it takes time?

A two-track approach is needed for our level one problem. Many Indian and Pakistani scholars, newsmen and military experts are agreed on this. Let the government bureaucrats of India and Pakistan go on holding talks along Track One. Their hardened mindsets, coupled with the South Asian penchant for red tape, will probably yield little tangible results unless the international community', led by the USA, leans on them. More fruitful results may be expected of scholars, journalists and NGOs, unbridled as they mostly are from 'official' thinking. Despite the country's dubious democratic credentials Pakistan's private media have often been astonishingly critical of the government. In sum, there is an absolute need for Track Two. Academics do not have to be shackled by official thinking and tow the government or any particular party line. Indeed, it is their obligation to come up with fresh ideas and solutions. Opportunity for a great deal of cross-border interaction via seminars, symposia, publications and media coverage should be provided for this second track. That would be an excellent way to build up a favourable public opinion. The latter in turn will generate pressure on the respective governments so that they start unhinging their fossilised mindsets. Also, more informed debate is needed within the legislatures of the two countries. The responsibility of academic, military and other informed groups is all the greater to 'educate' them as well as the layman.

The China Factor

Part of India's official justification for developing nukes and longer-range Agni series missiles is that China's Tibet-based nuclear arsenals, the upgraded CSS-5 missiles, also target India. Therefore, although China is technically located outside South Asia, India can ill-afford to overlook its growing nuclear potential. Without a solution to the potential Chinese nuclear threat, it will be difficult for India to denuclearise. This in turn will only act as a strong disincentive to Islamabad to take the path out of its NWS status. There is also an ambiguity regarding the Chinese position. Beijing extended no-first-use vis-a-vis non-nuclear states. Since India is now a NWS state, does or does not the Chinese NFU apply to the latter? Such cobwebs need clearing up. It may well be that the Chinese in turn will insist on a larger-scale US—and secondarily also Russian—nuclear disarmament down to a level which they perceive to be tolerable for their national security. So, serious effort at South Asian denuclearisation will involve not merely India and Pakistan but also the other three nuclear powers. One way out of the seeming impasse with Chinese nukes could be an internationally guaranteed NFU agreement between India and China.

Also, cooperative denuclearisation in South Asia must urgently address our level two, catastrophic terrorist threat scenarios. Traditional nuclear deterrence absolutely fails to deter die-hard kamikaze squads. The 11 September attacks on high-profile US targets merely underscored how vulnerable even the world's most powerful nation is to this type of new threat.

There is little time to lose. Both Track One and Track Two must be pursued vigorously with the goal that they ultimately converge. Bungling with a nuke whether by a state or a non-state actor like a terrorist gang will mean instant nirvana for all. There is no second chance with nukes the long-term effects of radiation on the survivor of a nuclear blast and the environment in which he lives are too gruesome even to contemplate. There is enormous scope for conducting research into methods of cooperative denuclearisation in the subcontinent followed by patient implementation. Scholars should turn their attention and energies to addressing this urgent problem. The time to act is NOW!

Notes and References

1. More discussion in Jyotirmoy Banerjee, *Nuclear World. Defence and Politics of Major Powers*, Manas, New Delhi, 2002, Chapter 9, pp. 192-227; Gurmeet Kanwal, "India's National Security Strategy in a Nuclear Environment, *Strategic Analysis*, New Delhi, Vol. XXIV, No. 9, Dec. 2000, pp. 1617-18; Instt. For Peace and Conflict Studies, New Delhi, seminar report, "Nuclear Testing in South Asia", Article 115, 12 June 1998 (henceforth ipcs.org); K. Subrahmanyam.

2. "Challenges to Indian Security", *USI Journal*, New Delhi, Vol. CXXX, No. 542, Oct.-Dec. 2000, pp. 541-62.

3. Nuclear doctrines in Jyotirmoy Banerjee, *Strategic Studies*, Allied, Calcutta, 1998, chapter IV, pp. 62-80.

4. "Issue Paper: Increasing Funding and Enhancing Implementation of US-Russian Non-Proliferation Cooperation", *Nuclear Threat Reduction Campaign (NTRC)*, Washington DC, 13 March 2002 cites facts and figures, including the Lloyd and Cutler report. On cooperative denuclearisation and attendant problems, see Graham T. Allison et al. (eds.), *Cooperative Denuclearization from Pledges to Deeds*, Harvard Univ., Cambridge, MA, 1993; *CNN.com Interactive*, "Cold War. The Bomb"; Harold A. Feveison (ed.), *The Nuclear Turning Point. A Blue Print for Deep Cuts and De-alerting of Nuclear Weapons*, Brookings, Washington DC, 1999, p. 91. An IAEA agreement, signed in 1980 but entering force 7 years later, fixes responsibility of nuclear transportation on states while the material is within their territory or aboard its ships and aircraft. Convention on the Physical Protection of Nuclear Material".

5. Feveison, *op. cit.*, chapter 11, p. 216; 10 April 2002.

6. Jang.com, 12 Sept. 2001, electronically accessed at *SandNet*, *nautilus.org* 17 July 2001, Vol. 2, No. 29; P.R. Chari, "Is a Nuclear Bargain Possible?" ipsc.org, article 032, dt. 1 Dec. 1997. On the Neemrana Group, Lt. Gen. Sardar P.S. Lodi, "CBMs Necessary to Prevent Accidental Nuclear War", *Defence Journal* online (Pakistani armed forces' website), Jan. 2002.

7. Minister of State for External Affairs Omar Abdullah's report to India's Parliament, "Delhi wants nuclear talks with Islamabad" *Dawn.com*, Internet (ed), 1 Sept. 2001. On the nuclear treaty, Javed Naqvi, "New Delhi slams speculation on nuclear site attack", *Dawn.com*, 23 Oct. 2001. Report of the seminar in *Times of India*, 27 April 2002, p. 6.

8. P.S. Suryanarayana, "Ready to formalise nuclear test ban treaty with India. Musharraf", *The Hinduonnet*, 12 Nov. 2001.

9. M.B. Naqvi, "More realistic thinking on the nukes", International. *The News* (online, Islamabad), 30 Jan. 2002; "Hit and Run", *India Today*, New Delhi, 30 July 2001, pp.19-27. In February 2002, Russia backed fully the Indian stand on Kashmir including the need for priority talks on cross-border terrorism from Pakistan. Text of the joint communique in Strategic Digest, New Delhi, Vol. 32, No. 2, Feb. 2002, pp. 235-336.

10. *Dawn Internet* News Alert, 2 January 2002; "Missile power states to continue proliferation talks", Jang.com, accessed via *SandNet Weekly* Update, nautilus org, Vol. 3, No. 8, 2 March 2002: Indo-Kazakhstan Joint Statement, New Delhi, 12 Feb. 2002, *Strategic Digest*, New Delhi, Vol. 32, No. 2, Feb. 2002, p. 234; TOI, 4, 21 Jan. 2002; Lodi, *op. cit.*

11. "Pakistans Musharraf droht Indien mit der Atombombe", Spiegel online, 5 April 2002, Der Spiegel interview with Musharraf). See also Stephen P. Cohen, "Nuclear Deterrence in South Asia: Strategic Considerations Reconsidered", *ipcs.org*, Nuclear and Disarmament Issues, Article 166, 12 Jan. 1999. The Pakistanis have been openly talking of resorting to the nuclear option ever since India responded to the terrorist attacks by mobilising its armed forces. See Pakistani Communications Minister Javed Ashraf's statement to a Kuwaiti newspaper, "Pak could use N-weapons if attacked: Minister", Hindustantimes.com report in *SandNet Weekly* Update, Vol. 3., No. 5, 1 Feb. 2002; TOI, 30 April 2002.

12. Within less than a fortnight after the attack on India's Parliament, US State Secretary Powell declared on 26 Dec. 2001

the Lashkar-e-Toiba (LeT) and the Jaish-e-Muhammad (JeM) as "foreign terrorist organizations" much to New Delhi's satisfaction. Two days later, Bush observed at his Texas ranch that Musharraf had already caused the arrest of 50 terrorists and expressed the hope that India noted it. *TOI*, 14, 27, 29 Dec. 2001. The fresh US look at India as an important power is argued in Stephen P. Cohen, *India: Emerging Power*, Oxford University Press, 2001; Ajaz Ahmad, "Back from the brink?" *Frontline Online*, Vol. 19, Issue 5, March 2-15, 2002. On India's continued skepticism, see the statement of the Indian Minister of state for External Affairs in Oslo that Islamabad had released terrorists on a large scale in Jan. 2002. FM 1 radio, Calcutta, 6 April 2002, 10 p.m. Agni II test in M.V. Ramana, "A Nuclear Wedge", Frontline online, Vol. 18, Issue 25, Dec. 8-21, 2001. *CNN.com / World*, however, reported on 26 March 2002 ("India rules out nuclear war") that Premier Vajpayee had assured his audience at a televised press conference in Shimla that there would be no nuclear war with Pakistan; India, after all, was committed to no-first-use and, according to him, Pakistan had expressed similar views. His Defence Minister, Fernandes was more outspokenly hostile to Musharraf and Islamabad' s hawks.

13. Naqvi, *op. cit.* on India 'winning' in a nuclear exchange, see also M.R. Srinivasan, "Indo-Pak nuclear asymmetry", *The Hindu*, 1 Aug. 2001. Two days after the devastating suicide attack against Kashmir's State Assembly, India's Deputy Home Minister I.D. Swami mentioned on 3 Oct. 'hot pursuit' as an option to SAB TV. "Strikes on camps in Pakistan an option, says India", *Dawn.com*, the internet Edition, 4 Oct. 2001; "Strikes on militant camps in Pakistan an option", International. The News (online), 4 Oct. 2001; Musharraf does not rule out N-option. Can India, Pakistan survive a N-war?" *TOI*, 14 April 2002, p.14; TOI, 4 Feb. 2002.

14. Naveed Miraj, "Indian nukes open to theft, sabotage", *The Frontier Post Online*, Peshawar, 2000. The study quoted was co-authored by instt. Director Dr. Shireen Mazari and Maria Sultan. In fact, the US field commander in Afghanistan, General Franklin Hagenbeck stated in March 2002 that the US forces could enter Pakistani territory, with Islamabad's permission of course, in order to deny fleeing Al Qaeda and Taliban fighters sanctuaries there. CENTCOM chief General Tommy Franks requested permission for this but Islamabad chose to remain publicly silent

so as not to stir up even more domestic turmoil. On 26 and 29 April 2002 *TOI* reported that US forces were covertly operating inside Pakistan; among the reasons were persistent rumours that Osama was hiding there and also that the US does not trust Pakistani forces, including the ISI, since they seem to contain radical elements among their ranks.

15. *Dawn.com*, "Law soon on nuclear threat reduction steps: US", March 11, 2002; Judith Miller and Michael R. Gordon, "US Review on Russia Urges Keeping Most Arms Control", nytimes.com, July 16, 2001; *"NTRC, "Issue Paper", op. cit* and "Issue Paper: A Working Legislation Agenda for 2002: The Nuclear and Terrorism Threat Reduction Act of 2002", April 9, 2002.

16. Feveison, *op. cit.*, p. 102, Note 2; "Convention on the Physical protection of Nuclear material", *iaea.org*, p.18; *TOI*, 19 April 2002.

17. Miraj, *op. cit*; Sumita Kumar, "Pakistan's Jehadi Apparatus: Goal and Methods", *Strategic Analysis*, New Delhi, Vol. XXIV, No.12, March 2001, pp. 2179-98.

18. "Gen. Pervaiz Musharraf. Absolutely Secure", *The Far Eastern Economic Review*, 20 Dec. 2001 (interview, electronically accessed); Sultan Mohammad Khan," Right choice for Pakistan", *Dawn.com*, 29 Sept. 2001.

19. Mariam Baabar, "Pak nuclear assets in safe hands: Sattar", *News International*, online, Islamabad, 2 Nov. 2001; Tahir Mirza, "US refutes reports about plan to take out Pakistan's nuclear arms", *Dawn.com*, 30 Oct. 2001; Seymour M. Hersh, "Watching the Warheads: The Risks of Pak's Nuclear Arsenal", *New Yorker*, 5 Nov. 2001; "Two retired nuclear scientists admit to meeting Osama bin Laden", Dawn.com, 12 Nov. 2001 quoting undated *Washington Post*. The General in charge of nuclear weapons security under a new strategic planning division is Khalid Kidwai, who is answerable only to the President. The N-sites have beefed up security with extra troops and anti-aircraft batteries guarding them, Ijaz and Woolsey, *op. cit.*; Musharraf interview, *The Far Eastern Economic Review*, *op.cit*.

20. Dr. Hasan Aksari Rizvi, "Nuclear assets are in safe hands", *Dawn.com*, 12 Nov. 2001; on Biden's statement Praful Bidwai, "Nuclear worries mount by the day", *Asia Times.com*, 3 Nov. 2001; Douglas Frantz, "US and Pakistan Discuss Nuclear Security", *nyt com*, 1 Oct. 2001.

21. Ijaz and Woolsey, *op. cit*.

22. "Law soon ?", *op. cit.*, Dawn.com, 11 March 2002.

23. *Strategic Digest, op. cit.*, p. 1603; *Pravda*.ru (online, English ed.), 22 Nov. 2001; Also *nyt.com report* (undated) carried by many Pakistani newspapers, *SandNet*, 13 March 2002. 25. *Times of India,* March 28, 2002.

26. P.R. Chari, *"Is a Nuclear Bargain Possible?"* ipsc.org. Article 032, dt. December 1, 1997.

27. Ijaz and Woolsey, *op. cit*; see also *Times of India*, 10, 2002; *The Telegraph*, Calcutta, February 14, 2002.

28. Text of the NSAB draft in *Strategic Digest*, New Delhi, Vol. XXIX, No. 9, September 1999, pp. 143942; Subrahmanyam, *op.cit.*, pp. 541-42.

14

Dilemma Behind Pak's Nuclear Programmes: Options Before India

Badruddin

Since the beginning of nuclear age over the last six decades the humanity has faced grave and horrifying threats. The effects of international organizations, global disarmament conferences, regional associations and NGOs have been far from complete in preventing the threats of modern wars. The advancement in the field of nuclear technology and politically motivated national interest has also strengthened the course of war. Besides, the growing separatist movement, war of cessation communication failure, relative deprivation lack of internal cohesion threats of external conflict has also added to the growth of modern arms race. The world of nuclear science is full of horror and secrecy.[1]

Today some nations are busy in acquiring weapons through indigenous technology while others through proliferation of varied means. Pakistan that dreams to be a symbolic superpower and the biggest rival of India has acquired the Weapons of Mass Destruction (WMD) through collaboration with China and North Korea. The critics widely believe that Jinnah's Two Nation Theory and the eventual partition of India in 1947 was directly responsible for political disaster and Pakistan's dissatisfaction with the partition. Since then it became a gateway for promoting militant nationalism. Gradual strategic consideration co-opted with Islamic sentiments prompted Pak officials to redesign the domestic as well as internal ideology that considerably promoted *Jihad* culture. Pak decided to align with power blocs blindly by abandoning the relevance of neutrality and non-alignment. Its policy makers aligned with USA, China and a number of Arab Nations. In return it received packages of socio-economic assurances of varied categories from the Arab World. The US also provided aid to Pakistan to modernize its defence programme. Pak, being an economically vulnerable and politically divided nation, relied heavily on its nuclear programme to get political concessions from the US and for exposing the nuclear proliferation network. The security initiatives were framed full of deception and disinformation.[2] Pak's tilt towards USA opened window of opportunity for it, India on the other hand opted for Pro-Soviet policy and non alignment. It was certainly a disadvantage for India which believed in "No First Use" or "Never Use" of weapons against humanity.

In the very beginning, Pak's Nuclear Programme was rather slow. The Indo-Pak war in 1971 resulted in the culmination of Bangladesh and it was also a serious shock to Islamabad. The divided and broken nation and its leaders made efforts to not only to redesign Pak's domestic political structure but also its evil designs against India. Pakistan's nuclear programme also started to take shape. Zulfikar Ali Bhutto, a radical democratic leader and a keen observer worked as a coordinated authority of Pak Atomic Energy Commission (PEAC). He secretly entered in agreement with China with a view to acquire Ballistic Missiles for name and fame. In one of the public speeches, he said: "If I am assassinated, I would be remembered..."[3] over the succeeding years China, assisted Pak in pursuit of the enrichment of missile and nuclear technology and violated international agreements including CTBT. Soviet intervention in Afghanistan in 1979 and the subsequent political developments threatened Pak's national sovereignty. The Soviet occupation of Afghanistan an "Evil Empire" in American terminology opened a new chapter of nuclear arms race in the subcontinent.

General Zia-ul-Haq, who replaced Bhutto in a planned military coup in 1977, was also a great supporter of Pak's Nuclear Programme. Even the leaders like Benazir Bhutto and Nawaz

Sharif too spoke in American language and became the true advocates of Pak's modernized Defense Policy. President Zia a keen observer and a great fan of 'Cricket Diplomacy' urged the need for possessing 'deterrent weapons' to maintain Pak's status in South Asia. Arab fundamentalists' ideological support to Pak's Lobby' assured President Zia of all possible help to protect the identity through promotion of Islamic Bomb. Characteristically, Pak's nuclear proliferation was promoted by egocentric fundamentalist policies. It inherited the blood of militant Islamic culture that was a part of geo-strategic consideration. It significantly helped Pak to patronize Taliban Al-Qaeda (soldiers of God) through network of transnational terrorist movements in the name of *Jihad* (holy war).[4] With the tactful bargaining within the shadow of holy Islam, these hardliners developed technical dimensions to promote terrorism. At this pretext, Pak freed itself to use weapons in the name of dislodging terrorism in South Asia where China and US openly supported Pak. The Muttahida Majlis-e-Amal (follower of United Community), a nexus of religious organization has been a logical corollary of Al-Qaeda network presumably responsible for 9/11 episode. US warning to Musharraf having secret information about Laden and his associates, and Pak's changing stand on Jammu and Kashmir is the clues that Pak has maintained Doubled Standard.[5] Consequently; the transnational links of Pak with terrorist organization and WMD are different to trace. It is clear that Pak can handle any kind of network without fear.

It is widely believed that Pak has wider network of secret nuclear plants. Dr. Abdul Quadir Khan, the founder of Khan Research Laboratories (KRL) and the father of Pakistan's Nuclear Bomb has been the brain behind the transaction of nuclear programme. Dr. Khan has been as popular as Gaddafi and Saddam Hussein and has worked in different capacities. He held highest administrative-cum-scientist-post in Pak and was conferred with topmost civilian award. A controversial Khan who was also believed to have been involved in secret supply of Nuclear Technology to North Korea, Iran and Libya continued to work under the pretext of civilian nuclear programme. The US Intelligence Agencies warned Dr. Khan and blamed Islamabad officials for not pursuing the norms of UN Security Council. The

US has assured Pakistan of assistance of every possible manner, provided it becomes a signatory to CTBT, morally accept the Additional Protocol and respect the legal binding of International Atomic Energy Agency (IAEA). The focus should be on safeguard and verification in case of Pak, what KRL has been doing, is a secret to the monitoring agencies. Pak's top most secret 'Kahuta Plant' the brainchild of KRL, probably near Islamabad, continues to remain under tight security of intelligence agencies. Kahuta complex is like 'Mini Science City' that has engaged hundreds of scientists, administrative staffs and researchers. Intelligence sources also suggest that its' network are spread in Libya, Iran and North Korea, what the US describes as "axis of evils" and "rouge states". Besides this, the unconfirmed reports also indicate KRL's engagement with 15 other countries including middlemen, front companies, and secret agents and manufacturing plants. The wider network of Kahuta-cum-KRL serves as Transit center despite global pressure not to acquire clandestinely transferred blueprint nuclear designs. It was also publicaly highlighted by the UN Nuclear watchdog in October 2003, that Western media and policy personnel continue to blame Pak for supplying sophisticated centrifuges to many nations linked with KRL. More recently Pak-China-Libya nexus over the exchange of Nukes-for-missile remain well known to National Command Authority set up by General Musharraf in 2002. But Pak's nuclear options remain ambitious as well as mysterious while President Musharraf, who has been repeatedly warned by the international community, suitably praised Khan's "heroic service". Even the Director General of IAEA El-Borade has said: "There is sophisticated worldwide network of Nuclear weapons. The guilty proliferators must be warned".[8] Probably, Pak is not free from such criticism. It shows the intention of Pak that exploded nuclear devices at the pretext of security. Take an example of Ghauri an Intermediate Range Ballistic Missile that was tested by Pak on April 16, 1998 having a capacity of 1500 km. Besides, Pak also conducted series of tests on May 28, 1998 that increased the possibility of nuclear arms race over the Indian sub-continent. Probably it is Pak's wish to follow the glory of Afghan ruler Mohammad Ghauri, who was famous for cruelty and who defeated Indian ruler Prithviraj Chauhan.

Although with the US pressures, Khan was arrested but also pardoned by General Musharraf much against the wishes of the US. This clearly shows that Dr. Khan had a role in proliferation of nuclear technology but due to the need of Pakistan's support for tackling the Al-Qaeda the US has preferred to overlook it. It also speaks for the duplicity of the US policy towards the nuclear proliferation which treats India and Pakistan differently. Pakistan's intensions of "going extra miles" to build cooperation and good neighbourly relations remain mysterious. The China-Pak nexus also appears to be countervailing force to India. But, definitely it is tragic that Pakistan is diverting much of its meager resources for unplanned nuclear programme. It makes little sense for Pakistan when resources are needed badly for socio-economic growth.

Options before India

The response of India has been one of the restraints because our domestic policy has no idea as what should be done. Weak Public opinion divided nationality and regional issues also work as obstacle for any response. There are interesting scenarios that have emerged in India:

1. The decision-makers have often been in dilemma whether India should stick to its peaceful nuclear policy or go ahead with the task of manufacturing nuclear weapon or government should draw a definite policy or adopt the doctrine of "No First Use". In case India opts to go for the nuclear weapon option there is definitely a heavy risk of Trade sanctions from the developed nations, including the conditions of WTO WB and IMF. Many ongoing developmental projects of India would suffer.

2. Policy analysts have suggested using Diplomatic Channels to dismantle the nexus of Pak with evil forces. India should attempt to have sanctions imposed on Islamabad. It should also use political lobby to cut off relations with Pak. During the post-Cold War era when there is no need of countervailing forces, India can knock the door of UN Officials and the global forums against Pak. The process has already begun.

3. India, being an economic power, respects the sentiments of economic programme and not the military. India has the largest number of Computer and Software professionals in the world. During the age of globalization the multinationals are ready to

make India as a base of global economy. In view of this it is also being felt that just the way China is able to counter US pressure why India is not able to control threats from Pakistan.

4. Being the most powerful economy is South Asia and having fifth largest military in the world, India could review its programme and develop missiles to counter Pak's threat without going to nuclear. It should bring body and soul together to modernize defense system besides maintaining its non-aligned position over the issue of nuclear disarmament. The aim is not to enter in arms race but to remain within striking distance. Even India is capable enough to neutralize Pak's nuclear programme by matching strength. Pragmatically, such strategy may not be an intelligent approach.

5. The cross-border terrorism is now being considered as a daily exercise. After, Kargil misadventure, India has been attempting best to guard its sovereignty. The post-Kargil scenario has witnessed alarming growth of terrorist activities including attack on Indian parliament, Akshara Dham temple, and sabotage of American Center Kolkata or killing of Hurriyat leader Abdul Ghani Lone. These have increased the threat of war. Despite repeated warnings from the USA and Britain to defuse the situation and peace initiatives by both India and Pakistan there is hardly any notable change in Pak's rhetoric activities and also no let up in cross-border terrorism. These crucial questions have raised doubts before India. Whether India should give up the 'No First Use' of nuclear weapons and stick to its traditional policy?

At a time when the international community is emerging in a form of global village, it is indeed ironical that India and Pak are still engaged in arms race. Despite the Confidence Building Measures to promote a stable environment and the reduction of unauthorized use of nuclear weapons the confidence is still lacking. Presently only a meaningful dialogue can promote mutual understanding between India and Pakistan. There is also a great need and realization to promote people-to-people initiatives. Prominent NGOs like Pakistani and Indian People's Forum for Peace and Democracy, People's of Asia Forum, India-Pakistan Friendship Society, Travelling Seminars, NAM Media and South Asian community have already come forward to rescue the situation.[9] More sincere efforts at the government level are required to change the scenario of mistrust, suspicion and hatred.

Notes and References

1. M.K. Narayanan: Politics of Proliferation. *World Focus* (New Delhi), Vol. 25, No. 2, February 2004, p. 21.
2. *Ibid.*, p. 22.
3. Matin Zuberi: Pakistan's Nuclear Dilemma. *World Focus*, Vol. 21, Nos. 10-12, October-December, 2000, p. 21.
4. Veena Kukeja: Pakistan, Taliban Al-Qaeda Nexus. *World Focus*, Vol. 25, No. 2, February 2004, pp. 14-15.
5. Kalim Bahadur: M.M.A. and the Nuclear Proliferation. *World Focus*, Vol. 25, No. 2, February 2004, pp. 18-19.
6. Garima Singh: A New Nuclear Non-Proliferation Initiative: American Hypocrisy in Pakistan. *Manistream* (New Delhi) Vol. XLII, No. 12, 13 March 2004, pp. 7-9.
7. See Commentary: Nuclear Proliferations and Western Responsibility, *Mainstream* Vol. XLII, No. 27, June 26, 2004, p. 3.
8. M.K. Narayanan: Politics of Proliferations pp. 21-22.
9. For details of NGOs of Pak: Beyond Boundaries. A Report on the state on Non-officials Dialogues on Peace, security and cooperation South Asia, University of Toronto, 16-18 December 1996.

15

Indo-Pak Relations: A Snake-Ladder Game

Jitendra Narayan

The immediate neighbour state in front was termed as ari (enemy) state by Kautilya, a great Indian Philosopher of 400 BC. And if this terminology is valid in the fullest sense of the term even today it is in the case of Indo-Pak relations. Pages of history of Indo-Pak relations remind us of a Snake-Ladder Game. Every step towards the game of foreign relations between the two countries ultimately becomes the victim of poison of prejudice and mistrust in spite of a good start. The legacy of communal antagonism, mistrust, suspicion and insecurity which originated before partition did not subside with the creation of India and Pakistan; it got transformed into Indo-Pakistan rivalry and conflict making them unable to live as friendly neighbours.

Partition of India was accompanied by several unfortunate circumstances. There were problems related to the division of assets and liabilities demarcation of boundaries both of the land and water and basically the feeling of suspicion and distrust, which got aggravated following partition.[1] The communal riots and large scale migration from both sides widened the differences between the two communities and the two countries.[2] This Muslim, Hindu and Sikh hostility precipitated an orgy of murder and savagery that consumed tens of thousands lives and loss of properties on both sides. Instead of joining together in celebration of their great victory over

European colonialism, the people of South Asia witnessed a blood bath, hatred and conflict. It was this communal issue and their failure to accommodate diversities, which influenced the course of relations between the two.[3] Moreover, the political system, which the two countries chose also, led to a gulf between the two. Pakistan always looked at India as Hindu-India", ignoring altogether its secular character, while the existence of Islamic state of Pakistan was bound to raise some misgivings in the Indian circle.[4]

The political power was transferred to the leaders who had undergone a long period of confrontation, strife and struggle. The memories of the cruel day hovered on the minds of the new statesman of the country.[5] The events preceding partition had coloured their views responsible for putting different policy goals by the leaders of Pakistan.[6] The suggestion offered recently by Lt. Gen. (Retd.) Nishant Ahmed of Pakistan on Jammu and Kashmir was revealing. He said "My sincere suggestion to our neighbour is that they cannot keep a people subjugated permanently through the use of force. At the times of our 'Golden Jubilee' the People of Occupied Kashmir are much more alienated than they were at the start of this half country, despite all of India's efforts and inducements. In the light of this evolving scenario, India needs to rethink as to the future that holds for it in Kashmir. I would also suggest to India not to confuse Kashmir with Punjab. The two situations are totally different. In the long run, the Punjab solution will not work, you may suppress a people's quest for freedom through brutal use of force temporarily, *but it will not alter the basic nature of a Muslim community's differences with you* (emphasis added by the author).[7]

What Ahmad suggested further had enough to reveal the mindset of those responsible to decide the destiny of our distant neighbour. He said that such traumatic surgery (partition) was unlikely to heal without complications and the British left India and Pakistan to deal with the consequences of this enormous and hastily carried out operation which resulted in the death of half a million to one million people and another two million were forced to migrate. *This seriously poisoned the relations between the two sides at the very outset and it would have taken the two people decades of peaceful living together to overcome the trauma.* But the relations between India and Pakistan became even more acrimonious due to the award of Gurdaspur to India by the Boundary Commission. This enabled India to move its forces into Kashmir and resulted in the first Indo-Pakistan war within a few months of India and Pakistan gaining their independence (emphasis added by the author)[8].

There are also people and organizations in Pakistan who have a dream to unfurl the Pakistan flag on the Red Fort at Delhi. General Gazi had promised during one of the general elections that if the Islam Jamhoori Ittehad (IJI) led by him was returned to power, its government would unfurl the Pakistani flag on the Red Fort at New Delhi. The leader of the opposition in the Senate Khurshid Ahmed who was also the Naib Amir of Jamaat Islami too had expressed the similar sentiments.[9] This psyche of a large section of the people of Pakistan has also not allowed their leaders to develop and maintain good relations with India. History reveals that Pakistan, since its birth took upon herself the role of "protector" of Islam and Muslims. They have exploited this factor in the field of international politics. Indeed, they left no stone untouched in making India feel that Muslims living in India are not getting a fair deal. Therefore, whenever communal disturbances occurs in India, Pakistan tries to establish that minorities, particularly Muslims are not safe in "Hindu-India". Pakistan's proclivity to assume the role of guardianship in respect of Indian Muslim is one of the major irritants between India and Pakistan.[10]

Infact, communally coloured view and poisoned mind of Pakistan has proved greatest hurdle in the way of good, friendly relations with India. Kashmir has also proved constant irritant between the two countries. During UN General Assembly debate in 1966 the Indian spokesman remarked that Kashmir was but a symptom of the deep malaise in their neighbourly relations.[11] Infact, till today Pakistan has not accepted the accession of Jammu and Kashmir (J&K) to Indian Union. Moreover, the way leaders of Pakistan have reacted to the issue of J&K reveals their mindset. Once, Jinnah told a deputation of the J&K Muslim Conference that, "Kashmir is in my pocket" because Jinnah had thought that Kashmir being a Muslim majority state would opt for Pakistan.[12] This mind set of Pakistan has not changed at all and the leaders of Pakistan while changing their language and strategy on J&K at different point of time want to see the dreams of Jinnah fulfilled.

J&K became an integral part of the Indian Union in 1947 through final accession in accordance to the legal framework determined by the British Parliament for the independence of the Indian subcontinent. But Pakistan refused to accept the accession of J&K and considered that it was based on fraud and violence. Pakistan continues to look upon the issue as the core of India's relations with Pakistan. This is manifested by Pakistan's pronouncements and its repeated aggression against India. Pakistan's attempt in 1947 to capture J&K using military force was successfully resisted by the Kashmiris with the support of Indian army but Pakistan could hold a portion under its occupation. Again in 1965 Pakistan's attempt to capitalize on local disturbance to foster insurgency led to war with India, ending with Tashkent Declaration of 1965. Once again in 1971 such attempts led to Pakistan's defeat and loss of its eastern wing and creation of Independent Bangladesh.[13]

In complete contravention of Tashkent Declaration of 1965 and the Shimla Agreement of 1972, signed after two wars, Pakistan which still aspires to wrest J&K by force, changed its strategy and embarked on a programme of sponsoring terrorism in the state. Since 1989 with over 20,000 people killed, Pakistan continues its proxy war against India. Even after the Kashmiris voted for democracy, elected their own government in 1996 and signaling their disenchantment with terrorist violence in 2004, Pakistan has not given up its policy of trying to disrupt the free democratic policy of J&K. Disappointed with the response of the Kashmiris to its calls for a "holy" war in J&K, Pakistan has taken recourse to sending in battle hardened Pakistani, Afghans and other mercenaries who have distinguished themselves only by drenching the soil with the blood of the very people whose interests they claim to champion in the name of religion.[14]

Since 1989 to spread fear a strategy has been adopted by the terrorists of selective killing of prominent persons, Hindu, Muslims and Sikhs as well as to suppress the differences of opinion, paralyzing the economy, press, judiciary and administration. Despite well-documented evidence Pakistan claims that it is only providing "moral, political and diplomatic support" to an indigenous Kashmiri uprising in J&K. But the truth behind the latest phase of Pakistani sponsored violence has been clearly spelt out in the book "Fateh" the biography of the former chief of Pakistan's Inter Service Intelligence (ISI), General Akhatar Abdul Rehman. His biographer Brigadier Haroon Rashid states "..The plan which General Akhatar Abdul Rehman has made for Kashmir's movement for independence was to come into effect in 1991. It appears that this plan was made with the struggle for the liberation of Afghanistan in mind, which it was thought would be achieved by spring 1989... However, the Kashmir plan was inaugurated in 1984...The Kashmiris were provided with some arms which were not suitable for the Afghan Mujahideen."[15] Some of the comments by columnists in the English media of Pakistan, though read by a minuscule minority are also worth noting. In a brilliantly argued write-up in Dawn Ayaz Amir, a former member of the National Assembly and distinguished columnist seeks to challenge the notion that the threats from the Indian side have put the "national honour" of Pakistan on the line". He says "It is this attitude that took Pakistan into the wars of 1965 and 1971. What is the nature of the present heightened state of tension with India? We are faced with no Indian diktat regarding any aspect of nation's sovereignty. India considering the circumstance propitious, is putting pressure on us to close the *Jehadi* outfits which have been waging war (or whatever) in Occupied Kashmir", he writes. M.A. Naizi, a senior journalist of Pakistan and Kunwar Idris, a former Chief Secretary of Sind has also revealed the same thing.[16]

The period of 1989-90 was marked by the targeted killing of government officials, media personnel, members of judiciary, minority Kashmiri Pandit (Hindu) community and Kashmiri Muslims who dared to question the terror tactics and excesses of the terrorists. One immediate effect between January and April 1990 was the resignation of the duly elected state government, the massive exodus of nearly 2,50,000 Kashmiri Pandits and over 50,000 Kashmiri Muslim from the valley with the Pandits settling in refugee camps in Jammu, Delhi and other cities in India.[17]

Infact, for two and half decades, a period that saw both military and civilian governments, Pakistan favoured *Jehad* (holy war) as an instrument of foreign policy, Pakistani newspapers at least the English media are full of commentaries on the "Bleed India" strategy adopted by Islamabad in the last 12 years. Some of the writings are so candid that India needs to no longer harp on evidence on the ground. A commentary on the dilemma faced by Pakistan, in the English daily *The Nation* by M.A. Niazi, best illustrated the point. It says: "Pakistan had followed a policy of "bleed India" and of engaging its forces there, by all out support for the indigenous Kashmir freedom struggle or *Jehad*. This was one of the reasons given for abandoning the Taliban to preserve the Kashmir policy. India made that impossible by the threats of going to war in six months."[18] Hijacking of Indian Airlines Flight IC-814 by terrorists for hostages' deal of Kandahar in December 1999 also exposed Pakistan thoroughly. What is abundantly clear is that the hijacking carried out by five professionally trained desperadoes almost all of them the Pakistani nationals, was a Harkat-ul-Mujahideen operation in which the Pakistani state had collusive hand. Such a fear of terrorism seemed designed to serve several objectives. The first and largely symbolic, objective was to humiliate the Indian state, demonstrate its softness and helplessness in the face of low-intensity terrorism in the guerilla mode. The second was to raise the level of Indian and international concerns over the Kashmir issue and also to raise the cost to Indian of holding on to its part of J&K in the face of international alienation and Pakistan aided extremism and terrorism.[19]

In 1999 over 1,000 Pakistan based militants and Pakistani regulars crossed the line of control into the Kargil area and seized Indian army outposts in a surprise attack.[20] The Indian army regrouped, driving the Pakistani forces back. As the Indians attacked, Pakistan prepared its intermediate range missiles for nuclear strikes, perhaps to deter Indians from attacking Pakistani territory. The US diplomacy helped persuade Pakistanis to pull its troops out of India and temporarily head off the full scale war.[21] Months later, General Pervez Musharraf, widely held to be the architect of the Kargil offensive deposed Nawaz Sharif. Tensions mounted again in December 2001, when five militants attacked the Indian Parliament forcing India to post its army along the Line of Control (LoC). Pakistan responded massing it forces and under international pressure, announcing a crack down on Islamic militants infiltrating from Pakistan to Kashmir.[22]

Even in this prevailing situation leaders of both the countries are found engaged in Confidence Building Measures (CBMs). With the coming to power of the United Progressive Alliance (UPA) government of Manmohan Singh, India-Pakistan relations have once again got off to a good start. The meeting between Manmohan Singh and Pakistani President Pervez Musharraf on September 24, 2004 in New York has given cause for optimism. Singh told the media that the Pakistani leader spoke with great sincerity and wanted to correct the notion that he was a man with a "unifocal vision". He added that during the talks both of them wanted "across the board progress on issues". He described the outcome of the talks as "very good". He further said that his meeting with Musharraf was "a significant step forward" as well as "historic in more ways than one". The Indian Prime Minister went on to add that the joint statement issued after his talks with the Pakistani President committed the two countries "to advance beyond what was agreed to in the January 6, 2004 statement both in terms of discussing CBMs as well as moving to discuss complex issues relating to the state of J&K.[23]

Earlier also on many occasions history has witnessed a good start off relationship between India and Pakistan. Even in the recent past Gujral and Vajpayee governments of India had adopted a set of confidence building measures. Lahore Declaration of 1997, Vajpayee's visit to Minar-e-Pakistan and "bus-diplomacy" were directed towards the goal of CBMs. These steps were also considered significant during that point of time. And at a press conference in Lahore, Vajpayee had also said that his visit was "brief" but "substantive."[24] But these steps became victims of prejudice, hate and mistrust and in place of good will and friendly relations earned Kargil war from Pak side in 1999.[25] Having moved to the brink of war in 2002-03, the two countries once again had to step back to make peace and a new start to resolve their differences. July 2001 Agra summit is a testimony to this fact. Indian Foreign Secretary Shashank and his Pakistani Counterpart Riaz Khokar agreed to step back to 1998 and pick up the threads from the composite dialogue in February 2004 interrupted by the Kargil war. The latest peace initiatives by both the countries are once again to construct the road map for the composite dialogue.[26]

However, the later developments in Indo-Pak relations can be explained in the context of perceived threat to the peace arising out of the nuclear capabilities acquired by both the countries (India and Pakistan) after 1989 and also in the backdrop of Kargil war of 1999 and terrorist attack of September 11, 2001 on America and also on Indian Parliament in December 2001. These incidents compelled USA to pressurize Pakistan to adopt a tough stand against terrorism. Under such pressure from Washington, Musharraf recently ordered a crackdown against Al-Queda elements said to be hiding in tribal areas bordering Afghanistan. Pakistan has physically handed over 500 odd members of the Al-Queda and Taliban, who were caught in crackdown across Pakistan. He has banned a number of sectarian and fundamentalists groups reputed to have links with terrorist groups and have agreed to a ceasefire with India. His announcement that Islamabad no longer insisted on a United Nations resolution on Kashmir was also an important development.[27] Tough going of Pak against terrorist and *Jehadi* elements in Pakistan which were earlier getting all kind of support from political military establishment of Pak was certainly a new and welcome development.

This new development provided space for a new chapter of CBMs between the two neighbours. For the first time in the history of relations between the two countries Pakistan initiated a unilateral ceasefire and it has been in place since November 26, 2003. After initial hiccups Islamabad accepted all the confidence building measures proposed by New Delhi including the ones related to a bus service between Muzaffarabad, the capital of Pakistan Occupied Kashmir (PoK) and Srinagar and the revival of the ferry service between Karachi and Mumbai and the train link between Sindh and Rajasthan. On the economic front, Pakistan spearheaded the campaign for the adoption of the South Asia Free Trade Agreement (SAFTA) and is actively engaged in convincing a reluctant Bangladesh to endorse the framework perhaps with an eye on the SAARC summit. Hardliners in Pakistan are unhappy over the government's stance on SAFTA and see it as a major reversal of its earlier position of having no trade with India until the Kashmir issue was resolved. Whatever be the motives, Pakistan is moving at a peace no one had dreamt of before.[28] In fact, in the post-September 11 era, there is a growing worry among political parties, the intelligentsia and civil society that after Iraq it could be Pakistan's turn especially in view of its status as a nuclear weapon state. The common refrain is that it is wiser to make peace with India than provide an excuse to the US and its allies to intervene in the internal affairs of the country. Ever since the Pakistani government decided to change its policy on Afghanistan within days of the American President George Bush's statement that "either you are with us or them," there has been a furious debate in a section of Pakistani civil society on the need to rethink seriously the Kashmir policy.[29]

It is against this backdrop that one would have to evaluate the shift in nuance on the Kashmir issue made by Musharraf in his interview to Reuters. Pervez, Hoodbhoy, a nuclear physicist at a Quaid-e-Azam University in Islamabad and a peace activist, is all praise for the pragmatism of Musharraf while talking about Pakistan's willingness to look beyond the UN resolutions on Kashmir in the quest for a solution. "It is true that plebiscite was indeed the solution mutually agreed upon in 1948 and that India had reneged on a solemn commitment. But the passage of five decades and drastically changed geo-political circumstances demand a reappraisal. Today, plebiscite is no longer the obvious way of determining the wishes of the people of J&K. For example, it clearly excludes a major section of Kashmiris who would opt for independence today but which in 1948, may not have wanted it... More frightening is the likelihood of a plebiscite igniting communal passion leading to horrific Gujarat style bloodbaths across the subcontinent. Moreover, at a practical level there is no agency including the UN, which is able and willing to implement a task, that all nations (except Pakistan) see impossibly difficult. Therefore to insist on plebiscite is the surest way of guaranteeing that a bloody stand-off continues", he writes in *Chowk* an Internet magazine dedicated to the promotion of peace between India and Pakistan. In effects the latest move of Musharraf could mean a preparatory stage in which inflamed nerves are soothed and the high-pitched, decades-old rhetoric is toned down. While the division of Kashmir is unfortunate it is better to accept this reality rather than live with endless suffering that has consumed nearly 90,000 lives since 1987. Hoodbhoy argues.[30]

Mushahid Hussain, former Information Minister of Pakistan also asserted that the dialogue process would not be derailed. Hussain besides being Secretary General of the ruling Pakistan Muslim League is a member of the Senate and Chairs the Foreign Affairs Committee of the Upper House. He said that the people of Pakistan had endorsed the peace process. As an illustration he mentioned the effusive welcome given to the Indian Cricket team in three different parts of Pakistan. US Secretary of State Colin Powell had also expressed the hope during his visit in March 2004 that "the spirit that we have seen in the last few days affects the whole comprehensive dialogue process between the two countries."[31] Out of the developments as explained above India-US relations have been exceptionally warm in recent past these can be said as perhaps the best ever. The US was initially unhappy with India's decision to back out from dispatching troops to Iraq. Even then the armies of both the countries have been holding joint military exercises regularly. The last joint exercise between the air forces of the two countries was held in February 2004 in India. The improvement through the Next Steps in Strategic Partnership with India, which includes expanded bilateral cooperation in civilian nuclear activities, civilian space programmes and trade in high technology, is being seen as a sign of further closeness. However, severe US restrictions are still in force on the transfer of dual use technologies to India. They were imposed following India's first nuclear test in 1974.[32]

But the warm feeling developed in the recent past between U.S. and India had to experience cold wave due to some recent developments arising out of the decisions of the US. These developments also have adverse effects on Indo-Pak relations.

The decision of the Bush administration to grant Pakistan the status of a Major Non-NATO Ally (MNNA) has obviously came as a surprise to the Indian establishment, which feels that the Bush administration has gone back on certain assurances. Some are even disturbed by the US waiver of the existing sanctions on Pakistan imposed purportedly in the larger interests of democracy. Theoretically an enhancement of military cooperation with the US on accounts of MNNA status will be a big boon to Pakistan.[33] The invoking of Pressler Amendment against Pakistan in 1999, consequently due to the evidence of its acquiring nuclear weapons capability led to a ban on all military sales to Pakistan and the termination of US Pakistan defence cooperation. A ban was imposed on the training of Pakistani military officers in the US exchange of visits by military officers were curtailed, equipment in pipeline (F-16s, three naval aircraft and so on) were frozen and a ban was imposed even on the supply of spare parts for equipment sold to Pakistan before 1990. Pakistan ceased to be eligible for concessional military supplies. There was an unannounced ban on exchange of visits by scientists working in the nuclear and military establishments. Advisories were issued to all US educational institutions and research laboratories to exercise care and caution against Pakistani scientists seeking admissions or invitations in respect of subjects relating to nuclear and missile development. But things have changed after Pakistan's recent elevation in to a MNNA status. Here it is important to note that Pakistan has been one of the closest allies of Washington since the early 1950s having been part of American military groupings such as the South East Asian Treaty Organisation (SEATO) and the Central Treaty Organisation (CENTO).[34]

These developments have a booster to the moral of political-military establishments of Pakistan. Changed tone, tenor and language of Pakistani leaders on Kashmir can be explained in the context of these most recent developments. Once again, the Pendulum had swung towards the Islamists. There is little indication so far that Pakistan is actually winding up support to terrorists as the then Indian Army Chief General N.C. Vij pointed out that the terrorist activities continued unabated, and no actual effort was being made to cap or dismantle their infrastructure.[35] Musharraf once again is back with his old face on Kashmir issue. He has once again stressed on the centrality of the Kashmir issue in his address to an Indian media conclave. Musharraf emphasized that those fighting in Kashmir were freedom fighters not terrorists. He said that until India paid serious attention to the Kashmir issue there would be no progress on the other issues. Pakistani Foreign Minister Khurshid Mahmud Kasuri considers Kashmir issue as the most important unresolved disputes on the international agenda. He had all the praise for Musharraf for putting Kashmir on international agenda in a big way. In this course Musharraf had outperformed any other leader in terms of services for the Kashmiri cause, he emphasized.[36]

Facts as analysed above suggest that the relationship between the two countries is yet to come out from the legacy of communal antagonism, mistrust, suspicion and insecurity. Mindset of Pakistan has still not changed and the game of a snake-ladder continues. The intervention of other vested elements has further complicated the situation. But the compulsion arising out of the latest nuclear positions of both the countries requires a more serious thinking in terms of their relationship. According to experts long-range missiles possessed by the two countries constitute the single greatest threat to the region. The time taken by a missile to travel between the two countries is the shortest among the nuclear powers .. four to six minutes. Another ominous fact is that India and Pakistan lack the technology that allows for the recall of missiles once they are fired.[37] Therefore one can only hope for a new turn in place of a snake- ladder game between the two counties, but the history suggests otherwise.

Notes and References

1. Jaswinder Kumar: *Irritants in Indo-Pak Relations*, Deep and Deep Publication, New Delhi, 1989, p. 18, also see Nishant Ahmed, Kashmir in the Pakistan-India Military Equation, in K.R. Gupta, (ed.) *India-Pakistan Relations with Special Reference to Kashmir*, Atlantic Publishers, New Delhi, 2003, p. 120.
2. Ibid. See Kuldip Nayar: *Distant Neighbours: A Tale of the Sub-continent*, Vikas Publishing House, New Delhi, 1975, pp. 136-40.

3. Jaswinder Kumar: *op. cit*, pp. 18-19, also see Kuldip Nayar, *op. cit.*, pp. 1-32, also see Nishant Ahmed: *op cit.*, pp. 120-22.
4. Kuldip Nayar: *op. cit*, pp. 64-100 also see Jaswinder Kumar: *op, cit.* p. 20, also see K.P. Gupta: *op. cit* p. 3.
5. Ajay Saksena: *India and Pakistan: Their Foreign Policy (Areas of Agreement)*, Anmol Publications, Delhi, 1987, p. 19.
6. *Ibid.*
7. See Nishant Ahmed: Kashmir in the Pakistan – India Military Equation in K.R. Gupta, *India-Pakistan Relations with Special Reference to Kashmir*, Atlantic Publishers, New Delhi, 2003, p. 127.
8. *Ibid.*, p. 120 also see N. Jayapalan: Indo-Pakistan Relations in K.R. Gupta: *op. cit* pp. 135-39.
9. Jaswinder Kumar: *op. cit*, pp. 161, also see Praveen Swami: Extending Terror, *Frontline*, Chennai, March 26, 1999, pp. 16-20.
10. *Ibid.*, p. 20, also see Aijaz Ahmad, Pakistan's Time of Reckoning *Frontline*, Chennai Feb. 1, 2002, pp. 22-26.
11. Ajay Saksena: *op. cit* also see Sukumar Murlidharan, The Subcontinental Stand-off, *Frontline*, Chennai, January 18, 2002 pp. 10-13.
12. Jaswinder Kumar: *op. cit*, p. 44, also see Embassy of India Washington DC, A Comprehensive Note on Jammu and Kashmir, in K.R. Gupta (ed.) *op. cit.* pp. 40-43.
13. K.R. Gupta: *op. cit.*, pp. 32-33.
14. *Ibid.*, p. 33.
15. *Ibid.*, pp. 54-55.
16. Sukumar Muralidharan: *op. cit.*, p. 15.
17. K.R. Gupta: *op. cit.*, p. 55.
18. Muralidhar B. Reddy: Alone at the Top. *Frontline*, Chennai, July 19, 2002, p. 114.
19. *Frontline*, Chennai, Jan. 21, 2002, pp. 10-14.
20. Shaun Gregory: Analysi: South Asia's Nuclear Brinksmanship "www.bbc.com. May 29, 2002 in K.R. Gupta: *op. cit.* p. 116.
21. Alan Sipress: et al., Report India Pakistan were Near Nuclear War in 99 *Washington Post*, May 15, 2002 in K.R. Gupta: *op. cit.*, p. 116.

22. Benjamin Friedman: India and Pakistan War in the Nuclear Shadow" in K.R. Gupta *op. cit.*, p. 116.
23. John Cherian: Bilateral Bonhomie, *Frontline*, Chennai, October 22, 2004, pp. 18-19.
24. John Cherian: Euphoria and Reality, *Frontline*, Chennai, March 26, 1999, pp. 23-24.
25. Sukumar Murlidharan: *op. cit.*, pp. 11-13.
26. Muralidhar B. Reddy: A Time Table for Talks, *Frontline*, Channai, March 12, 2004, pp. 30-31.
27. Muralidhar B. Reddy: The Jehadi Backlash, *Frontline*, Chennai, January 16, 2004, p. 125, also see Krishna Swami Sridhar: Double Speak on Terror, *Frontline*, Chennai April 23, 2004, p. 37, also see Muralidhar B. Reddy. A deal for peace. *Frontline*, January 30, 2004, pp. 9-12, also see Sukumar Muralidharan: General's maneuvers *Frontline*, Chennai February 1, 2002, pp. 4-6.
28. Muralidhar Reddy B.: Turning Over a New Leaf, *Frontline*, Chennai January 16, 2004, p. 121.
29. *Ibid.*
30. *Ibid.*, also see A.G. Noorani: War Benefits Neither Side, *Frontline* Chennai, January 18, 2002, pp. 4-6.
31. John Cherian: A Balancing Effort *op. cit.*, p. 47, also see John Cherian: India and Pakistan Clearing the Air, *Frontline*, Chennai, August 13, 2004, p. 130.
32. John Cherian: "Diplomacy A Shock From the West *Frontline* Chennai, April 23, 2004, p. 36, also see John Cherian: A Balancing Effort, *op.cit.* p. 47.
33. John Cherian: Diplomacy A Shock From the West, *op. cit.* p. 37.
34. Ibid p. 40, also see John Charian: A Balancing Effort, *op. cit.* p. 40.
35. Praveen: Jammu and Kashmir a Meaningful Course, *Frontline*, Chennai, February 13, 2004, p. 26.
36. Mohammad Shehzad: India and Pakistan, I hope this Opportunity is not Missed. *Frontline*, Chennai, January 16, 2004, p. 122, also see John Cherian: India and Pakistan a New Round with Hope. *Frontline* Chennai, July 30, 2004, p. 43.
37. John Cherain: World Affairs: Building Confidence, *Frontline*, Chennai, July 16, 2004, p. 45.

16

Sino-Indian Relations: Need for a Paradigm Shift

Roop Singh Bareth

India and China are the trans-Himalayan twins holding together roughly one-third of the world humanity. Both the countries represent a unique example of having two ancient civilizations of the world across the Himalayan regions, covering India, China and some neighbouring areas form an important cradle of human civilization and as such the civilizations in India and China are the twins emerging out from this cradle around the Himalayas.[1] Of course, the two ancient civilizations, after their initial phase had followed the separate path of development and had created two different patterns of livings and life styles. Yet the cultural interaction between the two continued down the ages and as K.M. Panikkar has rightly observed that cultural influence is always a two-way traffic for influencing and being influenced.[2] Rabindranath Tagore after his "great pilgrimage" had underlined the need for "cultural intercourse and friendship" between the two great Asian nations. In his message to the Chinese friends, Tagore appealed that "It is our duty today to revive the heroic spirit of that pilgrimage following the ancient path which is not merely a geographical one but the great historical path that was built across the difficult barriers of race difference and difference of language and tradition, reaching the spiritual home whose man is one in bonds of love and co-operation."[3] In nutshell, the Sino-Indian cultural relations present a rich historical background of their interactions and interrelationships, hence, there is a need to understand and analyze their bilateral relations independently through indigenous perspectives instead of looking at each other through the west.

At the dawn of the new millennium, perhaps nothing has confused our intelligentsia more than India's relations and responses to the outside world in general and to China in particular. The cold war era and now the post-cold war period has put litmus tests to India's foreign policy for protecting and promoting its national interests in the highly contradicting and complex global scenario. With the collapse of the Imperialist International System after the Second World War, India and China started their bi-lateral relations with a clean slate and forged a strong bond of friendship against imperialism, colonialism and for Third World solidarity. Now it is the part of history that the two Asia giants–India and China, rose to the 'Himalayan heights', in forging a bond of friendship and brotherhood (Hindi-Chini Bhai Bhai) had committed the 'Himalayan blunder' when fought a bloody war in 1962. Thereafter, the bi-lateral relations continued to be stressed and strained almost for the next three decades resulting into deep suspicion, misperception and misunderstanding. Now with the end of the cold war and the beginning of a new phase of globalization and liberalization not only the international scenario has substantially been changed, the domestic scenario within India and China has also undergone structural changes, hence it provides a vantage point to review and reconsolidate the Sino-Indian relations in the light of the growing socio-economic realties and responses across the Himalayas.

It is a strange fact that India's advent for democracy in 1947 coincided with the emergence of cold war politics which over clouded the Afro-Asian states at a time when they were struggling to establish their independent identities in the comity of nations. India's independence, thus, not only ushered a new era in Asia the Third World but also coincided with the drawn of a new epoch in the world history. Inaugurating the Asian Relations Conference (ARC) in New Delhi on March 23, 1947, Pandit Nehru, visualizing the changes, called upon the delegates that there was a widespread urge and an awareness that the time had come for peoples of Asia to meet together, hold together and advance together.[4] It was not a vague desire but the compulsions of events which forced the newly independent states to think along these lines. The old order of imperialism and colonialism was fast receding into the oblivion and a new international system, dominated by two rival hegemonistic superpowers as "prime movers of the world" had emerged on the world horizon. Equipped with the most deadly weapons of the time, the two superpowers plunged into the politics of bipolarization along with the formation of military blocs and political groupings in which the independence and security of newly independent states was put to severe threats and they were forced to make undesirable compromises and alliances.

Political Solutions to the Security Problems

Nearer the home, several significant developments had taken place which reoriented and refocused the problem of India's security into a new and altogether different rather difficult context. Notable among them were, the emergence of a hostile state-Pakistan in 1947 and the establishment of People's Republic of China (PRC) after communist revolution in 1949. The formation of Pakistan as a separate sovereign state after the partition would not have had as grave consequences as emergence of Pakistan as a "hostile neighbour" did.[5] Similarly, any political changes across the Himalayas would not have mattered much to New Delhi as did China's emergence as a communist giant more so at the time when the global environment was fully charged with politics of bi-polarization, in the bitterest form. The defence policy enunciated and very well implemented by the British Government was neither found functional nor desirable in the changed circumstances and therefore, it was indeed a Herculean task to prepare and practice a policy on the one hand to seek solutions for the security problems in the context of deteriorating domestic conditions and on the other hand outside the uncomfortable regional milieu over shadowed with the cold war politics.

It was in this global and regional milieu that independent India not only had to formulate its security strategies but also to recast and redefines its political perceptions and priorities accordingly. The principle of non-alignment, above all, was a political strategy to keep the cold war politics and military rivalries away from Asia so as to ensure "Asia for Asians". Similarly, Sino-Indian friendship established and expressed as "Sino-Indian axis" at Bandung was no less a collective endeavour to seek political solutions of the security problems not only in the sub-continent but in Asia at large. The diplomatic efforts through ARC for forging Afro-Asian solidarity, the initiation of solving J&K problem through the good offices of the UN or resolving Tibetan issue through Panchsheel, irrespective of their final outcomes, were enough to prove that in the initial phase, serious efforts were made by New Delhi to diffuse and dissolve the security- problems but it appears that no well thoughtout defense policy based on sound military preparedness and strategic calculations was formulated. All the political arrangements made through ARC or through Panchsheel were found incapacitated and the strategies of non-alignment also got exposed when Pakistan joined SEATO in 1954 and the cold war politics was dragged down to doors of India. Yet it is true that the 'wide spread urge' resolving security problems through political and not through military solutions, continues to remain relevant even today therefore, it provides a vantage point for the academicians to re-examine and re-establish its necessity in the conflict-riddled post-cold war global scenario.

The Sino-Indian Friendship

The military debacle in 1962 was the severest blow to India's foreign policy ever experienced. It rendered its defence policy and the defence installations totally exhausted and exposed. After this debacle Nehru became 'a broken man' who had no longer the capacity to recast and redesigns a new defence policy for a humiliated nation and he passed away quietly in 1964. There is no dearth of literature on the causes and consequences of the 1962 military debacle by different scholars with different viewpoints. The ostensible reason for the 1962 crisis was border dispute between the two states, however, it appears that border dispute was not 'the real cause'; it was made 'a cause' to humiliate India for political reasons.

The establishment of communist regime in China under Mao Zedong in 1949 was not a welcome development for New

Delhi. However, the government of independent India led by Pandit Nehru was of the view that friendship with Communist China despite the different political systems is not only possible but it was imminent also in view of the emerging post-Second World War global scenario. He also believed that Sino-Indian collaboration might emerge as a 'strong bulwark' against imperialism and colonialism and could become a rallying point for Asian solidarity. India could also emerge as a leader of the newly independent Afro-Asian bloc and get its 'due place' in the comity of nations. In view of the long range national interests, Pandit Nehru did not realize the problem of Tibet or the border dispute as damaging for forging an axis between New Delhi and Beijing in a world dominated by two superpowers.

The communist rule in China in 1949 also did not appreciate 'the bourgeoisie rule' headed by Pandit Nehru in New Delhi. However, during Mao's regime, foreign policy was not independent rather a part of Mao's holistic approach to the state and the emerging international setup. The basic postulations of Mao's holistic approach were 'anti-imperialism' and the objectives of making 'revolutions' within the states. In the world dominated by imperialist forces, Mao was well aware of the weakness of the revolutionary forces both within China and outside hence; he devised and demonstrated the strategy of 'united front'. In order to neutralize the challenges of imperialist Japan, the revolutionary forces in China under Mao forged a united front with the nationalists. After establishing People's Republic in China, Mao relentlessly made efforts to fight against the imperialist forces and evolved the strategy of joint front in which India occupied a pivotal place. India's unqualified stand against imperialism and colonialism carved out a significant place in Mao's strategy and acted as a cementing factor in Sino-Indian collaborations. As a part of the policy, PRC did not abrogate India's exercise of its erstwhile colonial rights in Tibet unilaterally as had been done in the case of rights of the other imperialist powers in China. Not only this, Mao attended the national day celebrations at the Indian embassy in Beijing in 1951 in the most unusual and symbolic gesture and called for unity with India in the common cause of "working for peace"[6].

It was under this background of recognizing each other's

importance in their respective perceptions that Sino-Indian collaboration scaled the new heights of friendship in a record time. The Panchsheel Agreement of 1954 was not only a milestone in their bilateral relations rather it was a model prescription containing 'a set of guiding principles' for all states to follow in their foreign behaviour in order to seek political solutions to their bilateral problems. Similarly, Bandung conference of 1955 was 'a grand-show' of Asian Solidarity against imperialism and colonialism and an overt expression of emerging Sino-Indian friendship. It is astonishing that those who prescribed it flouted the 'Panchsheel' and the Bandung was allowed to repeat.

The Triangular Relationship

It is noteworthy that in the later half of the fifties significant changes had taken place in the foreign policy perceptions of both India and China. In Chinese perception, the Soviet Union, the leader of the communist bloc, had started to loose its credentials as a champion of the 'communist revolution' as well as a leader against 'imperialism'. In Mao's perception, the Soviet Union under Khrushchev had abandoned the international agenda of fighting against the imperialism and was pursuing the new agenda of 'peaceful co-existence' and prevention of nuclear war in the international politics. This was not considered in consonance with the pursuits of 'communist revolution'. Any way, the net result was that the Sino-Soviet rift started to widen in the international politics ultimately posing both the communist giants as the bitter enemies against each other. It was strange that the initial phase of Sino-Soviet rift coincided with the period of Indo-Soviet friendship. When Mao was developing serious doubts about Soviet Union under Khurshchev, the later was pursuing serious plans to wean India away from China. It was a fact that Bandung was disliked by both the superpowers but Soviet Union, which was not allowed to participate on the ground that it's "mainland lies in Europe" resolved that Bandung be never repeated. The growing Sino-Indian friendship was considered detrimental to the Soviet Union's hegemonistic interests in the Third World particularly in Asia where India was emerging as a leader of the newly independent Afro-Asian bloc. This was the reason that in the end of same year i.e. 1955, the Soviet team comprising of its President Bulganin and Prime Minister Khrushchev arrived at New Delhi and laid down the solid foundation of Indo-Soviet friendship.

Soviet Union had provided an alternative model of development in the state and a new pattern of socio-economic inter-relationships within the society which fascinated many Indians especially the leftists. Pandit Nehru, though a liberal democrat, was a great admirer of the Soviet Union ever since he visited the Socialist State. However, independent India could not attract the attention of Moscow during Stalin's period and the bilateral relations continued to remain just normal. After the death of Stalin in 1953, a significant change took place in the Soviet foreign policy under Khrushchev both towards Washington and Beijing and in this process of reorienting and recasting the foreign policy; India emerged as an important state in the Soviet calculations.

At the time when Soviet leaders landed at New Delhi, India was facing a rough weather. Nehru's government was committed to the targets of 'quick economic and industrial development' of the state as its top national priority but the absence of any meaningful technological support from the Western countries, prevented the establishment of the basic industrial setup. At the external level, the situation was more alarming and appealing. Pakistan, after joining SEATO in 1954, became a recipient of full American 'moral and material support' and consequently gained full political and diplomatic support on J&K issue from the Western bloc. On this most hypersensitive issue, India got isolated both within and outside the United Nations. Though India had carved out a place within the newly independent Afro-Asian bloc and also cultivated understanding and friendship with Beijing but it was of no consequence because China herself was an 'out cast' in the comity of nations. At such a crucial juncture when India was all alone to face the Western onslaught particularly regarding J&K and full cooperation in establishing basic industrial structure the strong foundation of Indo-Soviet friendship was laid down and it is remarkable that this foundation witnessed no visible cracks till the demise of the Soviet Union.

India valued its growing relationship with China and cautiously continued to venture on the path of friendship in order to fight against the imperialism and to forge the Asian solidarity but incidentally a new factor the Soviet Union, emerged which was too important for India to ignore. As already mentioned that it was the same period in which serious differences arose between Beijing and Moscow culminating ultimately into a rift and a serious rupture in the monolith communist bloc. It was under this background that China started doubting India's credentials as a champion against imperialism and as 'a genuine non-aligned state' for the cause of Afro-Asian solidarity. In Chinese perception, India was playing politics and their worst fears were confirmed when Dalai Lama was granted political asylum in 1959. It is pitiable that for the reasons beyond their control, New Delhi could neither succeeded in reposing its faith and confidence in the Chinese leaders nor could fully appreciate and acknowledge the growing sensitivities and accompanying circumstances across the Himalayas. It was under this background of emerging triangular relationship between Beijing-New Delhi-Moscow that misperceptions and misunderstandings were formed and unfortunately Sino-Indian friendship turned out to be a casualty.

The last decade of the 20th century has witnessed one of the most rapid paces of changes in the global environment in the recent human history. Beginning with the fall of Berlin wall in 1989, a number of developments have occurred notably, the disintegration of the USSR in 1991, which has substantially altered the power-equilibrium in the international system causing serious consequences for the regional and sub-regional systems in the world. The end of the Soviet Union was not merely the demise of a state rather it was also the breakdown of the superpower dominated 'International bipolar system' and hence a "systemic collapse" with far reaching consequences. The new "poly-centric system" is still evolving and due to which the post-cold war international system is severely infected with the vices of unilateral interventionism, instability and so on. The beginning of the nineties coincided with the dawn of a new era of globalization, liberalization and privatization in the international economics and trade. The state economies, particularly in the developing countries, so far protected and confined within the state boundaries have been forced to globalize their markets and resources. The state control over its economic enterprises was forced to liquidate gradually and the MNC's and TNC's were given way to domestic markets and thus 'non-state actors' and the 'supra-state structures' started to redefine and redesign the emerging international economic and trade system in the world. In the field of science and technology, the 'Technocratic' and the Cybernetic' advancements have almost revolutionized the means and patterns of communications in the world rendering physical distances and national boundaries almost immaterial.

The Durable CBM-Trade

With these new transformations taking place at the global level, significant changes have also taken place within the domestic scenarios of the two states and now in the overall changed context, a new beginning seems to be taking place for the improvement of their bilateral relations. In the eighties and the nineties, the economic and trade systems in China and India have gone a sea change and in view of the emerging economic and technological realities mutual trade seems to be the most durable CBM in Sino-Indian rapprochement. Though compared to their size, the volume of their bilateral foreign trade is still very small but recently the border trade has substantially increased their traffic in goods and in people across the border. The two countries started a joint venture in steel production in Orissa (India) between India's Mideast Integrated Steel Ltd. and China's Metallurgical Import-Export Corporation (MIEC) in January 1993. Indian exports to China shot up from $ 181 million in 1992 to $ 417 million by the end of 1993 – an increase of 170 per cent which is remarkable. India's imports reached $ 259 million, up 63 per cent from the year before.[7] Two agreements signed in November 1996 on Maritime shipping and combating smuggling of narcotics and arms and other economic offences on Sino-Indian border will go a long way in boosting their mutual trade and confidence. The two sides have agreed for free trade in 15 local items such as yak-tail, salt, borax, China clay, China silk etc. This has not only increased the border trade rather it has resulted into the revival of various cottage industries on the either sides. For example in Pithoragarh district of India, the carpet weaving cottage industry which has been completely shut down as it depended entirely on Tibetan wool revived with the availability of the raw material from Tibet.[8] There are other uncharted areas of future co-operation such as aircraft, ship building, repairs, railways, tourism etc. which have enormous potentiality for mutual trade endeavours.[9]

The Chinese economy has remained as one of the most vibrant and the fastest growing economy in the world registering a growth rate in the range of 8.8 per cent in 1997 to 7.3 per cent in 2001. The Gross Domestic Products raised from $903.4 billion in 1997 to $1.19 trillion in 2001 and the foreign exchange reserves also increased substantially from 139 trillion Yuan to over 200 trillion Yuan in 2001. The foreign trade also jumped from $ 325 billion in 1997 to $462 billion by the end of 2001. These are indeed very impressive figures, which testify the economic accomplishments of China. But it is worth mentioning that China is also confronting serious domestic socio-economic problems[10] which have led to important changes in the party leadership and the political system. These have also are imposed serious constraints on the foreign policy formulations in PRC.

The Security Scenario

It is noteworthy that the military asymmetry between India and China in the sixties was the major 'immediate cause' behind the 1962 debacle that ruptured their relationship completely. In October 1964, after the Chinese nuclear explosion at Lop Nor in the plateau of Shanghai the power-asymmetry further got aggravated and hence the PRC with 'nuclear teeth' started to threaten and encircle India beyond the Himalayas. It is beyond doubt that the initial momentum to China's foreign policy towards South Asian countries came from its hostility towards India. Beijing continuously played its 'anti-Indian card' fairly for a long period of time through India's neighbouring countries especially Pakistan, Nepal and Bangladesh in fomenting 'hate India campaign' in the Indian sub-continent. In doing so, Beijing, naturally, found its greatest opportunity in Pakistan–a state with a population of over a hundred million, with a standing army ranking in the ten most advanced armies in the world and the state with the established anti-Indian credentials. China emerged as a major source of supply of arms and ammunitions for Pakistan over the years[11] to the extent that it provided covertly, "the critical assistance" for nuclear and missile technology to provide "nuclear teeth" to Islamabad. Apart from Sino-Pak collusion, China's bilateral relations with Nepal or with Bangladesh were mainly revolving around the axis of anti-Indianism. This has remained one of the most important reasons, which substantially deteriorated the security scenario in the sub-continent making it the 'grimmest' region in the world politics.

The nineties ushered not only a new era in the history of international system in the world but it also witnessed a new significant transformation in the security environment in the South Asia. Whatever may be the pros and the cons of the Pokharan II in the wider realms of international peace and security but this is true that it struck a "balance of terror" by imposing "the power-parity" between the two states for the first time, though this process was started with Pokharan I in 1974. This is one of the reason that in the new millennium both the countries have willingly pushed down 'the border dispute' which once caused a bloody war, under the carpet and are embarking, very confidently, upon the path of economic co-operation and technological collaboration. Hence, it appears that "power-parity" between the two Asian giants seems to be a pre-condition for "controlled peace" if not "complete peace" for the future co-operation. Being the established nuclear power with the latest killing capability, both seems to be quite conscious of the fact that the pattern and practice of their bilateral relationship will not only influence the socio-economic developments in their respective states but will also influence, decisively, the regional and the global politics in the future in evolving 'polycentric system' in which India and China both will certainly be the 'centers of power' to reckon with. Hence, there seems to be a U-turn in their relationship, which deserves an in-depth study to analyse and estimate their future course of relations and responses.

The two 'Asian giants' are back on the path of economic

co-operation and technological collaboration with full vigour at the dawn of the 21st century which indeed is a welcome move. The fast growing mutual trade has opened up new vistas of future co-operation and confidence between the two states. According to the Chinese Customs statistics the bilateral trade between India and China rose by 5.03 per cent in 1998. With New Delhi retaining the slot as Beijing's biggest trading partner in South Asia.[12] In the post-Pokharan II phase, the security scenario is substantially changed in the Himalayan region. India's successful explosion of the 'thermo nuclear device' has struck a balance in the killing capabilities between the two Asian giants and has significantly transformed the 'threat perceptions' and security-concerns' in the region. India's nuclear policy, which is aimed at maintaining "a minimum but credible difference", has come out for parity in their future course of actions. The 'new low' experienced in their bilateral relations on account of Pokharan II in 1998 has been successfully over come and now at the dawn of the new millennium their bilateral relations seems to be more matured and balanced. A significant hike in economic and trade collaborations, qualitative change in the security perceptions and an appreciable progress has been noticed in their political relations. Besides adopting a similar approach towards the many vexing international issues such as opposing unilateral interventionism, unipolarism, hegemonism etc. to advocate for polycentrism, environmental protection, NIEO in the international politics, both the states have taken resolute steps in improving their bilateral relations on many political issues. Both the states have successfully managed to keep the much troubled border-issues at 'low profile' and had maintained the complete 'peace and tranquility' at LAC to their credit. More recently, the Chinese pronouncements regarding Sikkim[13] are highly encouraging not only for resolving one more old issue of yesteryears but a very positive move for giving way to strengthen and boost border trade.

Need for a New Paradigm

The Chinese foreign policy has always remained 'Sino-centric' and hence proved to be the most 'prudent policy' in promoting and protecting its national interests in the comity of nations. They are the players of 'realpolitik' in which 'power-projections' and 'power-profiles' matter more than anything else in promoting and protecting their national interests may be at the cost of the other. Commenting on their foreign behaviour India's former National Security Advisor late Mr. J.N. Dixit had pointed out that 'the Chinese do not believe in pulling other people's chestnuts out of the fire."[14] India's relations with China in the past had proved that Chinese hardly hesitate in resorting to power mechanisms if their national interests so warranted. Therefore, India should evolve and implement a prudent foreign policy in relation to China to protect its national interests including the security and strategic interests. To keep their bilateral relationship 'balanced' and 'booming' they should resort to 'realities' rather than 'rhetoric'. On account of illusions neither the power parity nor the mutual interests be ignored.

Tibet had remained and continues to remain the most volatile cause of misperceptions, misunderstandings, suspicion and distrust. The issue has been internationalized in the past but now it appears that the new leadership in China under Hu Jintao is sincere enough to resolve it and in this pursuit India's willing co-operation is considered imminent in Beijing. As a matter of fact on the issue of Tibet, China's international image is much maligned and the world forces consider Tibet as a 'safe leverage' to pressurize China. China is also constrained due to its own limitations within Tibet and is conscious of the fact that the final resolution of the problem of Taiwan would also depend on the peaceful solution of the problem of Tibet. As China is preparing hard for organizing Olympics in 2008 to exploit it as an occasion to project its 'global image' particularly in the western world,[15] Beijing seems to be serious in preparing a road-map to stage a successful come back for Dalai Lama to finally resolve the issue and herein lies the political importance of India for the success of this diplomatic venture.

Keeping the pace of economic cooperation and technological collaboration at full swing, New Delhi is to play its diplomatic cards very carefully at least in this regard. The importance of Tibetan card should be realistically reassessed in the context of the new developments that had taken place in the nineties and in view of the emerging attitudinal changes taking place in the Chinese foreign policy towards India, particularly on Sikkim. The time has come when India should stop looking at Tibet through the eyes of the West and independently evaluates the issue in view of its own national interests. In this regard, if at all an occasion arises when Tibetan issue seems to be nearer to resolution, India should have little hesitation in accommodating Chinese sensitivities and in offering its good offices. But in such negotiations India should firmly stand for resolving the border dispute also and a strategy should be prepared in which both the issues could be resolved amicably. The territorial imperative had created a deadlock in the Sino-Indian relations for almost more than four decades. Now the time seems to be ripe for serious deliberations as Tang Jiaxum, the Chinese State Councilor has said that Russia and China has recently sorted out their border dispute once and for all. He made an optimistic observation that "being personally involved in the settlement of this question, I know very clearly that the boundary question between China and Russia was far more complicated than between our two countries.[16] The territorial issue needs to be amicable resolved through political dialogue and diplomacy within the ambit of national interests.

The emerging Sino-Indian relations ought to be understood under the wider context of the triangular relationship emerging between India, China and the United States. In the post-Pokharan II phase, Indo-US relations have improved considerably. Apart from the significant increase in the Indo-US trade, both the states have taken resolute steps in forging 'strategic partnership' through the Next Steps in Strategic Partnership (NSSP) since 2004. It appears that United States may not be directly involved in the bilateral issues of Sino-Indian relations, yet the US may also not appreciate any strategic alliance in the Asia-Pacific region particularly the Sino-Indian alliance with far reaching consequences. Hence, there is a need to pursue the national interests very carefully in the broader context of this triangular relationship between New Delhi, Beijing and Washington.

Notes and References

1. The direct ape ancestor of humanity – Ramapithecus was first discovered in 1932 at Rama at the Indian foot hills of the Himalayas now lying within Pakistan. In recent years, a large

quantity of fossils of this species has been discovered in Yunnan and this Chinese province has acquired a new reputation as the "home land of Ramapithecus". See also A Sino-Indian perspective for India-China Understanding by Tan Chung in *Across The Himalayan Gap: An Indian Quest for Understanding China* edited by Tan Chung (Gyan Publishing House, New Delhi, 1998).

2. K.M. Panikkar: *Indian and China*, Asia Publishing House, Bombay, 1957, p. 63.
3. Rabindranath Tagore's message to the Chinese friends dated April 23, 1957, p. 37.
4. J.L. Nehru: Changing India. *Foreign Affairs*, XLI(3), April 1963: p. 455.
5. Sishir Gupta quoted by Stephen P. Cohen, Security, peace and Stability in South Asia: An American Perspective. *Asian Affairs*, 1988, p. 37.
6. *Diplomacy of Contemporary China*, New Horizon Press, Hong Kong, 1990 p. 213.
7. V.P. Dutt: *India's Foreign Policy in a Changing World*, Vikas Publishing House, New Delhi, 1999, p. 220.
8. Rajesh Kandian: *Tibet, India and China*, Vision Books, New Delhi, 1999, p. 176.
9. Jasjit Singh: Future of Sino-Indian Relations. *The Strategic Analysis*, Vol. XVI, No. 11, Feb. 1994, p. 1512.
10. V.P. Dutt: India-China Ties, *The Hindu*, March 22, 2002.
11. Prime Minister Mohammed Khan Junejo acknowledged this while welcoming China's Defense Minister Zhang Aiping in Islamabad in July 1985 and said that Pakistan "today stands self-reliant in many of its defence requirements only because China had so generously transferred its technology and know how". *The Pakistan Times*, July 7 1985.
12. *The Hindu*: March 22, 1999.
13. C. Raja Mohan: Sikkim and the road to Lhasa, *The Hindu*, May 10, 2004.
14. J.N. Dixit: *India's Foreign Policy*, Picus Books, New Delhi, 2003, p. 83.
15. Merry Beth Markey, The Executive Director of the International Campaign for Tibet has highlighted it and expected that Beijing should initiate the talk to resolve the issue at the earliest.
16. Amit Baruah: China Backs India's Dialogue Policy on Kashmir, *The Hindu*, October 20, 2004.

17

India, America and Pakistan in the New Era: Challenges and New Equations

Annpurna Nautiyal

As can be assessed from the US policies that the spread of nuclear weapons, terrorism and the unresolved Kashmir issue has put South Asia in the list of very volatile and dangerous places in the world, which otherwise does not figure as an important region in the US priority. Actually the war against terrorism in the post-9/11 period which has moved to the top of the American policy agenda and the proliferation of nuclear weapons have emerged as the issues which not only are important and require immediate US attention but these have also secured a place for India in the US designs because India is also fighting cross-border terrorism since the last one decade. In view of the similarity of the threat perception the US intends to develop a close cooperation with India for confronting the challenges to peace, security and stability. Bush administration's policies of favouring democracies, acknowledging India as a rising power and responsible state with advanced nuclear technology on the one hand has provided a new outlook to the relationship between India and the US in the new era but on the other the soft policies of the US towards Pakistan despite its role in promoting cross-border terrorism and nuclear proliferation sometimes casts a shadow on the closeness and forces India to believe that it has to fight its war on terrorism alone or the terrorism in other parts of the world has different meaning for the US. As we ponder about the prospects of the triangular relationship between India, Pakistan and the United States, we find that although there is a change in the US outlook towards India, which is being regarded as historic in some quarters particularly after the recently concluded visit of the US by Indian Prime Minister Manmohan Singh. The latest ten year defence and full civil nuclear cooperation agreement with India as well as the US declaration to help India evolve as a major power in the 21st century indicate towards the changing tone but the duplicity of the US policies towards terrorism, refusal to support India's claim for the permanent seat in the UN Security Council, pressures on India for reviewing its relations with Iran to which the US considers a rogue state and desire to have a good working relationship with Pakistan is also intact. In view of this it can be said that despite some warming of relationship through NSSP (Next Steps in Strategic Partnership) and showing a keenness for enhancing cooperation in economic, defence, and strategic partnership and tackling terrorism, the US has not abandoned its even handed approach or putting India and Pakistan in equal pedestal in South Asia particularly in the politico security issues. In the opinion of Jeffrey E. Key [1] such approach means seeking close ties with India but also not isolating Islamabad or giving up its ties with it which clearly indicates towards the realism in the US policies that makes India apprehensive about the US intentions, despite the newfound warmth in its relations with the US.

Actually the trend of coming closer to India especially after the Kargil war between India and Pakistan started to take shape during the second term of President Clinton, who visited the subcontinent when his tenure was nearing to its end. Clinton's visit was important from the point of view that it took place after 22 years and that too with the sanctions on which had been placed on both India and Pakistan after the 1998 nuclear explosion. During the Kargil crisis the US took an exceptional and unexpected step by condemning Pakistan for having sent troops across the line of control and played a key role in brokering a cease fire agreement. It was seen as a shift in the US policy. India's opinion towards the shift in the US policy was once again reinforced when President Clinton during his visit in March 2000 spent only a single day in Pakistan and used this occasion also to reprimand Gen. Pervez Musharraf for having engineered the October 1999 coup. The US pressures on Pakistan against the violation of the LoC during the Kargil crisis and desire to improve relations with India by visiting the subcontinent though helped in developing a favourable atmosphere. But his emphasis on the four 'R' (1) Respect the line of control (2) Renew dialogue (3) Renounce violence (4) Restraint to be observed [2] and sympathy and concern for Pakistan despite its support to cross-border terrorism failed to woo India. It was viewed by the Indian think tanks as nothing new but revival of the old policy of either favouring Pakistan or India because these points though used as a warning to Pakistan to mend its ways ultimately applied on both the sides and made it clear that despite the growing disenchantment with Pakistan, the US was not willing to abandon Pakistan or its even handed approach in South Asia. Actually the US has always followed a policy of either favouring India or Pakistan depending on each President's attitude as well as the geopolitical necessities since the cold war days like Nixon's policy of tilt towards Pakistan during the 1971 Indo-Pak war or during Soviet occupation of Afghanistan and this policy is still intact.

In view of this it can be said that though the need to work closely with Pakistan had ended with the end of the cold war therefore Clinton wanted to extend a hand of friendship for India but with caution. Bush also followed the policies embarked by Clinton and wanted to accord priority to India because he was unhappy with Pakistan because of its unwillingness to sever its ties with the Taliban regime in Afghanistan. Bush also chose to ignore the issue of nuclear proliferation and some sanctions were also lifted. But the events of September 11, 2001 and the US war against terrorism once again forced the US to reexamine its policies towards Pakistan because of its extensive links with the Taliban. Moreover its geographical proximity to Afghanistan made its cooperation vital for the war against the Taliban regime and also Osma Bin Laden's Al- Queda terrorist network. Due to this reason the coldness by which America had treated the Pakistani President General Pervez Musharraf after he seized power in 1999, was replaced by a certain kind of warmth. Before the terrorist strike the Bush Administration had relegated Pakistan to the category of a rogue state because of its military dictatorship, its support to the Taliban regime in Afghanistan, its involvement in cross-border terrorism and acquiring nuclear and ballistic missiles from China and North Korea and suspected role in supplying it to others. But the 9/11 changed the situation and on account of its geographical location the US once again accorded importance to Pakistan. However, presently while maintaining good relationship with Pakistan the US also wants India's cooperation therefore the US administration is pursuing a policy of tilting both ways. In fact the US policies towards Pakistan in the aftermath of the terrorist strikes exhibited that even in this age of precision guided munitions, long range bombers and extensive missiles capabilities, the exigencies of geography still matters.[3] Since Pakistan's physical proximity with Afghanistan was crucial to carry out any war against Taliban regime therefore Bush not only showered Musharraf with praise, concern and attention, waived various economic sanctions, provided an aid package that exceeded $600 million in 2002 but also restarted US-Pakistani military cooperation.[4] On account of the support of General Pervez Musharraf and the Pak army in its war against terrorism the US had been following a policy of not paying serious attention towards the Indian demand of action against Pakistan which is quite annoying for India. As India feels that it has shown excessive tolerance and exercised restraint vis-à-vis Pakistan despite the continuing trans border infiltration of Pakistani trained terrorist but the US has done nothing to restrain Pakistan.[5] Such policies make India apprehensive about the US intentions because in the past also the US has sought to manipulate the balance of power in different regions by promoting certain countries as a means of checking others. In South Asia the US has been doing the same by preferring and promoting Pakistan and because of its strategic location and willingness to cooperate in all the US ventures including anti-terrorism.[6]

This can further be understood by the fact that despite criticizing Musharraf particularly after the evidence of the involvement of the Pakistani citizens in the terrorist activities in India, for not taking action against the banned terrorist groups, the US was not willing to isolate Pakistan or to shun its Pakistan bias in adopting new policies for South Asia even in the changed circumstances. The American policy of putting pressures on Pakistan to end support for militant organizations and on India to start negotiations with Pakistan on Kashmir simultaneously after the 9/11 could be seen as the new moves of establishing parity between India and Pakistan. Although the US has denied that it has a triangular relationship rather insisted that it has independent relations with India and Pakistan but the gestures of the Bush administration of appreciating Indian democracy and also the acceptance that the two largest democracies on earth are no longer estranged suggests that there are some linkages between the two policies.[7] It also clearly indicates that under the present circumstances while the Bush Administration is keen to court India with which it had a problematic relationship during much of the cold war but it also wants to keep Pakistan under its hold. Although putting India and Pakistan on equal footing and developing close ties with Pakistan serves the US interests in a better way yet the fear that the close relations with Pakistan could damage the carefully developed ties with India, therefore, to convince India about its intentions, the US officials always try to assure India that a close relations with Pakistan would not be at India's expense. The US necessity of maintaining close relations with both the countries has made the relationship more interesting because though the US wants to maintain equal relations, and parallel improvement of relations with both India and Pakistan and force them to adopt peaceful means in resolving the Kashmir issue by pursuing a policy of tilting both ways, it has also been carefully weighing how its policy towards one would affect its relations with the other. Due to such approach while taking any policy decision about Pakistan it is trying to keep India also in good humour. Consequently while providing help to Pakistan the Bush administration has also realized that besides exerting pressures on Pakistan to curb its support for the insurgents in Kashmir it would have to offer India some other sops. Therefore not only military to military cooperation with India was initiated but the discussion on the transfer of the dual use technology was also renewed. This can be understood in a better way from the US offer to India for supplying the F-18 as the F-16 fighter aircraft which are capable of carrying nuclear weapons are being supplied to Pakistan therefore to pacify India the US has offered to supply F-18 tc India.

Yet it is unclear how long Washington will be able to maintain this balancing act or the policy of keeping both happy. Though there is no denying of the fact that presently the relations between India and Pakistan have also improved but in view of Pakistan's attitude towards Kashmir and preference to use Kashmir as a threat and also for the proxy war, India has expressed its apprehensions against such supplies. In view of this it is clear that the policy of supplying weapons (on a wider scale accepting Pakistan's claim to nuclear power status) to both the adversaries at the same time and that too when Pakistan is not ready to demolish its terrorist base, serves the US interests best as in the past also the US had supplied weapons to the adversaries like Israel and Arab countries at the same time as it was beneficial for the US national interest. The US is also opposed to the Iran-India gas pipeline and has started pressurizing Pakistan to move out from this agreement because the US treats Iran as a rogue state.

It is apparent from the above that the national interests, economic compulsions and global power politics consideration has always guided the US foreign policy towards South Asia and being the only superpower the US can aggravate or ease the situation of insecurity in this region. In view of this India is not in a position to ignore the US pressures because the US has a capacity to deny India its rightful place and objectives in world politics. As a result of this India has no choice except following the US suggestions and accepting the US role in the solution of the Kashmir dispute. The Indian position indicates the helplessness through which India is undergoing because though Indian leadership has always denied the role and mediation of any third power in the resolution of Indo-Pak problems but the US has made it clear that the present spring time in Indo-Pak relations which led to the normalizations of relations became possible due to the efforts of the two countries themselves and the supportive role played by Washington. Although the former Foreign Minister of India Yashwant Sinha clarified India's position by commenting that "the US interests in our relationship is like the interests of a friend. They are talking to us like how a friend talks. That is where it stops. There is no other role for anyone.[8]" But it is obvious that the offer from India for the renewal of dialogue and restoring the other links with Pakistan despite knowing that Pakistan has not stopped the cross-border terrorism was clearly under the US pressure. In fact India cannot ignore the US pressures and role because by always appealing to the US to control Pakistan India has already accepted the US role in South Asia and therefore it has to act accordingly. On the other hand despite appreciating Pakistan the US also criticized Musharraf particularly after the evidence of the involvement of the Pakistani citizens in the terrorist activities like attack on Indian parliament and Akshardham, for not taking action against the banned terrorist groups and the latest moves of Pakistan towards peace with India also indicate that Pakistan has also been under the US pressure to move seriously in the direction of normalisation of relations with India. The state of the relationship being shared by these three is not only interesting but also requires further probing in view of the fact that presently Pakistan is under close scrutiny because of the reports of the revival of terrorist camps in its soil and its role in transferring nuclear technology to the rogue states against whom the US has waged a war of pressure tactics therefore all the eyes are focused on America's action against Pakistan because Iraq was attacked on the similar grounds. This provides a strong basis to understand the various issues and factors of the triangular relationship between India, Pakistan and the US in the post-cold war era but before analyzing this it is essential to briefly analyze the US policy toward South Asia.

US Policy towards South Asia: The Cold War Era

South Asia has always been awarded a very low status in the US policy priority list because it not only lacks vital natural resources and strategic location and more so the US also did not have vital strategic interest in South Asia. This can be verified from the fact that there was no senior official to deal with South Asia till the end of the Cold War. It was clubbed with the Near East and put under the charge of the Assistant Secretary for Near East and South Asian affairs.[9] It was only after the end of the cold war that it has been put under the charge of a full-fledged assistant secretary of state. Since the US policies were largely governed by the needs of containment of communism, therefore as and when the communist threat intensified the US became active in the region otherwise the

US did not take much interest in it. As the two major states of South Asia had developed mutually antagonistic relations almost immediately after their independence, therefore, preparing a policy that could satisfy both India and Pakistan was a great challenge and required immense skill which the US, being a new entry in the world politics lacked. With the result the US policy of tilting both ways failed in winning the trust of either India or Pakistan rather the image of an opportunist power became associated with the US.

The US policies towards South Asia, particularly towards Pakistan and India have been an example of carrot and stick diplomacy which can be divided into three phases (1) up to 1971 (2) 1979 to 1989 (3) 1989 to present.[10] In the first phase the relationship was totally based on the concerns of the power politics of the cold war era in which India's non-aligned policy and non-participation in the military alliances pushed the US towards Pakistan and a close relationship was developed with it. In fact, Pakistan became the major US ally in South Asia due to two reasons (1) Pakistan was eager to collaborate with the US (2) Its strategic location between the Persian Gulf and East Asia made it strategically important. As a matter of fact, the US policy makers held the view since the beginning that with Pakistan the Middle East could be defended and without Pakistan there was no way to defend the Middle East.[11] Moreover, once the US recognized the importance of Kashmir support to Pakistan's stand as well as entering into the military alliance with Pakistan became a strategic necessity and by doing this the US acquired an image in India "as a friend of Pakistan and opposed to India."[12] The image of the US as unfriendly friend has surfaced and resurfaced time and again and widened the gap between India and the US. The Pro-Pakistan tilt in the US policy, attitude towards Kashmir and arms aid to Pakistan had been the major sources of tension in Indo-US relations because the arms supplied to Pakistan were never used to meet the communist threat but against India in different wars. Interestingly, Pakistan is the only country in South Asia with its Islamic traditions which has participated in all the US led military alliances and coalitions from 1950's to present but its participation in the US led alliances during the cold war was largely for seeking security and strengthening its defence against

India not for the containment of communism. Actually, Pakistan never perceived a communist threat until the outbreak of the Afghan crisis in the late 1970's therefore; Pakistan had nothing to do with the ideological factor of the cold war; it only wanted security against India by acquiring the requisite military capability. The alliance with the US therefore fulfilled Pakistan's purpose of seeking security against India and the US aid starting with a programme of only $25 million gradually rose to $1.5 billion and during Afghanistan crisis it crossed a $2.5 billion mark. The US also established its electronic intelligence bases in the northern part of Pakistan to monitor Soviet missile tests in the Soviet Central Asia, although, such facilities provided valuable information to the US but these measures alienated India more.[13] The US decision to ignore the ground realities encouraged India to pursue its policy of non-alignment in ways that were not appreciated by the US. Historian Stanley Wolpert has labeled the US military alliance with Pakistan "surely the worst single blunder in US South Asian policy and easily the most costly."[14] Robert Hardgrave an expert on South Asian affairs opined, "with little sensitivity to the impact of the American actions on regional stability, the US contributed to deepen Indo-Pakistan enmity and encouraged India to seek closer ties with the Soviet Union."[15] which not only provided economic and military assistance to India but also supported India's position on Kashmir. Meanwhile India also learned how to exploit its policy of non-alignment for aid from both the superpowers.

The US policies towards Pakistan also led India to believe that the US was not only arming the enemy but was also trying to put Pakistan in a client status so that it might be used to put pressure on India. By providing military aid the US thus helped in increasing the hostility between the two. The US policies towards South Asia also revealed the different perceptions of security being shared by the US and the South Asian states because while the US believed that the main threat for the Indian subcontinent emerged from the communist countries, India and Pakistan looked upon each other as the main threats to their security. In view of the relationship with Pakistan, India has all the reasons to believe that the US military assistance to Pakistan since the 1950's has not only destabilized

South Asia but has also hampered the evolution of a natural regional balance of power in which India would enjoy its rightful position of unchallenged supremacy.[16] The US policies have also produced a psychological problem in Indian policy makers who think that the US policy makers not only treat India and Pakistan equally, but also give less importance to India. The denial of a proper status to India and patronizing Pakistan by the US has also been an irritant in the Indo-US relations.

Although despite India's policy of non-alignment during the first phase (1947 to 1979) aid was also provided to India particularly during the 1962 Indo-China War. The US economic assistance to India increased considerably and reached about $400 million during 1961-62. India was also seen to be in a unique position to help the US to contain China's aggressive ambitions in Asia. During this period due to the convergence of interests the irritants in the Indo-US relations were ignored. But the US military aid to India was not appreciated by Pakistan and despite the fact that it had received between $1.2 billion to $1.5 billion in military aid from the US, besides $3 billion in economic aid during 1947-65, Pakistan became apprehensive of the US policies and by following the theory of enemy's enemy becomes friend it began to cultivate close friendly relations with China.[17] In 1963, it entered into an agreement with China and a large area in Kashmir was provided to China. At the same time Pakistan also began to develop close relations with the Soviet Union. It was a reflection of Pakistan's disillusionment with the US despite the aid received and also exhibited a change in Pakistan's perceptions particularly related to security vis-à-vis India. But the phase of lukewarm relationship in US-Pakistan and Indo-US relations existed for a short period because the aid provided to India during the China war could neither remove the old doubts nor cement the bond of friendship between India and the US. Since this aid was largely provided to meet the challenges of communism therefore, it not only remained inconsistent and ineffective but also decreased America's reliability as a partner in India's eyes. The US policy of stopping and resuming aid at will also became a source of irritation because aid was provided during the 1962 war but the embargo imposed during the 1965 war was not liked by India and forced it to believe that the US had been favouring the aggressor and treating India as equal to Pakistan.[18]

As the US was deeply bogged down with the Vietnam problem therefore during this phase it did not take much interest in the sub continental matters but as the later events exhibited that the US disinterest was short- lived because the changes taking place in the communist bloc once again aroused the US interest in South Asia. The necessity to establish relationship with the communist China in the wake of the growing differences between China and the Soviet Union provided reasons for the US to establish close friendly relations with China. The need of developing close relations with China forced the US to tilt in favour of Pakistan as it acted as a channel for China opening. The Nixon-Kissinger Pro-Pak tilt during the 1971 Indo-Pak war not only deteriorated Indo-US relations to its lowest ebb but also motivated India to develop more closer, relationship with the USSR so that a proper strategy to meet the challenges generated by the creation of a triangular axis of Pakistan-China and the US could be evolved. As the later events exhibited that India's policy of moving closer to the USSR allowed India not only to achieve its goals in the 1971 war but also the creation of Bangladesh. The security environment due to the triangular axis also gave a momentum to India's nuclear programme, which was mainly driven from a phenomenon of energy to security programme. India's refusal to sign the NPT, its nuclear programme and test of a nuclear explosive device in 1974 also became a source of permanent irritation between India and the US because it called for sanctions by the US on the export of the high technology to India.[19] Since then other states and coalitions of nations like the Nuclear Suppliers Group have also been pressurized by the US to not to assist India or to transfer nuclear technology. India's nuclear test made Pakistan more insecure and desperate to develop its nuclear programme as it was considered the only way to counter the threat from India. Pakistan's nuclear programme also called for sanctions under the Symington Glenn amendment and economic and military aid to Pakistan was totally cut off in 1979, which made Pakistan once again suspicions about the US and their relations also deteriorated.

But the US apathy and distance towards Pakistan could not remain for a longer period because the occupation of Afghanistan by the Soviet forces in 1979, once again provided the reason for the US to work closely with Pakistan and also to arms aid worth $3.2 billion.[20] Pakistan also used this opportunity to build up its nuclear programme, which was overlooked by the US because it was felt that it would not be a serious obstacle to close relationship with Pakistan. It is therefore, believed that Pakistan became the nuclear threshold country with the full US knowledge. On the one hand the Soviet occupation of Afghanistan and Pakistan's role as a frontline state not only cemented the bond of friendship between the US and Pakistan but on the other hand India's policy towards the Soviet occupation and the diplomatic support to Moscow backed regime in Kabul came as a shock to the US and increased the differences between India and the United States.[21] By providing military aid to Pakistan the US inadvertently increased hostility between the two: India complained of the growing threat from Pakistan and the likelihood of using weapons against it. The US aid to Pakistan continued till the end of 1980's at an annual rate of approximately $600 million, however with the withdrawal of the Soviet troops from Afghanistan, Pakistan's importance as a frontline state once again receded. With the US President's failure to certify that Pakistan did not possess a nuclear explosive device all economic and military aid to Pakistan was stopped in October 1990 under the provisions of the Pressler Amendment. The suspension of aid worsened the US-Pakistan relation further.[22] Infact, the Pressler Amendment became the sharpest symbol of American maltreatment in the eyes of the Pakistani public because in their opinion it ignored India's nuclear programme and imposed penalties on Pakistan only.[23] Pakistan's resolve to maintain its nuclear programme became stronger as a reaction against the US pressures. Although, during this phase (1979-89) Pakistan had a four-fold importance for American geo-strategic interests: as a sympathetic player in the Gulf and Iran, as a friend of China, as a key factor in Afghanistan and as a possible target of further Soviet expansions. India figured nowhere in all these calculations but a certain opening up and warming of relations between India and the US was also witnessed.[24] In the 1980's both sides began to view their relationship with a long-term perspective and some American scholars also began to see India as the emerging regional power and a possible alternative to the growing power of China.

India's desire to move from primarily a public sector dominated economy to private enterprises, opened up opportunities for the US business community for investment and profit and this also increased India's value. In 1982, President Ronald Reagan and Prime Minister Indira Gandhi signed the Science Technology Initiative, which enabled a transfer of US technology to develop India's light combat aircraft. The high technology initiative of the US was taken with the view to balance the military and economic assistance to Pakistan and also to increase the US influence over India's military programme.[25] It was also considered a suitable way to curtail the Soviet influence. Since India was aware of its over dependence on the USSR for military hardware therefore, it also wanted to move closer to the US. But these efforts were not long lasting, as there were disagreements over specific types of systems and technology to be exported. With the implementation of the MTCR in 1987 exports became more difficult and India's test of Agni intermediate range ballistic missile produced sufficient bitterness in the relationship. Interestingly these considerations became important only after the end of the Soviet occupation. But India always believed that that the US policy of initially providing certification that Pakistan did not possess a nuclear explosive device and there after refusing this certification provided a greater legitimacy and credibility to Pakistan's nuclear programme and its success in manufacturing nuclear weapons. The above account clearly suggests that during the cold war the US policy in South Asia was totally based on its geo-strategic calculations and intensity of the communist threat. Due to this the US policy has never been principled and consistent rather it represents opportunism in the US policy, even in the post cold war era the US policy lacks consistency.

Triangular Relationship: The Post-Cold War Era

The end of the cold war and the subsequent disintegration of the Soviet Union in the early 1990s saw a reverse trend in this triangular relationship with an upward movement in Indo-US relation and downward movement in US-Pakistan relations. Essentially this has been a regular feature of the US foreign policy because sometimes it looks favouring India and sometimes Pakistan, however most of the time it has shown a tilt in favour of Pakistan. It was felt that in the absence of the irritants of the cold war era like India's non-alignment and close ties with the former USSR and stoppage of the US military aid to Pakistan, a new relationship could emerge between, India, Pakistan and the United States. The needs of globalization and market economy also paved the way for bringing the world's two largest democracies closer, as India's vast market potential, adoption of open economy had become quite lucrative for the US business community. The US started to view South Asia particularly India on account of its liberalization measures, as a region of intense economic growth, potential, opportunities and development but on the other hand its tensions and problems also made it a region full of challenges. India was placed in the category of the 10 big emerging markets by the US Department of Commerce, which was also seen as an indicator of India's growing importance as an economic partner to the US. Unfortunately, despite the growth and development in economic relations, much change could not take place in the politico-security issues in the last one decade. A close look at the US policies in the post-cold war era reveals that the basic tenets of the US policy are still unchanged and its relationship with India and Pakistan in which the later has generally been preferred as a dependable ally and a frontline state vis-à-vis the West Asia is still unchanged. The national interests of the US not only still require Pakistan more than India but it also finds to deal with Pakistan easier than India in terms of its diplomatic and security calculation. The US military industrial complex also favours Pakistan. Lee H. Hamilton has provided the following reasons for the continued US support to Pakistan even in the post- cold war era (1) It is the 7th largest nation in the world and the second largest Muslim state (2) Its strategic location near the major countries like China, Pakistan, Iran, India, Middle East, the Persian Gulf and Central Asia (3) Pakistan has been an active supporter of the UN peace keeping activities.[26] It was also accepted by Stephen J. Solarz in an interview that the US policy towards Pakistan is not guided by any attraction but the US have some important mutual interests which require a measure of constructive cooperation between the US and Pakistan. In his opinion, "these interests include containing Islamic extremism, facilitating a measure of stability in Afghanistan, combating the production and use of drugs, controlling international terrorism encouraging economic development and reform and bringing stability in South Asia. Pakistan is in a position to affect the US interests in South Asia therefore it is a country which we can not afford to ignore."[27] Thomas P. Thornton has also commented, "Pakistan should never be considered a negligible quantity in any geopolitical calculations. It plays an important role in South Asia and South West Asia. But its curse it geography, for it is overshadowed by India and its political shortcomings are judged against India's relative success."[28] With the collapse of the Soviet Union, Pakistan has developed a particular interest in Central Asia as an area in which it can exercise its influence, gain a share of growing Central Asian markets and develop closer cultural, economic, ideological and security ties with its Muslim neighbours. Due to this the US interests in Gulf and Central Asia also identify Pakistan as a bulwark against the Islamic fundamentalism of Iran and their ties revolve around the containment of Iran.[29]

In view of the geopolitical importance of Pakistan the US policies towards Kashmir, cross-border terrorism and nuclear issue indicate that the global power politics has not produced a drastic shift in the US outlook towards Pakistan and despite problems in Pakistan the US is not willing to abandon it for the sake of developing close relations with India. Earlier also with the US administration's active support to Brown Amendment the way was opened for the supply of military equipment worth $370 millions to Pakistan in 1995 including P-3C orions aircraft and weapons which Pakistan had ordered prior to the imposition of the Pressler sanction in 1990.[30] The Brown Amendment also made it clear that the US did not have an India policy rather a South Asia policy and the President and the Congress would continue to equate India and Pakistan. It also implied that the US was once again acquiescing to Pakistan's equation of nuclear capability and overlooking the China-Pak missile connection. India therefore has reasons to believe that despite her efforts to increase economic and political cooperation and minimize confrontation over the Kashmir issue, the US has never abandoned its policy of equating India and Pakistan and also a double standard between India and China both of which deny the status of a major regional power to India.[31] Moreover, the two-country rule theory also still requires the senior US officials to visit both the capitals on official trips to the region and it also gives the impression of granting Pakistan equal status with India which is not liked by India.[32] Even Clinton also did not change this rule during his South Asia visit in which besides India, Pakistan and Bangladesh were also included. India strongly wants that the US should not equate India and Pakistan, because India is a democratic state, strong believer in the individual rights, freedom and justice, on the other hand Pakistan has been unable to develop a stable political system even after 57 years of independence and largely being termed as a failed state due to its mounting economic problems. But even if Pakistan violates all the principles of democracy and promotes terrorism the US preference for Pakistan indicates that it continues to serve the US strategic interests and also signifies that Pakistan would remain as an important factor in Washington's scheme of things as long as it continues to hold its special geographical position towards Afghanistan, Central Asia, Middle East and continue to act as a factor in Indo-US relations.[33]

Though there is no denying of the fact that the developments in the Indo-US relations particularly after the Kargil conflict indicated towards the emergence of a new equation in Indo-US relations. However the US stands of putting pressure on Pakistan for withdrawing its forces from Kargil or restoring democracy or resuming dialogue with India did not indicate a shift in India's favour. Because as per India's request the US not only refrained from declaring Pakistan a state promoting terrorism but also wanted to maintain close working relationship with Pakistan's undemocratic military regime. Interestingly, India and the US have never had a good relationship with one another on account of sharing the values of democracy, freedom, justice and equality rather the US has always preferred Pakistan or the military dictatorships worldwide because for promoting national interests the consideration of democracy has never been important for most of the US administrations. Since the US has always found it easier to deal with the dictatorships, therefore it has not totally discarded its old perceptions about Pakistan but under the changing scenario some kind of softness in its attitude towards India can also be felt because it needs India's cooperation too. In view of the changes the Clinton administration aimed towards increasing the level of bilateral cooperation with India, wiping all the sanctions and building strategic cooperation with India, Pressurizing India and Pakistan to sign the CTBT, NPT and keeping their nuclear programmes under control and converging with India to tame the belligerence of Islam in Afghanistan and Iran.[34] Cohen[35] has also suggested that the US foreign policy in South Asia in the post- cold war era should aim for promoting more economic liberalization, preserving and expanding Indian democracy, encouraging strategic normalization between India and Pakistan, helping India and Pakistan to manage their nuclear weapons and developing strategic cooperation with India. In view of the continued conflictual relationship of India and Pakistan Clinton, who had commented that "the most dangerous place in the world today is the Indian sub-continent and the LOC" [36]did not appreciate the 1998 nuclear tests by India and Pakistan because he believed that besides making the situation of nuclear proliferation in South Asia more alarming it had also increased the possibilities of the adjacent countries getting the nuclear technology from Pakistan. Therefore Clinton administration's foreign policy focused on motivating India and Pakistan to curb their nuclear and missile proliferation and also to restrict the growth of their nuclear weapons. Actually in the post-cold war era the nuclear proliferation issue, the US reluctance to accept the expansion of the membership of the nuclear club, and policies of overlooking the Pakistan-China nuclear and missile connection and dual policies in tackling terrorism have emerged as major irritants in Indo-US relations and hampered the development of closer ties.

The Post -9/11 Triangular Relations

The 9/11 terrorist attacks on the US allowed it to understand the plight of India in a symphatic manner as India has also been fighting cross-border terrorism since long. In view of the similarity of the threat perception the US exhibited its interest in developing close cooperation with India for confronting the challenges to peace, security and stability. As the former US ambassador to India, Robert Blackwill has also opined that no other countries than India and the US face the three intense challenges: advancing Asian stability based on democratic values: confronting daily threat of international terror and slowing the further proliferation of WMD.[37] This view has also been authenticated by the US's latest Patterns of Global Terrorism report[38] which brings out the stark reality that India continues to be the worst victim of terrorism. It says that during 2002 India had to grapple with far more terrorist strikes than any other country by Pakistan based groups. Extremist violence in Kashmir fuelled by infiltration from Pakistan across the line of control threatened to become a flashpoint for a wider India-Pakistan conflict during most of the year. According to this report 67 of the relevant incidents occurred world wide were in India that too mostly in Kashmir whereas the number in other countries was less Israel 9, Pakistan 8, and West Bank 7. It also said that though Pakistan remained a key ally in the anti-terrorism effort, offering support to the US operations in Afghanistan, implementing close law enforcement cooperation and cracking down on domestic terrorist and transferring nearly 500 suspected Al- Queda and Talibani Terrorists to the US but it has not shown willingness to control the terrorist operating from its border areas against India. In view of this the report has highlighted that like the US India also faces a significant threat because the militants are opposed to continued Indian rule over the disputed territory of Kashmir. This shows that though the US also shares India's concern about terrorism and wants India's cooperation in defeating terrorism. But despite the convergence of interest, the initiation of the NSSP, assurances for cooperation in the civil and defence technologies, the doubts still persist because of the duplicity of the US policies like ignoring the cross border terrorism being supported by Pakistan, China-Pakistan cooperation in nuclear and missile proliferation, transfer of nuclear technology to North Korea and putting pressures on India. As Colin Powell has opined that "though the two largest democracies on earth are no longer estranged but at the same time we have also been able to advance our relations with Pakistan-a country with domestic challenges of its own. We have since been trying to turn our parallel improvement of relations with India and Pakistan into a triangle of conflict resolution. Although, we do not impose ourselves as a mediator but we do try to use the trust we have established with both sides to urge them toward conciliation by peaceful means."[39] It clearly indicates that though the US wants to develop good relations with India but Pakistan has also an important role in its calculations became clear when the US preferred to ignore the policy gestures of India like welcoming in 2001 the Bush Administration's declaration of going in for the National Missiles Defence, and offering Indian military bases and facilities to the US in the aftermath of the World Trade Centre attack when the US readied to attack Afghanistan. While such bold policies exhibited India's willingness for developing close relation with the US but the geopolitical needs and interests of the US which required Pakistan's military dictorship more than India in tackling the Al-Queda terrorists did not allow it to grab the Indian offer. Since the Musharraf government had allowed FBI to operate from within the country and carry on its investigations therefore the US believed that no other government in Pakistan would be able save its interests in a better way and if Pakistan became a failed state it would seriously threaten the stability and security of the entire region therefore the survival of the Musharraf government became necessary for the US.[40]

As Pakistan was extending full cooperation to the US therefore while putting pressures on Pakistan to curb the cross-border terrorism, a policy of not giving serious attention to Pakistan's activities against India was also adopted and on the other hand India was pressurized to negotiate with Pakistan to resolve the basic issue of Kashmir so that the root cause of cross-border terrorism could disappear. In view of this in some quarters it is being felt that despite the talk of a strategic partnership with India to counterbalance China's rising power, the inability of the US to frame a policy on India without bringing Pakistan into picture, such partnership could not materialize till date. The US decisions to wave the coup related sanctions against Islamabad and the determination that Pakistan's nukes for missiles swap with North Korea do not deserve the imposition of sanctions supports the pro Pakistan bias of the US policies. It also suggests that as long as Pakistan serves the US interests and cooperates with US forces in their hunt for Al-Queda terrorists, the USA would not take any action against it for proliferation or continuing to support the terrorism against India.[41] The preference for Pakistan and necessity to involve it in the anti terror coalition has in fact forced the US to view the terrorism being faced by India from a different angle.

Although there is no denying of the fact that in order to improve relationship with India the US has also made some policy moves which indicate the good intentions of the US towards India. The recent agreement for ten year defence partnership with the US which aims to expanding defence trade and increasing opportunities for technology transfer, collaboration, co-production, research and development, maintenance of security and stability, defeating terrorism and preventing the spread of weapons of mass destruction and protection of free flow of commerce via land, air and sea lanes through a panel called the Defence Procurement and Production Group[42] signals the US decisions to befriend India. These developments are good and indicate the changing nature of relationship however these not only require to be taken seriously and implemented into policies but also call for caution on the part of India in view of the asymmetries in the military, political and economic power between the both as in the past also India and the US had signed such defence related agreements which could not cut much ice. Moreover the slow pace of the so called Next Steps in Strategic Partnership and the three separate bilateral dialogues indicates towards the reality because India's access to US technologies still remains far more constrained than China's. This also suggests that for being important like China and seeking respect from the US India needs to accelerate its growth in economic and military power.

Actually there are several examples which highlight the vagueness and duplicity of the US policies vis-à-vis India. Like the announcement to help India becoming a major power in the

21st century came the same day Bush made the controversial decision to sell F-16s to Islamabad which was regarded by Condoleeza Rice the US Secretary of State as a means for maintaining military balance in the subcontinent. It clearly reflected that it was just an exercise to divert attention of the Indian public. The granting of the MNNA (Major Non NATO Ally) status to Pakistan also shows the US preference for Pakistan. The US offer of selling F-18s fighter jets to India also seems to be a move to pacify the Indian public opinion over its rearming of Pakistan as India has already expressed its apprehensions towards such sales to Pakistan. In view of its past experiences India has all the reasons to believe that the F-16s with the P-3 Orion maritime reconnaissance aircraft, TOW anti tank missiles and Phalanx defence systems will be aimed against India. Such policies have strengthened the belief of the Indian defence analysts that the stringent technology controls against India and patronizing Musharraf not only encourages the military mullah complex that runs Pakistan but the supply of the major combat systems and multi billion dollar aid also encourages not to dismantle the state run terror complex against India.[43] A fact that was also stressed by India's Defence Minister Pranab Mukherjee during his recent visit to the US by saying that "the infrastructure of terrorism in Pakistan and Pakistan controlled territory, remains. We do not hear of operations like the ones being conducted by Pakistan in cooperation with the US, against the war on terrorism at its western frontiers, towards its eastern borders with India."[44] The recent terrorist attack on the Ram Janambhumi in Ayodhya further confirms the apprehensions of India about the possible role of Pakistan in such activities aimed to destabilize Indian polity and society. The former Indian Army Chief and defence analyst General V.P. Malik has also stressed that "Pakistan has not dismantled the terrorist infrastructure. It is only calibrating terror with talks."[45] India's Foreign Minister also confirmed that the terrorist camps in Pakistan had been revived and Pakistan is fast emerging as a epicenter of terrorism. The attack in Ayodhya also confirms the apprehensions of the security analysts that Islamabad could be scheming militants' attacks to keep up pressure on India to hasten the Kashmir talks while retaining the terror card as an option in its back pocket.[46] More over the India-Pakistan peace process has not changed the ground situation too much in the Kashmir valley as the militants have not abandoned their goal of freedom. Actually the terrorists have increased their sphere of activities and new targets like the Indian Military Academy Dehradun or headquarters of Infosys and Wipro have been included in their list. This fact has come into light by the modules of Lashkar-E-Toiba busted by the Delhi Police Special Cell recently. An attack on these or similar other establishments could be very disastrous for India. In view of the continued terrorist activities India feels that if terrorism remains unabated the peace process with Pakistan might also suffer. Unfortunately, despite direct or indirect signals from India about Pakistan's role in cross-border terrorism the US has preferred not only to overlook such signals but also putting pressures on India to make peace with Pakistan which India is unable to ignore hence the peace process is going on with basic problems in tact.

Conclusion

The US stand towards India and Pakistan in the post-9/11 suggests that US is neither pro-Pakistani nor pro-India but works only for the augmentation of its national interests which lie in peaceful atmosphere in the Indian subcontinent and for this it wants to keep both India and Pakistan happy by offering various sops. The US is keen to maintain good relations with both the countries simultaneously because it requires both for its global designs and interests. While the US shares India's concern about terrorism, wants India's cooperation in defeating terrorism, aspires to develop closer economic and defence ties, needs the support of democratic India for its strategy against China but it cannot afford to ignore Pakistan also due to its geopolitical importance, its willingness to join war against terrorism and its clout in the Islamic world. The Bush administration has made it clear that besides building strong bilateral relations and involving both India and Pakistan in its war against terrorism in South Asia the US also aims to resolve the Kashmir problem peacefully and prevent a nuclear exchange between India and Pakistan. This clearly exhibits that for the US its national interest is more important than anything else. This has allowed the US to adopt a selective approach towards terrorism in other parts of the world and lets it to react in a different way. Such approach is not very fruitful in curbing and controlling terrorism because there cannot be different parameters for identifying terrorists like my terrorist and your terrorist or my terrorist first and then yours. It is being generally felt that on account of such faulty responses towards terrorism and pointless and brutal war in Iraq and earlier in Afghanistan the US has created hatred and terrorist where there were none.[47] The spurt in terrorist attacks in India, London and Egypt also supports this argument. These attacks have strengthened India's argument that Pakistan is responsible for all terrorist activities and the threat to world peace does not arise from Iraq or Iran but from Pakistan hence suitable actions against it should be taken. With the evidence of the involvement of the people of Pakistani origin in the bomb blasts in the London Metro stations and as well as the reports of revival in infiltration of terrorists in India, though, the US has reiterated that Pakistan should close all militant training camps and block all infiltration across the LoC in Kashmir but still much needs to be done to restrain Pakistan.

But notwithstanding the ambiguity in the US policy it is also commendable that despite its need for Pakistan Bush has cleverly managed to avoid a rift with India also with the result both India and the US are scaling the heights of a new kind of closeness in their relationship which was unthinkable a decade ago. Actually the end of anti Americanism in India with the fall of the Soviet Union has made the US task of engaging India easier. The Bush Administration has involved India within the anti-terror coalition and to a framework of strategic partnership even while holding Pakistan's military dictatorship also very close with the other arm and in spite of differences about Pakistan's role the US and India have managed to navigate carefully because they have a common interest in fighting global terrorism, maintaining peace, promotion of democratic rights and economic growth.[48] The movement of two democracies towards developing defence and strategic ties as well as a desire for integrating trade, investment and technology transfer is not only creditable but also shows the progress in their bilateral relationship regardless of differences, which is a good sign. In view of the present scenario the US think tanks and experts on South Asia have also reiterated the need to taking India seriously and enhancing cooperation in civilian nuclear energy, space and high technology. In a recent report entitled India as a new global power: an action agenda for the United States prepared by the Carnegie Endowment for International Peace has advocated the need "to integrate India as a friendly nuclear weapon state into the evolving global nuclear regime."[49] The former US Ambassador to India Robert Blackwill also feels that the war on terror, weapons of proliferation and the rise of China calls for close Indo-US relations in the new era.[50] In a major policy decision the US President Bush besides acknowledging India as a responsible state with advanced nuclear technology also agreed to extend civil nuclear energy cooperation and trade with India[51] during the Indian Prime Minister Man-mohan Singh's recent visit to America. President Bush has also pledged to work with the allies like the Nuclear Suppliers Group and Congress to reduce the curbs and sanctions against India, which has never signed the Non proliferation Treaty. This is being seen as a very significant development in the Indo-US relations in the post-Cold War era and suggests the end of the US policy of sanctions against India being pursued by the US since long. However, it is also being felt in many quarters that these commitments would be hard to implement as it would be difficult for Bush to persuade Congress to change the Nuclear Non-Proliferation Act (NNPA) enacted to target India for its nuclear blast in 1974 more so it would allow other states also to claim for such status.[52] Even in India also the opposition and the left parties have started to express their apprehensions towards this agreement as they believe that by putting all the civil nuclear facilities under international monitoring and inspection of the International Atomic Energy Agency India has also implicitly accepted its protocol to allow international inspectors' access anywhere and anytime. They believe that as India's nuclear military capability comes from the civil nuclear programme therefore it would be difficult for India to refuse the pressures of the monitoring agency and such position would seriously undermine India's nuclear policy being pursued since 1974. Nevertheless under the present environment of good will it may be concluded that undoubtedly the movement of the two democracies: India and the US generates hope for the future however, in view of the past experiences and also the present response of the US towards India's claim to permanent membership in the UN Security Council as well as cross border terrorism India also needs to be cautious enough so that it may safeguard its interest without any undesirable compromises.

Notes and References

1. Jeffrey E. Key: Beyond Tilting both Ways; A New Post-Cold War South Asia Policy, *Asian Affairs*, Vol. 25, No. 2, Summer, 1998, p. 116.
2. *The Hindustan Times*: March 26, 2000.
3. Sumit Ganguly: India and Pakistan in the Shadow of Afghanistan. *Current History*, April 2002, pp. 147-52.
4. Jeffrey E. Key: See No. 2, p. 97.
5. Brahma Chellaney: The Lessons from Iraq. *Hindustan Times*, April 21, 2003.
6. Fouad Ajami, Iraq and the Arab's Future, *Foreign Affairs*, Vol. 82, No.1, Jan-Feb. 2003, pp. 2-18.
7. B.K. Srivastava: Indo-American Relations and the Issue of Terrorism. *World Focus*, Vol. 22, No. 10-11-12, Oct.-Nov.-Dec. 2003, pp. 35-36.
8. We Facilitated Indo-Pak talks: US. *Hindustan Times*, February 19, 2004.
9. Anirudha Gupta: Issues in South Asia; Geo Politics or Geo-Economics. *International Studies*, January-March 1997, Vol. 94, No.1, p. 20.
10. Ashok Kapur: Western Biases, *The Bulletin of Atomic Scientists*, January-February, 1995, p. 41.
11. Rekha Dutta: US Security Policy in India and Pakistan and the Question of Nuclear Proliferation. *Journal of South Asian and Middle Eastern Studies*, Vol. XXI, No. 2, Winter 1998, p. 29.
12. B.K. Srivastava: The United States and South Asia. *South Asian Survey*, January-June 1997, Vol. 4, No. 1, p. 402.
13. Selig Harrison: The United State and South Asia Trapped by the Past, *Current History*, Vol. 90, No. 614, p. 402.
14. Kul B. Rai, David Walsh, Paul J. Best: *America in the 21st Century*, Prentice Hall Inc., 1997, p. 144.

15 Robert L. Hardgrave: *India Under Pressure :Prospects for Political Stability* Boulder Co .Westview Press, 1984, p. 203.

16. Selig Harrison and Geoffrey Kemp: *India and America after the Cold War*. Carnegie Endowment Study Group on US-India Relation in a Changing International Environment, 1992, p. 7.

17. Arun K. Banerjee: The US and South Asia. In Shankar Ghosh and Somen Mukharjee (ed.) *Emerging South Asian Order, Hope and Concerns,* Calcutta, 1995, p. 130.

18. *Ibid.*, p. 130.

19. Virginia Foran: The Case for Indo-US High Technology Cooperation. *Survival,* Vol. 40, No.2, Summer 1998, p. 74.

20. Dennis Kux: *Estranged Democracies India and the United States-* 1941-91, Sage Publications, New Delhi 1993.

21. Virginia Foran: See No. 19, p. 74.

22. P.R. Chari: *Indo-Pak Nuclear Stand off: The Role of the United States,* Manohar Publishers, New Delhi, 1995, pp. 72-73.

23. General Mirza Aslam Beg: Pakistan's Nuclear Programme: A National Security Perspective, In John Gjelstad and Olav Njoestad (ed.) *Nuclear Rivalry and International Order,* Sage Publication, New Delhi, 1996, p. 169.

24. Stephen P. Cohen: *The Reagan Administration and India*. In Harold A. Gould and Sumit Ganguly, (ed.) *The Hope and the Reality-US Indian Relations from Roosevelt to Reagan,* West View Press, 1992, p. 144.

25. Virginia Foran: See No. 19, P. 75.

26. Statement of Representative Lee H. Hamilton: *Hearings Before the Sub-Committee on Near Eastern and South Asians Affairs,* March 7-9, 1995.

27. Stephen J. Solarz "We cannot afford to ignore Pakistan", *The Hindustan Times*, November 9, 1995.

28. Thomas P. Thornton: The New Phase in US-Pakistani Relations, *Foreign Affairs,* Summer, 1989, p. 143.

29. Ram R. Subramaniam: Nuclear Proliferation in the Third World.Region Specific Case of India Vs. Pakistan. *Brown Journal of World Affairs,* Winter/Spring, 1997, Vol. IX, Issue I , p. 98.

30. Jeffrey E. Key: See No. 1, p. 97.

31. Francine R. Frankel: Indo-US Relations: The Future is Now, *Washington Quarterly,* 1996, p. 130.

32. Jeffrey E. Key: See No. 1, p. 97.

33. Annpurna Nautiyal: Pakistan Factor in the Post-Cold War Indo-US Relations. *Journal of South Asian and Middle Eastern Studies*, Vol. XXII, No. 4, pp. 32-48.

34. Bhabani Sen Gupta: Vajpayee's Foreign Policy, *World Focus*, October-December,1999, p. 17.

35. Stephen P. Cohen: The United States and India: Recovering the Lost Grounds. *SAIS Review*, Winter-Spring, 1998, p. 100.

36. Brahma Chellaney: The Clinton Doctrine. *The Hindustan Times*, July 14, 1999.

37. Robert D. Blackwill: The Quality and Durability of the US India Relationship, Remarks delivered November 27, 2002 in Calcutta.

38 .US Report: India Worst Victim of Terror in 2002: *Hindustan Times*, May 2, 2003.

39. Colin L. Powell: A Strategy of Partnerships. *Foreign Affairs*, Vol. 83, No. 1, January/February 2004, p. 31.

40. B.K. Srivastava: Indo-American Relations and the Issue of Terrorism. *World Focus*,Vol. 22, No. 10-11-12, Oct.-Dec. 2003, pp. 35-36.

41. Brahma Chellaney: Is the United States Taking a Pro-Pakistan Stand. *Times of India*, New Delhi, April 27, 2003, p. 12.

42. *Hindustan Times*: June 30, 2005.

43. Brahma Chellaney: See No. 42.

44. Peace with Pak not Firm: Pranab, *Hindustan Times*: June 29, 2005.

45. Subhash Mishra, Ramesh Vinayak and Sandeep Unnithan: Terror in the Temple. *India Today*, July 18, 2005, p. 28.

46. *Ibid.*

47. Vikram Sood: Democracy Battles Realpolitik, *Hindustan Times*, July 10, 2005.

48. Sumit Ganguly: See No. 3. pp. 147-152.

49. US should let India have the tech it wants, says report. *Hindustan Times*. July 17, 2005.

50. *Ibid.*

51. Making History: *Hindustan Times* (ed.) July 20, 2005.

52. Brahma Challaney: N. deal: Tough task ahead, *Hindustam Times*, July 21, 2005.

SECTION-III

HUMAN SECURITY, GOOD GOVERNANCE AND REGION SPECIFIC ISSUES

18

Terrorism as Weapon

D.B. Shekatkar

"At the heart of every terrorist act there is a cause, a political goal, a perceived injustice or denial of liberty that is as concrete to the activist as any prime minister's motion of justice or freedom. No political rhetoric can disguise this fact. No opponent of terrorism should forget it."

Expression of dissent and resistance to an established order is an age-old phenomenon in the history of mankind. Mankind has practiced violence since the days of caveman who fought for his animal needs, or the gratification of his emotions and passions or indeed for self-preservation.

Terrorism is a distinctive disorder of the modern world. It originated as a term and has come into the spotlight of global conflict in our lifetime. Individuals and groups who felt aggrieved or oppressed resorted to violence when they could not achieve their aims by political means. Though subversion and terrorism have been known for centuries, it is in recent years that the subject is receiving greater attention the world over. All over the world such conflicts have proliferated, particularly, in developing countries like India. These have often been inspired, aided or abetted and directed by external factors to achieve political and ideological goals. Terrorism above all, is an expression of ideas including political protest is paradoxically accompanied by a sense of powerlessness by many people in controlling their own destinies. Terrorism looms as a major threat to free societies. The growing number of terrorist attacks, the increasing destructiveness of terrorist weapons, and the siege atmosphere around some of the government buildings and houses of political leaders are constant reminders that terrorism is limited neither by distance nor by choice of targets.

Political terrorism on international scale represents the emerging low cost, high pay-off alternative to other known forms of trans national violence. It is increasingly being used by the disaffected the world over as a means of projecting their influence beyond boundaries of nation states into submission of physical violence and fear psychosis. Since it seems to be paying-off, terrorist activities are showing exponential growth rate. Democracies of the world are practically bedeviled by the menace although even autocratic states are not totally immune to it. A complex web of interaction and relationship between terrorists of various organizations in different parts of the world is gradually but surely surfacing while counter measures on international scale through cooperative efforts among affected are hardly perceptible. This is perhaps yet another example of institutional inertia in the face of minority deviant behaviour and manifestation of the incapacity of modern democratic states to react to group violence with speed and effect.

Whatever are the causes for this gap between action and response, terrorism has exploded on the world scene as an epidemic with no sign on abating. Only its intensity and scale are growing. Groups with little or no direct political power have demonstrated repeatedly in recent years that by employing certain tactics, central to which is the use of direct terror, they can achieve effects on a target community which are out of all proportions to their numerical or political power. Such tactics attract worldwide publicity; create widespread panic or apprehension and causes national governments to concede to demands for the understanding of the use of terror for political ends. While on the one hand political terrorism is perhaps the most topical issue today on the other hand it is also perhaps the least understood phenomenon of our times. Media abounds in terrorist stories but treats them simply for their sensational value. Terrorists benefit from such publicity and symbiosis becomes complete.

Serious debate on genesis of political terrorism particularly resulting in proper understanding of origins, causes and concepts of terrorism so essential to devising effective means of combating it. In attempting such an undertaking it is desirable first to ascertain the substance of the threat to separate the reality from the media image. To ascertain whether current terrorism is an outgrowth of past use of terror or a unique phenomenon generated by new political force. In addition to understanding its general and contemporary motivation there is a need to ascertain whether new developments such as transportation, communication and weaponry give the use of terror more leverage than the past forms of terror and therefore result in a greater threat than in the past. Analytical study of the problem and prospects of terrorism reveals that it carries within itself; the seeds of its own destruction and in the seeming helplessness of the democratic states and the institution of the civilized world order do lay a viable solution to the problem. In India, too, the problem of the political terrorism can be solved if appropriate measures are taken, policies formed and properly implemented well in time.

Definition

In order to appreciate the nature of terrorism it is necessary to look at the definition and concept of terror and terrorism, and to examine its often ambiguous status to other forms of civil, military or political violence and criminal behaviour. One of the problems in defining terrorism lies with the subjective nature of terror. We all have different thresholds of fear and more terrifying to each of us than others. Because of the complex interplay of the subjective forces and frequently irrational individual response it is very difficult to define terror.

The dictionary defines a 'terrorist' as one who uses terror-inspiring methods of governing or of coercing the government, or community. Political terrorism may be defined as the threat or use of deliberate violence, indiscriminately or selectively against either enemies or allies to achieve a political end. The intent is to register a calculated impact on a target population and on other groups for the purpose of 'altering the political balance in favour of the terrorist'. Thus terrorist activities, when directed against democratic states with a plethora of minority groups or against states that contain historically antagonistic people-seems to be aimed at discrediting the existing government by provoking it to concentrate its coercive power on a particular segment of the population with which the terrorist try to identify.

Origin

Terrorism has its roots in tyrannicide, which has been known since the dawn of history and has been universally recognized. It is therefore of noble birth as the slaying of tyrants to rid society of the scourge was always regarded as an honourable act and to that extent political terrorism cannot be faulted with as the legitimate duty and right of the oppressed. History abounds in examples of tyrannicide. Some of the greatest men in human history were honoured not because they put up with injustice but because they chose to take arms to wrest for themselves and for their fellow men, dignity, honour and freedom and the society has been the better off for it.

When the legitimacy of recourse to arms by individuals to rid the society of tyrants is extrapolated to the level of organized violence by a group of disaffected people with a view to replacing the government in power, it gets classified as struggle for liberation of the oppressed and finds justification among the radicals, no nation can ever ensure full satisfaction of all aspirations of all its constituent members especially when it packs within its geographical boundaries diverse ethnic groups as we find in India. Some or the other communities or groups invariable feel discriminated against or deprived, throwing up a group leader who in the absence of legitimate power to match with power of the state, propagates the cult of violence. We have been witnessing this phenomenon in Assam, Punjab, Jammu and Kashmir and North East India.

Trends

India is passing through a phase of her development and progress, in which a number of political, social and economic problems have emerged. These issues have created discontent and have resulted in people resorting to violent actions and agitations in various parts of our country. In India the unchecked population explosion, mass unemployment, increasing industrialization and urbanization have generated social, economic and political disparities leading to erosion in values, ethics, heightening aspirations and corruption across the board.

The process of modernization has caused tremendous economic pressures on our traditional societies who are keen to retain their regional, tribal affinities. Criminalisation of politics, lackadaisical attitude of bureaucrats and attitude of law enforcing agencies deny the fulfillment of people's aspirations. All these factors are causing discontent, frustration, and compelling people particularly unemployed youth to perceive that they have no future and are being discriminated. The perceived discrimination and sense of injustice lead to formation of groups around specific issue of discontent, sometimes imaginary and inspired. The issues and problems resulting in emergence of terrorism in Punjab, J&K, Assam, North East, Andhra Pradesh, Maharashtra, Bihar and Madhya Pradesh are different; however they have one thing in common, the "use of terror". When peaceful means fail to resolve discontent, violence is resorted to. The degree of violence is often determined by the degree of perceived injustice and discrimination.

Terrorism is philosophy of premeditated violence; it is being used by a group of misguided youth to achieve social or political ends about which the participants themselves are not very clear. It will be seen that the phenomenon of terrorism has been part and parcel of human existence, but the modern technological and industrial advances have given it a boost and modern youth in many affluent countries of the world have taken recourse to it under the false belief that by using terrorism as a weapon against the society they would be able to change to their way of liking a much easier said than achieved ideal, for obvious reasons. Terrorism is cheap in terms of efforts and resources. It is well-known that dramatic terrorist acts can be accomplished by a few men with little training or logistic support. However organization, secrecy, discipline and conviction are all much more important.

There is no doubt that by and large terrorism has grown out of urbanization, industrialization and the resultant affluence coupled with frustration set in the youth because of non fulfillment of their expectations from the present day society. As far as India and other developing countries are concerned the roots of terrorism can be traced to the destruction of traditional moral values, present day pace of life and unemployment among the youths; unscrupulous behaviour of some political parties and lack of character shown by their leaders and so on. The younger generation, which is backbone of terrorist organizations, is attracted towards it, because life outside is unbearably hard and monotonous. If conditions are so created and pressures so exerted that life within the terrorist organization too loses charm and becomes equally dull, disintegration creeps in. To a young terrorist there can be nothing more frustrating than lack of action. Overt or covert, an extremist/terrorist/militant organization requires nourishment in order to hold its members together, keep up their morale and not to let their enthusiasm wane. So long as the goal appears achievable, the organization thrives. More idealistic the make up of its members more egoistic are the needs. A larger majority of terrorists remain at lower runs of psychological and safety needs. Money and women are their main attraction. Those who qualify for higher social and esteem needs, obviously look for publicity and status of heroes. A terrorist has strong propensity for publicity and would go to any extent to make his presence felt. It is for this reason that high-risk targets are increasingly sought for and held an attraction. It has become a fashion to own responsibility after nefarious act of large-scale killings and sabotage. Aim is to inspire awe and create panic. It also helps in placing law-enforcing authorities in disrepute.

The basic reasons for the lack of international cooperation in tackling terrorism are the patronage, support, finance, refuge, training facilities, hideouts, intelligence, and access to media that many countries are prepared to provide to the terrorists operating in the neighbouring countries. Growing cooperation between the terrorist organizations in India and abroad also bring within the reach of terrorists more destructive weapons which further enhances the dramatic impact of their activities. Sophisticated small arms, grenades, explosives, remotely controlled mines, rockets and several other variants of this deadly array are freely and abundantly available to the terrorists. Weapons and equipment supplied by the US to Pakistan for Afghan Mujahideens have ultimately reached the terrorists in Punjab and J&K. Perhaps the most frightening dimension of this free access to modern weaponry to the terrorists is the likely extension of his reach to the chemical and biological or nuclear weapons. It is very terrifying to even imagine as to what impact a few nuclear tipped missiles, bombs, or other highly lethal poisons in the hands of a few terrorists will have on the target.

It was 'Chanakya' who in his treaties on statecraft had advocated the covert dispatch of trained men in various garbs and guises to create dissension, disaffection and disorder leading to the extinction of the adjoining state and its eventual merger and/or annexation. The wheel has however moved a full circle and Pakistan is now using terrorism in J&K as a fine art though in a different pattern. However, Pakistan must recognize that terrorism in worst form will return to Pakistan in near future. It is only Pakistan, which can prevent the return of terrorism on its land.

Response and Remedies

Civilised world's response to terrorism has been slow, indifferent, apathetic and callous. The responses have ranged from those of appeasement, palliates, accommodative to a display of vehemence and rhetoric which have failed to discourage the terrorists or to promote the confidence of people in the democratic states or in their capacity, political will, determination or ability to wipe out terrorism. The most important aspect, which we must consider is that no child, is born as terrorist, fundamentalist, militant, or an insurgent. It is the treatment in family, in school and by society, which hardens the attitude of an individual towards governing system, a foreign power or any one else. If no wish to combat terrorism let us remove the causes, let us not create breeding grounds for the terrorists, fundamentalists, or insurgents.

Difficulties in Combating Terrorism

Combating terrorism whether by infringement of individuals liberty, diplomatic negotiations or reprisal raids is complicated by several problems:

(a) It is difficult to agree on a definition of terrorism with its many manifestation from criminal to political to insane.

(b) Often anti-terrorist acts may be more objectionable and oppressive than those acts they wish to prevent, creating martyrs and often improving the credibility of the threat.

(c) The adoption of anti terrorist safeguards and punishment must be universal. For example, it is no use to have an expensive efficient system in USA or France to prevent nuclear theft if potential terrorists can smuggle in the materials from other countries. Global dependence requires that each nation depend on others to deter terrorism through punishment and strict security measures. The problem is that many governments do not oppose all terrorist acts.

(d) It is difficult to institutionalize programme to combat terrorism because most nations do not want to abandon the principle of asylum. In the past some western countries have accepted many refugees who have clearly committed illegal acts under law of some other country. They have allowed terrorists to seek asylum.

(e) Any response to terrorists' activity must consider domestic political implications.

We must recognize and accept that terrorism is indivisible. To combat terrorism there is a need to evolve and adopt a comprehensive approach to include, destruction of training camps, facilities, infrastructure, finance, drug connection, political diplomatic, moral and economic support as well as other measures against states/regimes, which sponsor terrorism.

The global threat of terrorism will require a global response. Some of the important elements of such a response are as follows:

1. If terrorism is a global menace, then global protocols to fight terrorism should gradually and steadily replace US-centric understanding arrived at bilaterally between the USA and various countries and groups.

2. The political response must include international and diplomatic consensus building.

3. The economic response must strike at and eliminate or cut off the financial network.

4. The legal response must include an effective legal and regulatory framework against terrorist activities.

5. The military response must include the defence and security forces. Experts in the field must replace bureaucrats in the expert groups and forums.

6. Elimination of nuclear/WMD capacity of states capable of sponsoring terrorism. Short-term agreements will be no substitute for long-term guarantees and safeguards.

7. The United Nations must be strengthened and made more effective. The credibility of UN, which is being questioned and undermined, must be restored in the overall interest of the world.

8. The educational response must include developing a modern and accommodative outlook, tolerance and respect for each other's existence. Draining out the renege and hatred from the Madarsa propagated philosophy is also necessary. A clear message must reach humankind that "do not believe in the alliance of money and machinegun, because your children will inherit not the money, but the machinegun which will destroy not only the children but every one else."

In conclusion, it is sufficient to state that the war against terrorism is as complex as the human mind itself. The war against terrorism has to be focused on the imperative to protect the value of co-existence of the people of different cultures, faiths and languages, which form the bedrock of India's secular polity. It cannot be made conditional on a particular person, a group, a faith or a country.

In our highly competitive, greed-driven age coupled with national ambitions of domination of the world it would appear that the dangers posed by terrorism are likely to continue unless we change our outlook and attitude. India and the neighbouring countries including South-East Asia and Central Asia, even China will witness the emergence of more terrorist organizations and groups in the near future. Some of our neighbouring countries and their protectors would not like India's development and prosperity. These countries could continue to exploit the communal and religious sentiments and vulnerability of minority groups and encourage terrorism in India. We must therefore be prepared to cope with terrorist acts that will almost certainly occur in different parts of our country including big cities. No doubt some will argue that there is no way to guard against the unknown and unseen and will oppose strong action and expenditure for preventive measures. This sort of fatalism can result in terrorist incidents that will be both costly and embarrassing to the government and the entire nation. It would be unwise to pretend that the tide of sabotage, killing, bombing and hijacking can be totally turned back. But if we are not to surrender to lawlessness, we must expand our present efforts to make terrorism less effective and less attractive.

Chanakya laid down four percepts of state policy viz. Saam (diplomacy), Daam (monetary incentives), Bhed (creation of differences and internal problems) and Dand (use of force). There can be no better doctrine than what Chanakaya laid down more than two thousand years ago. When confronted with the problems of terrorism or militancy, the government has a wide choice in the adoption of these methods. Each situation will have a unique solution. However the problem must be considered from the point of view of "national interests" and not that of narrow short-term political gains.

19

Globalization, Communication, Media and Terrorism in India

Sanjeev K. Sharma

One of the most serious problems of the modern societies these days is terrorism, as its has become the most dangerous enemy of the civilized society and the democratic system. It destroys the soul of the society by creating and recreating a state of permanent fear, provoking and legitimizing authoritarian answers. Terrorism has been a strategic threat to the internal security and even survival of countries. It is now being seen as a threat to the security of the whole international community. One of the greatest concerns of all the civilized cultures is the alarming incidence of violent crimes in today's world. There is a worldwide consensus that democracy is not only the best but also the only legitimate method of organizing modern politics. But the problem and menace of terrorism is all against the democratic way of political systems. Terrorism has transcended international boundaries, and thus, has acquired a global form. This problem has been affecting almost all countries in all the regions. Hence, the threat of terrorism is no longer limited to a particular country or region. The study of terrorism essentially involves the study of global politics and violence. There is much apprehension about journalists, government bureaucrats, and law enforcement officials being objective and scientific in their observations. This is true about most of the academicians also. Terrorism is the problem of the modern world and is said to be a bye-product of the New World order. Modernization, development, and communication revolution are considered to be the main sources of this menace.

Globalization and Terrorism

Global structures of production, trade and communication have brought rapid and revolutionary changes in the world order. Advancements in technology and communication have facilitated the groups and states sponsoring terrorism to extend the reach and the organization of their subversive activities through flow of funds from abroad and foreign sanctuaries. Spectacular terrorist activities have stimulated, alienated and frustrated individuals and groups to undertake their personal ward in order to settle their grievances. Some of the critics of globalization have tried to establish direct and manifest relationship between the phenomenon of globalization and the rising graph of international terrorism. "Globalization processes are multidimensional, encompassing diverse domains of cooperation such as trade and finance, multinátional corporations, cultural trends, environmental changes as well as emerging forms of political governance."[1] A few writers have analyzed the economic aspect of globalization with an eye on a better understanding of the problem of terrorism. Poverty being the repressive inhuman face of globalization has been construed as a powerful source of terrorism. "The passive helplessness and hopelessness is transformed into active extremism and fundamentalism which constitutes the broad social base of small terrorist groups. In addition, the aggressive globalization driving forcefully the world into a uniform cultural mould, inevitably provokes violent reactions."[2] But the fact remains that whatever the sources of terrorism, the problem has acquired a dangerous form. The world political community must unite itself against this heinous crime against humanity and make sincere, concerted and well calculated efforts to contain and diminish the occurrence and effects of this problem. It is in this backdrop that terrorism has been defined as "the unlawful use of force or violence against persons or property to intimidate or coerce a government, the civilian population, or any segment there of, in furtherance of political or social objectives".[3]

Terrorism has been categorized into three kinds: objective terrorism, which is meant to make known to the world the objective of the terrorists, demand terrorism, which is meant to achieve a specific demand, and punishment terrorism, which is meant to punish an identified enemy. Under the objective and demand terrorism, the terrorists identify themselves and their objectives or demands, as they want the world to know that they were behind the act of terrorism. Under the punishment terrorism, they leave the victim guessing as to who could have been behind the act.

Role of Communication and Media in Terrorism in India

The Indian sub-continent has long been witnessing terrorist campaigns waged by Islamic fundamentalist group based in and supported by Pakistan. The escalation of endemic ethnic conflicts in this nuclearized region of South Asia poses a serious threat to the internal stability and the inter-state relations as these conflicts have transcended national borders. The proliferation of the menace of drug trafficking and narco-terrorism has been influencing the internal security and domestic politics of India. The ramifications of the terrorist activities against India have been manifold. Exacerbated Indo-Pak tensions may be attributed as the foremost among them. The preceding years have witnessed increasing involvement of Pakistan-based terrorist organizations and the ISI in terrorist activities, not only in J&K but in other parts of the country as well. The pattern of proliferation in increasing fatalities in local confrontation has reached disturbing levels in India. The dynamics of narco-terrorism is also posing unforeseen implications for peace and security in this region. Rapid technological advancement and information revolution has also been unfortunately, facilitating the escalation of conflict and violence. "India has been the victim of state sponsored terrorism for the last two decades. There is not even an iota of doubt that the Pakistan government in collaboration with the ISI uses proceeds of illicit narcotic drugs and small trade to fund terrorism in India. Pakistan also aims to create ethnic division in the social fabric of the country by exploiting the religious sentiments and economic backwardness of Muslims in the bordering states of Jammu and Kashmir, Rajasthan, Punjab, Assam, Nagaland, Manipur and other states. The ISI allures the poverty ridden Muslim population of these states; at times others as well, into illicit narcotic drugs trade to fund terrorist activities in India."[4]

Several analysts have found a direct and close relationship between terrorism and Islam and the terrorist incidences in the west in general and United States in particular in the last decade has confirmed their conclusion. Pakistan sponsored cross-border terrorism in Indian states and also bordering Bangladesh further confirms the connection between Islam and terrorism. The northern state of India, Jammu and Kashmir has been infected with the cancerous disease of terrorism for more than two decades. The profile of terrorist violence in Jammu and Kashmir is presented in table 1:

Table 1
Terrorist Violence in Jammu and Kashmir

Year	*Total Incidents*	*Attacks on SF*	*Attacks on Others*	*Explosion and Arsoh*	*Other Incidents*
1988	390	6	1	142	241
1989	2154	49	73	840	1192
1990	3905	1098	485	1810	512
1991	3122	1999	321	611	191
1992	4971	3413	507	744	307
1993	4457	2573	539	900	445
1994	6895	2675	1594	1774	852
1995	6819	2570	1836	1633	780
1996	5523	1473	2133	1260	657
1997	3421	1212	1299	672	457
1998 (Oct.)	2405	996	905	510	57
Total	**55062**	**18064**	**9793**	**10896**	**5691**

Source: Ministry of Home Affairs.

The table clearly shows that there has been a series of attacks on security forces as well as civilians. It is indicative of the fact that out of more than fifty thousand incidents of terrorism faced by the state of J&K in a decade, one-third of them are attacks on security force personnel. The worst period of terrorist activities in the state was 1994-96. It may also be noted that around twenty per cent of these incidents include arson.and explosion. These acts involve targeting innocent citizens of the state and thereby, creating fear and panic among them. This has evidently led to large-scale exodus of Hindu population of the state from the valley. It is unfortunate that the citizens of a country have to lead a life of refugees in their own country. It is also evident from the table that the terrorist incidents have increased significantly after 1989 when V.P. Singh was the prime minister. Some of the hardcore terrorists were released from jails in lieu of the release of the abducted daughter of the then home minister. The incident inadvertently provided impetus to the terrorist activities in the valley and encouragement to the morale of the terrorist outfits. It is sad note on the state of affairs of India that this weakness of the state has continued to be manifested in several incidents of terrorism irrespective of the political party holding power as a result the number of terrorists acts in last few years has risen significantly. Again, any statistical decrease in the number of terrorist activities is not an indicator of the fact that the lethality of these acts has not increased dramatically.

Table 2
Killings in Terrorist Violence

Year	*1988-91*	*1992*	*1993*	*1994*	*1996*	*1997*	*1998*	*Total*
Sf Personnel	331	177	216	199	185	186	197	1725
Govt. Officials	123	36	34	26	67	26	11	369
Top Pol. Leaders	1	-	2	6	5	-	-	15
Politicians	37	4	8	6	29	20	8	124
Judiciary	5	-	1	-	2	-	-	10
Pressman	3	1	1	2	1	-	-	10
Hindus	228	67	87	95	110	55	150	891
Muslims	1121	706	841	858	1217	828	622	7176
Sikhs	18	10	7	5	3	-	1	46
Others	28	35	40	73	30	9	-	270
Militants	798	873	1330	1596	1209	1075	776	8989
Foreign Tourist	1	-	-	1	-	-		3
Total Killed	**2693**	**1909**	**2567**	**2867**	**2758**	**2199**	**1765**	**19626**

The Table 2 clearly shows that though there is an increase in the number of terrorists being killed in encounters with the security forces, the number of security personnel killed in these incidents has also risen significantly. The Table. 2 also shows evidently that the number of Muslims killed in the terrorist incidents is maximum as compared to others. This emphatically makes clear that despite the claims of religious 'Jehad' against Indian government in J&K, the militant outfit have not discriminated among the citizens for the purpose of targeting them and creating fear among the masses. Providing financial assistance, ideological support and solidarity, training and education, sanctuary, weaponry and motivation – all the essentials of terrorism have been facilitated by Pakistan to the terrorist organization to spread endemic violence in India and thus destabilize the internal security of the nation. Major active terrorist groups connected with larger pan Islamic terrorist network operating in India are:- Laskhar-e-Tiaba, Harkat-ul-Mujahadin, Jaish-e-Mohammad, Al-Badr-Mujahideen. There are many foreign groups that are mushrooming all over India. Most of these foreign groups are based in Delhi, Mumbai, Kolkata, Chennai, Bhopal, Indore, Bangalore, Hyderabad, Patna, Pune, Nagpur and other major cities of India. The Prevention of Terrorism Ordinance (POTO) has listed the groups considered as terrorist organizations in its Section 18. (See Table 3).

Table 3

1. Babbar Khalsa International.
2. Khalistan Commando Force.
3. Khalistan Zindabad Force
4. International Sikh Youth Federation.
5. Lashkar-e-Tiaba/Pasban-e-Ahle Hadis.
6. Jaish-e-Mohammad/Tahrik-e-Furqan.
7. Hizb-ul-Mujahideen/Harkat-ul-Ansar/Karkat-ul-Jehad-e-Islamic
8. Hizb-ul-Mujahideen/Hizb-ul-Mujahideen Pir Panjal Regiment
9. Al-Umar-Mujahideen
10. Jammu and Kashmir Islamic Front
11. United Liberation Front of Assam (ULFA)
12. National Democratic Front of Bodoland (NDFB)
13. People's Liberation Army (PLA)
14. United National Liberation Front (UNLF)
15. People's Revolutionary Party of Kanglcipalk (PREPAK)
16. Kanlapk Communist Party (KCP)
17. Kanglei Yaol Kanbakup (KKKL)

18. Mainpur People's Liberation Front (MPLE)
19. All Tripura Tiger Force.
20. National Liberation Front of Tripura
21. Liberation Tigers of Tamil Eelam (LTTE)
22. Students Islamic Movement of India (SIMI)
23. Deedar Anjuman

Sponsoring terrorism is an expensive affair and money for killing, kidnapping and sabotage does not come through proper channels. It comes through illegal and unofficial channels. "It is ironic that global terrorism, the phenomenon of terrorists operating against several nations simultaneously, was facilitated by globalization and now it has become the biggest challenge to globalization."[5] One of the most important weapons of the terrorist groups is propaganda through media and other sources of information like internet. The media and terrorism hold a special relationship. It has been suggested that "behind the media attention to terrorism is, of course, public interest in it."[6] Bhawani Singh has blamed media for catering support basis to the terrorist organizations. To him, "wide media coverage creates around them a halo of hero and evokes martyrs responses and quite a few terrorists become legends in their life time and martyrs after their assassination."[7] Ideally the media must contribute to the maintenance of democracy but the role of media in spreading propaganda and fostering fear in the name of freedom of expression requires serious attention. The communication media must understand that only democracy has provided them freedom of expression and this freedom has to be handled with care therefore it should behave responsibly in the wake of any crisis.

Strategies for Tackling Terrorism

India has played a major role in strengthening international consensus against terrorism in various international organizations. India is party to all major international conventions against terrorism and has also incorporated them in domestic legislation. The inappropriateness of the responses to this cancerous disease has been attributed to at least three reasons:

1. Insufficient explanations of the phenomena of terrorism.
2. Inconsistent application of the term.

3. Inability to comprehend deeper ethnic, social and cultural roots of this menace.

The ignorance, insensitivity and indecisiveness of the authorities instill a sense of indifference among the citizens towards the decision makers. This results in the terrorist groups holding the control over the media.[8] It has been observed and several events illustrate that "to achieve political goals, though not clearly defined but motivated by certain ideological leaning, derived and defined by fundamentalist doctrines, terrorism prevails."[9] The post-cold war period has witnessed a considerable increase in the number of terrorist activities reaching baffling proportions and attracting wide spread national and international concern. Terrorism entails systematic use of violence for attaining political, social, philosophical or religious goals by an organized group. Ethnic, ideological, and religious differences, availability of support structures by latent and manifest sources, failure of democratic means of conflict resolution, perceptions of socio- economic injustice and indifferent governance are the main reasons that contribute to the emergence of terrorism in most of the countries.

It has been argued that there are only three ways of winning a war against terrorism: appeasement, discouragement, and extermination. Violence is morally repugnant to the majority of Indians for religious reasons. Discouragement or destroying the morale of the terrorists is the most difficult method. Extermination is next to impossible. Even then, most of the countries attempt to use a combination of these two approaches while dealing with the terrorist problems. Appeasement or negotiation sometimes may encourage the problem.

The true alternatives to the present dangerous course of events lie in the combination of:

1. Alliance against social, cultural and political roots of global terrorism;
2. Strengthening the international judicial institutions and procedures; and
3. Restrained security policy response including military and police operations against terrorist organizations.

More international cooperation among the governments is required to monitor flow of information, people and money across border. Again, all the states initiating terrorist attacks, executing these attacks by proxy, or providing ideological, economic, military or operational support to terrorist organization, must be identified and branded as state sponsors of terrorism. Additionally, those states that provide terrorists with safe heavens and refuse to extradite them should also be included in this list. The states, which allow the terrorists and their supporters to recruit activists and collect money within their territory, or incite others to commit terrorist acts or to support terrorist activity, must also be branded as state sponsors of terrorism.

Notes and References

1. David Held: *Re-imagining Political Community* (eds.) Daride Archibigi, David Held and Mastur Kohler, The Polity Press, New York, 1998.
2. Radmila Nakarada et. al.: *The Tragedy of a Global Terrorism and Repressive Globalisation* in Transnational Foundation for Peace and Furture Research, Sweden 2001 (via internet).
3. F.B.I. Islam –Terrorism, Inc., Part I (via internet).
4. Kshitij Prabha: *Narco Terrorism and India's Security*, IDSA, New Delhi (via internet).
5. Muqtedar Khan: *Terrorism and Globalization*, Global Eye (Online Magazine).
6. Charles Kegley: *International Terrorism*, St. Martin's Press, New York, 1990, p. 158.
7. Bhawani Singh: Terrorism in Asia the Indian Variant, *Political Sci ence Review*, Jaipur, Vol. 26, Nos. 3-4, July-Dec. 1986, p. 78.
8. S.K. Sharma: Understanding Terrorism in India, *The Meerut Journal of Political Science and Public Administration*, Vol. 2 No. 1 July-Dec., 1996, pp. 1-7.
9. JK Pundir: Pan Isalmic Organizations and Terrorism in India, paper presented in National Seminar on Terrorism, Department of Sociology, Gorakhpur University, Gorakhpur, Nov. 20-22, 1999.

20

International Terrorism India's Perception: Support from Russia

Nalineet Ghildial

Relations between India and Russia are built on a very strong foundation and it is advantageous to both sides. In fact there is a long history of time-tested relationship since the days of the former Soviet Union. Even though ideologically different, India and former Soviet Union had convergence of interests uncommon in the relationship between any other groups of countries. Geo-political considerations, power politics and pragmatism brought democratic-socialist India and communist Soviet Union closer. It is important to note that Soviet Union acted as a shield for India in the Security Council on the issue of Kashmir. By virtue of its presence as a permanent member, it frustrated Pakistan's anti-India overtures. Soviet Union was also a major supplier of defense equipments and spare parts to India—at times even ignoring its close East European allies.[1]

Contrary to the suspicious nature of Indo-US relationship, which was a necessary outcome of their divergent views on many crucial issues of global concern, Indo-Soviet relations were based on confidence and mutual trust. Soviet Union's disintegration was, therefore, bound to come as a shock for India, which was also reflected, to some extent, in New Delhi's confusion and delay in responding to the abortive coup in Moscow. Immediately after it's emergence as Soviet Union's successor, and inheriting a plethora of problems—socio-economic, ethnic, political, and strategic—which were a natural outcome of the disintegration, Russia found itself engulfed in finding ways to deal with it's pressing problems. Moscow's unsuccessful attempts to seek financial assistance from the United States by toeing the American line on foreign policy issues, and it's lackluster and at times even indifferent attitude vis-à-vis it's traditional allies and a close friend like India, should be seen and interpreted in this perspective. The very fact that Russia very soon realized the significance of its relations with prominent Asian country like India, spoke of the continuing relevance of close Indo-Russian relationship. As an Indian scholar had observed in an interview to me, "Russia, with its plus and minus points is there and so is India. Therefore, both these countries are bound to return towards a close partnership."[2] It was also argued that since the ground realities of world politics have not changed much ever since Soviet Union's collapse and with the emergence of new threats and challenges, there would be an even greater need for co-operation and co-ordination between countries like India and Russia.

Thus, when India and Russia resolved to open a new era in their bilateral relations, they took note of the new challenges both were facing and were likely to face in the years to come. The fall-outs of their economic liberalization programmes and the threats to their plural societies emanating from the extremist elements were common to both. When Russian President Boris Yeltsin came to India in January 1993, India and Russia not only resolved many of their bilateral issues, like settling the matter of rupee-rubble arrangement, supply of Russian defense spare parts as also the crucial Russian support on the Kashmir issue. And now when both these countries are placed more or less on the same footing as far as adoption of market oriented economic policies is concerned this adds to the potentiality of greater co-operation between them. Both are dynamic economies with great potential for growth. India, with a large size, a pool of human resources and a large, growing market offers much for Russia which, in turn is abound with enormous natural resources as also acknowledged scientific and technical excellence. Both have been striving to get their rightful place in the global economy. There is a consensus in both the countries on the need to develop stable and strong relations with each other and this is what makes Indo-Russian relationship unique.

Apart from the existing traditional areas of co-operation like cultural, trade and defense, new areas like co-operation for the peace and stability of the region in and around the Central Asia, and to meet the most serious threat at present to global peace and security, i.e. international terrorism—all call for more intimate and fruitful interaction between the governments of India and Russia today and in the time to come. Their commonality of approach on 'new areas of tension and conflict in the post-cold war period' finds expression in every document signed between them, be it the Treaty of Friendship and Cooperation of 28 January 1993, Moscow declaration on Protection of Interests of Pluralistic States of 30 June 1994, the Declaration on Strategic Partnership of 5 October 2000, the Moscow Declaration on International Terrorism of 6 November 2001, the Delhi Declaration on Further Consolidation of Strategic Partnership of 4 December 2002, the Memorandum of Understanding on Cooperation in Combating International Terrorism of 4 December 2002 and the Moscow Declaration on Global Challenges and Threats to World Security and Stability of 12 November 2003.

Joint Working Group on Global Challenges

India and Russia are both victims of terrorism. India is facing the brunt of cross-border terrorism in the Jammu and Kashmir and Russia in the Caucasus where it is fighting the Chechen rebels. Quite naturally, therefore, the fight against terrorism has been a cornerstone of their domestic policies[3] and they have firmly expressed strong condemnation of all acts of terrorism wherever they may occur and whatever may be their motivation.[4] They believe that terrorism is a crime against humanity and, therefore, the states that aid, abet or shelter terrorists are as guilty of committing gross violation of human rights as their perpetrators. Long before the issue of international terrorism acquired the centre stage in world politics, India and Russia had already taken note of the "new threats and challenges in the form of aggressive nationalism, religious and political extremism, terrorism and separatism, which strike at the unity of pluralistic states", in the post-cold war era. The sixteen page Moscow Declaration on the protection of the Interests of Pluralistic States, 1994, had reaffirmed "the readiness of India and Russia to co-operate bilaterally and with all other states in combating terrorism and international crimes".

During his visit to Russia in November 11-13, 2003, the then Prime Minister Atal Behari Vajpayee highlighted this point in an interview to Russian newspaper Izvestia: "..those attacks (September 11, 2001) awakened the world to the reality of international terrorism, a scourge which both India and Russia had been suffering from, and were warning the world about, for many years.." India and Russia are also agreed on the definition of terrorism–that terrorism "constitutes a gross violation of human rights, particularly the most fundamental right – the right to life – and is a crime against humanity."[5] They are, therefore, committed to "firmly condemn all acts of terrorism wherever they may occur and whatever may be their motivation" and advocate that those who support terrorism or finance, train, harbour or support terrorists and states that aid, abet or shelter terrorists are as guilty of committing gross violation of human rights as their perpetrators."[6] This point was further reiterated firmly by the then Indian Prime Minister Atal Behari Vajpayee during his visit to Russia in November 2003 in an interview to Russian newspaper, "Nezvisimaya Gazeta". To a question: "Which one of the two – terrorism and religious extremism – poses the biggest threat to your country?" his answer was "... India is a secular country where all religions of the world are represented. Secularism is an essential principle of life in India, which is also enshrined in our Constitution. We reject extremism of any kind. Both India and Russia are multi-ethnic, multi-cultural and multi-religious pluralistic democracies, which are particularly vulnerable to terrorism. Terrorists have no religion, as no religion prescribes violence against innocent people. In fact, our battle is against those extremist elements, which misuse and misinterpret religion to justify terrorism and incite violence."[7]

In response to a similar question posed by another Russian newspaper, Indian Prime Minister rejected any linkage between terrorism and religion: "We totally dismiss the proposition that any religion is a source of terrorism. Such arguments seek to discredit one of the great religions of the world. No religion prescribes violence against innocent people. Our battle is against extremist elements, which misuse and misinterpret religion to justify terrorism and incite violence."[8] Since they are clear about the concept of terrorism, it follows that India and Russia favour a unified campaign to tackle the evil and express concern over the attempts to adopt a 'selective approach' to terrorism, which is a global problem.[9] "There can not be good and bad terrorists, our terrorists and others", warned Russian President Vladimir Putin adding, "all those who have resorted to arms in order to resolve political disputes, all those organizations, all those structures and individuals who carry out those policies should not be tolerated". Similarly, the following remark of the former Prime Minister Atal Behari Vajpayee holds significance in this context: "... international terrorism is today a global monster, which knows no national boundaries or territorial limits of operation. It exploits the openness and freedoms of democratic societies. It uses modern technologies and unorthodox techniques to achieve its destructive objectives. It can only be countered by global, united and comprehensive effort. We cannot afford selective approaches, which sacrifice the long-term goal for short-term interests. Differing standards cannot be applied for judging terrorism..."[10]

The co-operation and understanding between India and Russia on the issue of fight against terrorism, it may be noted, is not confined to the bilateral level alone but it is an international approach. It underlines the importance of joint efforts for establishing 'solid international legal basis for co-operation in combating international terrorism. The formation of a Joint Working Group on Combating International Terrorism for regular bilateral information exchanges and another Joint Working Group on Global Challenges are examples of bilateral initiatives. In addition to these mechanisms the ongoing regular contacts and exchanges at all levels have helped India and Russia to constantly upgrade bilateral cooperation and to work closely together to meet the various regional and global challenges facing both as plural democracies.

At the global level, India and Russia have advanced the adoption by the United Nations Security Council's two conventions–the Indian project on Universal Struggle against Terrorism and the Russian Project on Countering Nuclear Terrorism. They also achieved agreement on joint actions on the world scene to work out legal international documents determining the common legal notion of terrorism and terrorists. "This is a very important issue for terrorists are moving from country to country and national laws are not common everywhere", said Deputy Secretary of the Russian Security Council, Oleg Chernov during his visit to India.[11] In the fight against international terrorism the role of the United Nations is very crucial which represents the independent, sovereign countries of the world and is responsible for the maintenance of global peace and security. India, as a founder member of the UN and Russia as a permanent member of the UN Security Council are concerned about the challenges before the world body in the 21st century. They agree upon the need for a greater role for the UN to deal with the new threats and challenges effectively. Both favour reforms in the world body to make it more democratic and representative of the world community. Russia supports India's claim for a permanent seat in the Security Council. Earlier during Russian President Vladimir Putin's visit to India in 2002, India and Russia, in their joint statement, "confirmed their determination to contribute to the establishment of a just, multipolar world based on the principles of respect for the UN Charter and international law in the interest of removing threats to international peace and security."[12]

In an indirect attack upon the Unites States for resorting to a policy of unilateral use of force to settle problems of worldwide ramifications, India and Russia, in their joint statement issued at the end of Russian President Vladimir Putin's visit to India (December 3-5 2002) "strongly opposed unilateral use or threat of use of force in violation to the UN Charter, as well as interference in internal affairs of other states. It was stressed that a comprehensive settlement of the situation around Iraq is possible only through political and diplomatic efforts in strict conformity with the rules of international law and only under the aegis of the United Nations..."[13] It was emphasized that "the counter measures against this menace should be taken on a comprehensive and sustained basis. Such measures should be directed also against those states, entities and individuals who support, fund or abet terrorists or provide them shelter or asylum to engage in cross-border terrorism. There should be no double standards in the fight against terrorism. Both sides also reaffirmed the relevance of the Moscow Declaration on International Terrorism of 6 November 2001. They stressed the importance of strict implementation of UN Security Council Resolutions on the fight against terrorism, in particular Resolution 1373. They also advocated intensifying efforts to finalize in the United Nations the draft International Convention for the Suppression of Acts of Nuclear Terrorism and the draft Comprehensive Convention against International Terrorism. Roots of terrorism, which lay in their common neighbourhood posed a threat to their security interests. Both sides would take preventive and deterrent measures in meeting these threats and cooperate in this regard. Both sides declared their determination to enhance collective and bilateral efforts to prevent and suppress terrorism.'[14]

Both sides discussed in detail the current situation in South Asia. They stressed the importance of Islamabad implementing in full its obligations and promises to prevent the infiltration of terrorists across the Line of Control into the State of Jammu and Kashmir and at other points across the border, as well as to eliminate the terrorist infrastructure in Pakistan and Pakistan controlled territory as a prerequisite for the renewal of the peaceful dialogue between the two countries to resolve all outstanding issues in a bilateral framework as envisaged in Shimla Agreement of 1972 and the Lahore Declaration of 1998.[15] The Declaration of the Russian Federation and the Republic of India on Global Challenges and Threats to World Security and Stability signed on 13 November 2003 paid more attention on how to tackle the problem of terrorism than anything else. It reads like this: 'The Russian Federation and India are united in their fight against the evil of international terrorism. They actively cooperate with each other and with other countries in anti-terrorist activities. Both countries resolutely declare that international terrorists, whatever are their stated objectives and the causes they espouse, will never succeed in bringing the world to its knees. The Russian Federation and India believe that most urgent and essential steps in effectively and comprehensively dealing with the threat of international terrorism should be:

- Creation of environment for total rejection of terrorism and absolute unacceptability of any of its forms;
- Consistent and uncompromising approach to terrorism and giving up "double standards";
- Preventing the flow of funds for terrorist activities;
- Effective implementation of the UN Security Council Resolution 1373 aimed against those who support, fund, or abet terrorists or provide them shelter or asylum to engage in cross-border terrorism;
- Promotion of confidence between members of the anti-terrorist coalition by, *inter alia*, due consideration of interests of each one of them and ensuring that the fight against terrorism is strictly based on rules of International law and principles of the UN Charter;
- Reinforcing national and international legal instruments for countering terrorism, making the existing antiterrorist Conventions genuinely universal, and earliest completion of negotiations on the draft Conventions in the UN, including the Comprehensive Convention against International Terrorism submitted by India and the International Convention on Suppression of Acts of Nuclear Terrorism submitted by the Russian Federation;
- Steadfast cooperation to prevent terrorists from acquiring weapons of mass destruction, their means of delivery and materials and technology related to their manufacture;
- Improvement of mechanisms of legal assistance and extradition in order to ensure the inevitability of punishment for terrorist crimes;
- Efforts to promote coexistence of different religions, cultures and civilizations by stressing greater mutual understanding and respect amongst them, especially the idea that

terrorism cannot be identified with any particular religion or ethnic group.[16]

Conclusion

Thus, India and Russia present a good example of countries in the forefront of global fight against international terrorism. Both recognize that for the promotion of international peace, security and stability, it is essential that the countries concerned should enter into dialogue, consultation and cooperation. As strategic partners, they reaffirm their commitment to cooperate bilaterally and at the multilateral level on strategic issues and to evolve a universal effective system of countering global challenges and threats of the 21st century. In this respect, they stress upon the need to revamp the United Nations in order to play a leading and effective role in the settlement of global problems in an impartial and effective manner.

Russia understands India's stand on the issue of state-sponsored terrorism in Jammu and Kashmir. It respects India's commitment to discuss all outstanding issues with Pakistan peacefully through bilateral dialogue in accordance with the Shimla Agreement and the Lahore declaration and that for any meaningful political dialogue; cross-border terrorism has to stop. India's stand that terrorism and talks cannot go hand in hand finds favour with the Russian leadership. The Indo-Russian approach on terrorism is, it may be argued, a global one. They had been voicing concern on the attempts by some countries to adopt a 'selective approach' to tackle the menace. The recent disclosure by no less a person than the UN General Secretary, Kofi Annan that the US decision to attack Iraq was illegal confirms the dangers of a unilateral approach to global problems. Earlier, in the post-First Gulf–War in 1991, the then Secretary General of the United Nations, Boutros Boutros Ghali had also alleged that the world body had been sidelined by the United States.

It appears that US will take some more time to realize that the perpetrators of terrorism cannot be the partners in it abolition. Pakistan, which had been the main inspiration behind the creation of terrorist groups like Taliban, and which has been actively supporting, and abetting terrorism in Jammu & Kashmir, happens to be one of the main allies of United States in its fight against terrorism. This is what makes India uncomfortable and suspicious about US intentions. The stand taken by India and Russia, on the other hand, is a responsible one – that terrorism is a global problem and hence, requires a global solution; that terrorism cannot be justified on any ground whatsoever – religious or otherwise for it incurs a denial of the basic right to life and is, therefore, liable to be termed as a crime against humanity requiring to be dealt with accordingly; that not only those who unleash terror on innocent people but also those abetting, financing, or encouraging terrorism are to be treated at par ; that there should be a unified action against this evil and in this the United Nations has to play a leading role rather than any single country or group of countries assuming to itself the role of the so called 'peace maker' and above all that the nexus between terrorism and narco trafficking, development of weapons of mass destruction, etc. also needs to be taken note of. Such a stand is bound to get the backing of the world community as and when it realizes the inadequacy of the self- regulatory approach of some powerful countries to the serious issue of international terrorism.

Notes and References

1. For a detailed study of Indo-Soviet relations see, Peter J.S. Duncan, *The Soviet Union and India*, London, Rutledge, 1989; V.D. Chopra (ed.) *Studies in Indo-Soviet Relations*, Patriot Publishers, New Delhi; P.N. Haksar, *Studies in Indo-Soviet Relations*, New Delhi, Patriot Publishers, 1986; Zafar Imam, *Soviet Foreign Policy, 1917-1990*, New Delhi, Sterling Publishers, 1991; T.N. Kaul, *Stalin to Gorbachev and Beyond*, New Delhi, Lancer International, 1991; J.A. Naik, *Russia's Policy Towards India: From Stalin to Yeltsin*, New Delhi, M.D. Publications Pvt. Ltd.,1995; Ramesh Thakur and Carlyle A. Thayer, *Soviet Relations with India and Vietnam: 1945-1992*, Delhi, Oxford University Press, 1993; V.P. Dutt, *India's Foreign Policy*, New Delhi, Vikas1985; S.P. Singh, *Political Dimensions of Indo-USSR Relations*, New Delhi, Allied Publishers Pvt. Ltd.,1987.
2. Author's interaction with Prof. Zafar Imam, an authority on Indo-Soviet Relations.
3. For comments see Indo-Russian Axis to Fight Terrorism, *Pravda*

(On Line), January 21, 2003.

4. For comments on the issue see, Ajay Patnaik, Cross-Border Terrorism and Indo-Russian Cooperation, in Shams-Ud-Din, ed. India and Russia: Towards Strategic Partnership, New Delhi, Lancer Books, 2001, pp.129-136; O.N. Mehrotra, Indo-Russian Strategic Partnership in the Current World Order, in the same book, pp. 73-80.

5. Delhi Declaration on Further Consolidation of Strategic Partnership between India and the Russian Federation, December 4, 2002, Documents of the Embassy of Russian Federation in the Republic of India.

6. *Ibid.*

7. *Documents of the Embassy of Russian Federation in the Republic of India.*

8. Interview to Russian Newspaper: *Rossijskaya Gazeta*, November 2003, Documents of the Russian Embassy in India.

9. Alan Elsner and Sayed Salahuddin, India, Russia Decry US Double Standards on Terrorism, Rense.com.

10. *Interview to Russian Newspaper : Rossijskaya Gazeta , November 2003.*

11. *India, Russia to Develop Cooperation In Combating Terrorism,* Pravda *(On Line), January 16, 2002.*

12. India - Russia, Joint Statement, December 4, 2002, Documents of the Russian Embassy in India.

13. *Ibid.*

14. *Ibid.*

15 Russia asks Pakistan to end Terrorism for talks with India, Indian express.com December 1, 2002.

16. Declaration of the Russian Federation and the Republic of India on Global Challenges and Threats to World Security and Stability, November 13, 2003, Documents of the Embassy of Russian Federation in India.

21

Armed Rebellion in Nepal: A Challenge to Security of Nepal and India

Nalini Kant Jha

Nepal continues to remain one of the most volatile countries in the region amidst continuously expanding influence of the Maoists, political uncertainties and growing international interests. Recent developments have confirmed, once again, that while the Maoists have been successful in gradually pushing their agenda through violence and intimidation, the lust of power of the present Monarch, King Gyanendra, has aggravated the domestic turmoil in Nepal. From the moment the King dissolved Nepal's Parliament on May 22, 2002, that country began a long crawl away from democracy. He hurtled his kingdom into the abyss of absolute monarchy on 1st February 2005, when dismissing prime minister Sher Bhadur Deuba, he clamped emergency, suspended fundamental rights and assumed all executive powers in the name of "bringing back peace and effective democracy." Though the King has announced the lifting of emergency in Nepal on 29th April 2005, i.e., soon after his meeting with the Indian Prime Minister Manmohan Singh, in Jakarta, he has not withdrawn the draconian executive orders suspending fundamental rights, the King is governing the country directly and incarcerated political leaders continue to languish in jails. Under the circumstances, chances of restoration democracy appear remote.

As this internal turbulence in Nepal has serious security and political implications not only for Nepal, but also for its neighbouring country, India, which shares a long and open border as well as close socio-cultural linkages with that country, the present paper aims to examine the policy options available before India to deal with domestic turbulence in Nepal. In order to discuss India's policy options, it is relevant to briefly discuss origin, evolution, objectives, strategies and magnitude of Maoist insurgency in Nepal and the response of the King and political parties to this problem to understand challenges posed to India's foreign policy makers.

The Origin and Evolution of the Maoists Insurgency

Armed overthrow of the Nepalese State and establishment has been a long-cherished goal of the communist movement in that country. The only dispute they have had was about its timing. This was one of the factors that kept them divided ever since the foundation of the Communist Party of Nepal in 1949. When, for instance, the Panchayat system was introduced in Nepal after toppling of democracy in 1960, the Communists were divided on the course of political action. The radicals among them, who wanted an end to the Panchayat system, demanded the formation of an elected constituent assembly to draw up a new Constitution for Nepal. By the late 1960s, taking inspiration from the Cultural Revolution of China and fraternal linkages with the Naxalites of India, a small group of radical Communists began a violent movement aimed at exterminating the "class enemies". It was, however, suppressed that forced the group to renounce violence and change strategy, which helped it to emerge a nationwide but still a radical Communist force. In 1974, the group of radicals held a convention, known as the Fourth Convention. But it again suffered a setback in 1983, when one of its founder members, Mohan Bikarm, formed another party called the Communist Party of Nepal (Mashal).[1]

Though various Communist factions came together to form the United Left Front in 1990, yet in November the same year, opponents of the mainstream Communist Party formed a new party called the Unity Centre. The Communist Party of Nepal-Maoist (CPN-M) was born out of the Unity Centre in 1994, when a split took place and the faction led by Pushpakamal Dahal (popularly known as Prachand) decided to boycott the mid-term polls in Nepal and opt for armed struggle. The party was formed underground and the details about its organization and leaders were kept secret. It adopted a resolution to overthrow the existing constitutional system through armed revolution and establish a republic based on a Maoist-Leninist and Maoist prototype.[2]

The CPN-M got a boost in 1996, when the Samyukta Jana Morcha or United People Front of Nepal (UPFN), led by Baburam Bhattarai, a Ph.D from Jawaharlal Nehru University of India, who had captured nine seats in the 1991 general elections by participating in the mainstream politics as a political front of the Unity Centre formed by the coming together of four extreme Left groups, left mainstream politics and joined hands with the CPN-M. The UPFN, which considered itself the precursor of the revolutionary movement in Nepal, had participated in the election to "expose the deficiencies of the multi-party system." However, it was soon disillusioned when the Left forces under Man Mohan Adhikari formed a Government in 1994, which, he said, had digressed from the Marxist goal of creating a classless society. The UPFN thus left mainstream politics and joined hand with CPN-M in 1996 to start a "people's war."[3] Of late though ideological division has again emerged between the Maoist leaders Prachanda and Baburam Bhattarai. But this is not going to cripple the insurgents, as the former heads the CPN-M, the "People's government," and its armed wing, the People's Liberation Army; whereas the later has only the face of the Maoist movement.

Politico-Economic and Scio-Cultural Backdrop

Like other movements of similar nature, a combination of political, economic, and socio-cultural factors have facilitated the growth and spread of the Maoists in Nepal. For a start, economic factors like unemployment, under-employment, lopsided development and concentration of wealth in few hands have alienated the vast majority of poor Nepalese from the state apparatus. Since Nepal is predominantly an agricultural country with 80 per cent of population still dependent on agricultural land for their livelihood, the agriculture sector has become critical to the economic development.[4] But the successive Governments failed to make any significant headway towards land reform measures as well as to create avenues to generate employment in other sectors and divert people from the agricultural sector to other sectors for gainful employment. Not surprisingly, 71 per cent of the wealth even in relatively well developed capital is in the hands of the top 12 per cent of the household, and only 3.7 per cent of the national income reaches the poorest 20 per cent of the country's family. The per capita income in Kathmandu averages Rs. 20,939, while it is as low as Rs. 5,000 in the poorest district in the northwest region.[5] It is estimated that with an average economic growth, approximately four per cent per year for the past five years, it is insufficient to absorb the estimated 5,00,000 young people who join the labour force each year.[6]

But the country's political class failed to pay attention to these challenges of development. Instead, they continued to pre-occupy with political squabbling and survival of regime. The crisis of governance, especially virtual absence of governance in rural Nepal, indifferent Monarchy, subservient and self-serving Governments that refused to look beyond Kathmandu's corridors of power, widespread corruption and lingering political instability thus contributed to general dissatisfaction. Within few years of the multi-party democracy, the administrative short-comings became so apparent that the expectations of the people for better governance slowly diminished. If the principal Communist Party Government led by Man Mohan Adhikari failed to deliver on the land reform front, the political instability syndrome manifested in coming and going of eleven prime ministers in Nepal within twelve years eroded any hope of implementation of any long-term policy for the amelioration of the weaker sections of the society.[7] Lack of confidence and trust among the political leaders, the King and the military thus helped only to make the situation worse and the Maoists to grow.

Finally, marginalisation of the ethno-linguistic minorities leading to their alienation also played an important role in the rise of the Maoists. The cohesive structure of Nepali society was shaken in 1990 when the new Constitution declared Nepal a Hindu State and Nepali the only official language. Minority groups like the Tibeto-Burman community, questioned the propriety of declaring Nepal a Hindu State, as they do not consider themselves Hindus. Though pre-domination of the dominant groups and castes in education, employment, etc., was prevalent during the Panchayat regime as well, the commencement of democracy and the new Constitution brought the problem to the fore by guaranteeing freedom of expression and thereby giving voice to the people who were earlier silent spectators. This enabled ethnic groups in Nepal to organize themselves against socio-economic and political discrimination including the imposition of Sanskrit as compulsory subject in schools or Nepali as the country's lingua franca.

Promises and Methods

As the Maoists were quick to feel the pulse of the vulnerable sections of the Nepalese society, they promised these people a better future. They hijacked the basic agenda of economic development, which should have been a concern of the political parties. Their assurance to remove the Monarchy and the servile Government and replace it with a Communist State, which would end the exploitation of poverty stricken farmers and labourers in remote Nepal, attracted people, who are mostly from the poor and socially marginalized class.[8] They further proclaimed that they would establish a 'people's Government' thorough a 'people's war' in line with the ideology of Peru's Shining Path group. To form a 'people's Government,' the CPN-M, which bases its ideals, aspirations and course of action on Mao's style of dictatorship of the proletariat, adopted the "strategy of surrounding the city from the countryside."[9]

In the initial stages, they made symbolic attacks against some police posts and such installation as the Small Farmers Development Project, which provided loans for small farmers giving the impression that they had liberated them from the loans. But their main targets were the grass-roots workers of the Nepali Congress and teachers who were supporters of the NC. The Maoists were therefore able to neutralize possible resistance from the cadres of other political parties. Consequently, political parties could not develop an approach compatible with this problem. Even the NC, which was in power most of the time, was divided on handling this challenge. It helped the rebels tremendously in unabatedly growing both in organization and actions. By acts of threats of kidnapping, torture, killing and so on they first weakened the organization basis of the NC.

Crippling the NC apart, the insurgents targeted the local informers of the intelligence unit. Most of the victims of the Maoist violence were these local informers. Needless to add, this helped them to sabotage and destroy the intelligence network of the police.

Thirdly, the Maoists began to use the ethnic cleavage to its advantage by promising self-rule and autonomy to ethnic minorities in areas where they are in majority. They also vowed to recognise culture and language of ethnic minorities. In a pamphlet distributed on February 13 1996, they declared: "To maintain the hegemony of one religion (Hinduism), language (Nepali), and nationality (Khas) the State has for centuries exercised discrimination, exploitation, and oppression against other religions, languages and nationalities' and has conspired to 'fragment the forces of national unity that is vital for proper development and security.'[10] The Maoists therefore appealed to these indigenous ethnic groups to join the people's war, which got favourable response from groups like the Khamuan Mukti Morcha.

To achieve its objectives, the Maoists declared in February 1996 the inevitability of bloody war. In the same month, they submitted a 40-point memorandum to the Government then led by Prime Minister Sher Bahadur Deuba, demanding the abolition of royal privileges, promulgation of a Republican Constitution, and abolition of the Mahakali Treaty with India, etc. When the Government failed to pay heed to their demands, they carried out simultaneous attacks on different parts of Nepal on 13 February 1996. Since then, the guerrillas have attacked Government installations, indulged in loot and arson and killed local bureaucrats, village headmen and influential people especially in the western, central hill areas and the western terai. The Army, left untouched in the initial stages of what the Maoists call 'peoples war', became a target later on. They adopted methods like blowing conch shells to gather their supports. In Nepal, this has been the traditional means of communication across the mountains and valleys for centuries. Beginning with confiscation of land from the wealthy persons and its distribution among the peasants, the Maoists have in the course of time assumed multifarious Governmental functions. They levied taxes, set up schools, run parallel administration and held kangaroo courts to settle dispute, much to the relief of the hapless populace.

Spread and Support Base

By the time, the Maoists began to make major attacks on police posts, killing a large number of police personnel and seizing their weapons, they had grown beyond the control and capacity of the police. Beginning from six western districts—Rukum, Rolpa, Jajarkot, Salyan and Gorkha—and Sindhuli in the east in 1996, their influence has spread to 73 of Nepal's 75 districts, particularly in the poverty stricken, economically backward western parts of the country, where Maoists leaders are treated with reverence. According to Government's own admission, 32 districts were the hit where guerrillas roamed freely and organised open mass meetings. They have killed more than 10,000 people and destroyed roads, bridges and schools[11] By the late 1990s, in many of the hill and mountain districts of western and mid-western Nepal, they virtually rendered the State apparatus ineffective and assumed control over the rural areas with their own system of governance. Socially, championing the cause of minorities and weaker sections has enabled the Maoists to gradually extend their traditional social support base from the Brahmins, Kshthris and Newars combine to new groups such as Rais, Limbus, Burungs, Magars, Tamangs, etc.[12] This forced the former Nepalese Prime Minister, Deuba, to acknowledge that the "Maoists are successful in attracting frustrated people."[13]

The number of Maoist guerrilla fighters was estimated to be around 2,500, backed by 10,000 or more militia in the end of the year 2001. Their strength is rapidly growing since the intra-palace regicide that took place in 2001. According to Royal Nepal Army sources by the end of 2004, the Maoists had more than 6000 trained fighters with several times more active cadre who could be mobilised as a crude fighting force at a short notice. They are largely recruited from the rural poor though many criminals have also joined the Maoists on the promise that they will be protected from the Nepali police. Interestingly enough, one-third of the guerrilla squads are women. Every village has a revolutionary women organization. There are usually two women in each unit of 35-40 men, and they are used to gather intelligence and act as a courier.[14]

The main source of funding for Maoists have been through bank robberies, voluntary donation, extortion from rich businessman and tax collection in areas under their control. According to reports, the Maoists have looted more than Rs. 250 million from banks and other institutions. They have collected around Rs. 5 billion in the form of 'donations' and 'taxes.'[15] Thus despite their manifest ideology, the Maoists have not desisted from crime to fill their coffers, before resorting to more lucrative option of "asking" businessmen, contractors, civil servants and professionals to pay token sum as contribution every month.

As regards their sources of arms, ammunitions and training, Maoists are said to have procured arms from three sources, namely, raids on police stations, purchases from the illegal arms market, and locally made improvised explosive devices. The possibility of Nepalese Maoists getting arms and ammunitions from their fraternal comrades in India such as Maoist Coordination Centre (MCC) and People's War Group (PWG), who are operating in Indian provinces like Bihar and Andhra Pradesh, etc., cannot be ruled out. Coming the source of training, the Nepalese Government sources suspect that the well-trained Gorkha soldiers, who have retired from the British and Indian Army and are residing in the Maoist infected area, as well as retirees and deserters from the Nepalese Army are involved in providing training and combat manpower to the Maoist guerrillas.[16]

The Governmental Response

Not surprisingly, the Maoist armed rebellion has generated immense concern within Nepal about the politico-security fall-outs of this armed uprising. The Nepalese State has, therefore, used force as well as persuasion and negotiation to tackle the Maoist challenge to its security and integrity. But any strategy has hardly proved effective so far. The police proved ineffective against the better-armed and better-organised Maoists because for instance when the insurgency began in 1996, the police launched "Operation Romeo," in which it arrested and tortured a large number of insurgents. Though the police managed to contain the insurgency temporarily, the operation alienated a large segment of the rural population and thereby gave a new lease of life to the insurgents. The Governmental efforts to initiate talks with the Maoists failed to make any headway due to several precondition set by them, including release of all party activists from jails and withdrawal of police from the insurgency affected areas.

In 1998, the Government launched another offensive in areas known to be rebel strongholds. And operations were carried out in as many as 18 areas . The Government, however, failed to re-establish its writ in areas under Maoist control. This forced the Government to once again plead peace with the rebels by forming the Ganesh Man Singh Peace Campaign in July 1999. But this mechanism to persuade the guerrillas to give up arms did not make any breakthrough. A combination of 'carrot and stick' policy applied by G.P. Koirala Government too proved to be futile.[17] Given the magnitude of the Maoist revolt, the Nepali Army was not inclined to take charge of the counter-insurgency operations without declaration of an emergency. Unfortunately, the full-scale mobilization of the security forces and measures on the part of the Government had always been a matter of political controversy among the political parties. The Maoist took full advantage of the lack of commitment, determination and coordinated action on the part of the Government to strengthen and consolidate both in terms of arms and political influence. It was against this background that Prime Minister G.P. Koirala, who did not get the Army's assistance in curbing the Maoist menace at a time when they launched a major assault in Holeri, resigned in July 2001.[18]

Sher Bahadur Deuba, who was voted to power as prime minister in July 2001 following the shock of the royal assassinations made a serious attempt to buy peace. Even before taking the oath of office, he offered cessation of hostility and peace talks with them. In fact, this peace initiative on his part at a time when there was a widely articulated desire for peace was one of the factors that helped him at the hasting. Besides, the criminal activities of Maoists had put them in danger of being isolated losing their "Robinhood' image. This not merely followed on the widespread public outpouring of grief over the royal assassinations, but in the remote villages and outlying areas people were tired of the rebel's methods. There were reports of villagers confronting the Maoists and their demands. The killings of policemen even after their surrender to Maoists had led to abhorrence among people.[19]

To take wind out of Maoists' sails, Deuba timed his offer of talks with a series of legislative measures pertaining to land reforms, untouchability and gender discrimination. These measures included: a ceiling on landholdings, entry to low caste people in places of worships, giving women rights in parental property, granting of land and housing to bounded labourers *(kamatiyas)* freed one year before, and promising of a 25-year project for the uplift of ethnic groups of Mongoloid stock *(janjatis)*. Further, some Marxist leaders were pardoned as a precursor to the talks. Three rounds of talks were held between the Government and the Maoists. While the first and second rounds of talks were considered as confidence building, the third round was intended to discuss substantive issues. The Maoists had three principal items on their agenda, namely, the establishment of a Republic, framing of a new Constitution, and formation of an interim Government, though while entering into the third round they dropped on of the major items on their agenda, viz., demand for a Republic.[20]

But they changed their tune soon after and announced the formation of a People's Liberation Army and proclaimed themselves ready to launch an armed struggle. Since the Maoists leaders knew that Deuba was not in a position to concede any of their major demands, they used these talks only for making public appearances and holding well attended rallies, while continuing to strengthen their muscle power. Ending their four-month-old ceasefire, the Maoists attacked more than 35 districts in November 2001. The army barracks were attacked for the first time. According to press reports some 1,000 Maoist guerrillas attacked the Lamahi barracks in Dang district, which along with Sangja district was the scene of bloodiest battles on the first night and looted 300 guns, and a huge quantity of ammunition. They also killed 14 army personnel including a Major. On November 25, they attacked police office and Chief

District Officer's residence at Salleri, and the nearby air-tower. They also killed 11 army men and13 policemen.[21] Moreover, the Maoists declared the formation of a 'Revolutionary Government' with its capital in Rolpa, in western Nepal, and set up a 37-member United Revolutionary People's Council to run it.[22]

This left the Deuba Government with no alternative, but to advise King Gyanendra to proclaim an emergency. Accordingly, on 26 November 2001, the king declared emergency and gave a carte blanche to the army to cope with the insurgency. The Nepalese Army, which was so far lukewarm to get involved in civil war, now swung into action using helicopter gun ships among other equipments. The declaration of emergency was followed by a clampdown on the Maoists and their sympathisers in particular the media close to them. Since the fundamental rights of the citizens were suspended, the emergency regulations empowered the Government to detain people without trial, though a day after the emergency was declared, Prime Minister Deuba, assured that the civil rights of the citizens would not be curtailed. The Government made the emergency order more effective by the exhaustive conceptualisation of terrorism in a parallel exercise. The Terrorism and Disruptive Activities Control and Punishment Ordinance (TADO) promulgated by the Government left little to the imagination or the interpretative skills of the authorities.[23]

Although the Army had some success in fighting back the guerrilla attacks, the inadequacy of its operation to contain the Maoist insurgency was brought to the fore on 16 February 2002, when thousands of Maoists attacked the Mangalsen Army barracks and Sanfebagar airport in the far-western district, killing 55 members of the 58-man army contingent, 71 policemen, and five civilians, including the Chief District Officer. It was the single most reverse suffered by the security forces since the Maoists began their armed campaign in 1996. Critics said the incident exposed the hollowness of the Defence Ministry's claim that the Maoists were beleaguered and on the run, and led them to the unavoidable conclusion that "Nepal may have played its card of last resort—the Army—and failed to quell the Maoists militants."[24] While the Government may get solace from the fact the Maoists were at the "hit and run" stage, and nowhere close to raising a "People's Army" capable of occupying territory and holding it in the face of Army's counter attack, the Army too did not appear to be winning the war, as it failed to establish the Government's writ in large parts of the country, where the Maoist guerrillas call the shots.[25]

That the Maoists area in stronger position became evident when they refused to talk to the Deuba Government, which was re-installed (after its dismissal by the King in October 2002) in June 2004. They instead favoured direct negotiation with the King and reiterated their demand for an election of a new Constituent Assembly under the UN auspicious. This strengthened the King and as stated at the outset he used the inability of the Deuba Government to tame the Maoists to once again dismiss this government and impose emergency in February this year.

External Response

The gravity of the Maoists challenge to the State of Nepal generated widespread concern among major world capitals especially after the terrorist attacks on the US on September 11, 2001. Kathmandu promptly seized the opportunity provided by the post-11 September developments to muster its strength both in political and military terms. The US, Britain, China, Japan and many other friendly countries (including India of course) condemned the Maoists and expressed their unequivocal support and sympathy for Nepal's fight against the armed Maoist rebels. Within a very short period, Nepal witnessed hectic political, diplomatic, and security activities manifested in the visits of high-level dignitaries and other officials having political and security consultations.

The US Secretary of State, Colin Powell, visited Nepal in January 2002, the first ever visit to the Kingdom by any US Secretary of State, and held talks with the Government authorities about how the US could help Nepal to overcome the Maoist menace. During this visit, Powell assured support with defensive military equipment. He also promised both military and economic assistance.[26] The economic assistance was supposed to focus on "high impact job creation programme and upgrade the living standards of the rural people." Later on Washington condemned the Maoists attacks as similar to those of other terrorist organizations like Al-Queda, and reiterated its support for the Nepal Government's right to "protect its citizens and institutions from terrorist attacks.[27] On May 1, 2003, the US included the Maoists in its list of international terrorist organizations.[28] Washington, moreover, provided aid to Nepal worth US $17 million to turn the parade-ground Royal Army into an anti-insurgent force, inviting criticisms from the rebels, that aid from Washington was converting the Royal Nepalese Army into the Royal American Army.[29]

The British Government organized an international conference in June 2002 to mobilize international support for Kathmandu. Britain and Nepal apart, India, China, Japan, France, Germany, Russia, Norway, Denmark, Finland, Switzerland, Australia, and representatives of the World Bank and UN Development Programme attended this meet and expressed concerns over deteriorating security and human rights situation in Nepal. Likewise, the embassies of the European Union expressed concern at the worsening security situation in Nepal and continuing violence and brutal attacks against civilians by the Maoists. It urged them to return to the negotiating table "in good faith to achieve a peaceful and sustainable political solution of the present crisis."[30]

Similarly, soon after the end of the Maoist ceasefire in November 2001, the Chinese foreign minister telephoned Prime Minister Deuba, on 8 December to express Chinese "support to all the measures including the state of emergency initiated by the Government to maintain peace and stability in the country." He clarified that "neither within the Communist Party nor any entity of the Government of the People's Republic of China has any links with the support for the terrorists of Nepal." The Chinese Ambassador to Nepal referred to the Maoists as "anti-Government elements" and accused them of having misused the name of the Great Leader of China.[31] At the very start of the Nepalese King Gayendra's visit to China in 2002, the Chinese leadership reiterated its utter contempt for the anti-state activities of these "revolutionaries" who have usurped the name of chairman Mao Zedong. Significantaly, unlike in the past, Beijing has not made a single adverse remark about the growing Indo-Nepal cooperation to combat the insurgents. The Maoists have thus been pushed to defensive.

Implications for India

India has had been among the forerunners in extending both moral and material supports to the Nepalese Government in its fight against the Maoist menace. Soon after the collapse of the ceasefire in Nepal in November 2001, Prime Minister Atal Behari Vajpayee, talked on telephone to his Nepalese counterpart, Deuba, on December 8. He assured India's full support and cooperation to Nepal at all levels in meeting the challenges posed by the Maoists. New Delhi declared, including the Indian Maoist groups, as terrorists and increased action against them. India supplied helicopters that the Nepali security forces required immediately in meeting the challenges. The border areas were kept on "high alert" to check the movements of the Maoists. Their possible hideouts in the border districts and towns were searched, and some of the Maoist activists, who were undergoing treatment, were handed over to the Nepali police. Prime Minister Deuba, visited India in March 2002. Both the countries decided to intensify their efforts and cooperation to combat terrorism and cross-border crimes including sharing intelligence and information regarding the terrorists' movements.[32]

Indian concern over the Maoist rebellion is not surprising, as this country cannot remain unaffected by any upheaval in Nepal in view of the fact that the border between India and Nepal is even more open and porous than that between the US and Canada and links between peoples on both sides of it are also strong. This is especially true in the context of Nepal's Maoist rebels, who have an anti-India bias. The document adopted at the third plenum of the CPN(M) central committee in March 1995 declared that the armed struggle was specifically against "Indian imperialism." It also voiced opposition to the recruitment of Gurkha soldiers in the Indian Army. It is alleged that the Maoists are being trained by the ex-Gurkhas of the Indian army. Further, the Maoists demand the abrogation of India-Nepal Treaty of 1950 and the Mahakali Treaty.

Moreover, the Maoists, masquerading under various names such the People War Group (PWG) and Maoist Communist Centre (MCC), are very active in Indian States, namely, Andhra Pradesh and Bihar respectively. The timings of the attacks by the PWG in Andhra Pradesh after Maoists ceasefires in Nepal (November 2001 and August 2003) are noteworthy. The PWG, for instance, attacked the Andhra Chief Minister Chandra Babu Naidu, in October 2003, i.e., after the breakdown of talks between the Maoists and the Nepalese Government. It is said that the Maoists got electronic detonators and explosives from the PWG, while pistols, ammunition and high-quality detonators were provided by the MCC. Of late, they have established their foothold in West Bengal and Bangladesh also. As the Nepali Consulate General in Kolkata pointed out to the West Bengal chief minister that the Maoists not just from India and Nepal but also from Bangladesh have been holding conclaves in places like Silliguri in the narrow 'neck' in Indian territory that separates Bangladesh from Nepal. Besides, there are reports to indicate that Maoists are providing bases to insurgent groups such as the United Liberation Front for Assam (ULFA) in India's Northeast and getting arms and tactical training in return. The other side of the coin is that the Nepali Maoists, as and when under pressure from the army, try to escape to adjacent Indian territories and seek sanctuary in the hideouts of their soul mates.[33]

Not surprisingly, Nepal is emerging as the conduit for illegal arms brought from India, which are smuggled back again to India. By establishing its linkages within India, the Maoist in combination with the PWG and MCC is in a position to pose security threat to at least four Indian mainland States. They are in no way embarrassed by their cynical exploitation of the anti-Indian sentiment in the Himalayan kingdom that assumes outlandish proportions sometimes. The hijacking of IC-814 Indian Airlines flight from Kathmandu in December 1999, anti-India demonstration in that country over an unproved and repeatedly refuted statement of an Indian film star and the assassination of the royal Nepalese family in the summer of 2001 clearly brought to the fore a realignment of political forces, which pose a serious challenge to India.[34]

Indian Response

The socio-political turmoil in Nepal has thus a spill over effect in India. As instability knocks at the doors of Nepal, India has limited policy options to meet its security concerns. With political turbulence rocking Nepal and political parties decaying, the National Democratic Alliance (NDA) government in New Delhi believed that India's interest could be served by preserving the institution of Monarchy as stabilising force in the restive Himalayan State. The Nepalese Government's action of arresting the editor of a leading Nepali daily, with the apparent nod of the present king, for publishing a "seditious" article written by a top Maoist leader has signalled his inclination to check the Chinese influence in the Himalayan kingdom. India's then Minister for External Affairs and Defence, Jaswant Singh, therefore, took a right decision to visit Nepal in August 2001 to establish personal rapport with the new King Gayanendra. Besides, India rightly extended diplomatic support to declaration of emergency in Nepal in November 2001 and condemned violence by the Maoists.[35] More importantly, both the countries have not only reinvigorated the traditional system of joint management of border, but also when the Chief of Staff of Nepal Army visited New Delhi in November 2001 and discussed with his counterpart, he went back with a message of India's fullest sympathy and support, of what ever the Nepalese Government requires and asks for from India.

When the then Nepalese Prime Minister Sher Bahadur Deuba, visited India in March 2002, New Delhi offered him help to face the ongoing insurgency in Nepal, but at the same time clearly expressed its desire to see him address its concerns about misuse of Nepalese territory and hospitality by some forces inimical to India's national interest. The Nepalese leader reportedly showed his sensitivity to India's concerns about the Himalayan kingdom's vulnerability to penetration by some anti-India forces.[36]

Besides, India's fear of the Nepalese Maoists and Indian Left-wing extremists carving a corridor linking their movements all the way from the Dankaranya to the Himalayas has led it to supply its INSAS rifles at heavy discount of nearly 70 per cent and trained officers and soldiers in various Army-run counter-insurgency schools. The then Indian Deputy Prime Minister L.K. Advani, warned that the Government of India had an integrated programme to get rid of the trouble one and for all.[37] In response to Kathmandu's request, India rounded up Nepali citizens who have allegedly been in cahoots with the terrorists and sent them back home.[38] The NDA government thus saw no hesitation in endorsing the steps taken by the Nepalese Government to contain the Maoists.

The United Progressive Alliance (UPA) government, which came into power in India in June 2004 continued with the policy of the previous government. This government had to face the dilemma when the Nepalese King imposed emergency in Nepal in February this year. Since this step invited the ire of the Maoists as well as all democratic political parties in Nepal, the present regime in New Delhi rightly suspended military aid to Nepal. This was in consonance with India's long cherished tradition of opposing autocratic rule in India's neighbourhood. At the same time, this policy enabled India not only to align with democratic parties and intelligentsia in Nepal, but also needlessly alienating the Maoists. As the UPA government rightly realised that Maoists cannot be tamed by military action alone, it did not hesitate to abandon its half-century old policy of bilateralism in its dealing with Nepal and built a common front with the US, UK and European Union to bring additional pressure to bear on the King to restore democracy and allow the political leaders to resume negations with Maoists.[39]

Within three months of this bold move to use its leverage in Nepal to make the King see reason, the UPA government, however, made a U-turn in its Nepal policy. Not only Prime Minster Manmohan Singh, met King Gyanendra in Jakarta in April 2005, he even promised to expedite the delivery of arms suspended at the time of the royal coup. But what India got in return? As stated earlier, though the King announced lifting of emergency, he did not annul draconian executive orders suspending fundamental rights. Worse, the two countries learned about the U-turn in India's policy only from the King, who chose to make public Manmohan's assurances to him during their Jakarta meeting. It took the Government of India 17 days to confirm something that the Nepalese monarch had already announced. While constraints of time and space prohibit us from going in to reasons for this volt face in India's Nepal policy,[40] suffice is to point here that this dangerous flip flop is a betrayal of the Nepalese political parties struggling for the restoration of democracy. It is a shot in the arms for the King. Spurred on by New Delhi's benediction, the Nepalese security forces are likely to go all out to find bloody 'military solution' to the Maoists question, and intimidate democratic opponents and critics into the bargain. India's decision to go back to playing ball with King Gyanendra could increase disarray in the democratic camp. This is why the King was so eager to go public about the Indian U-turn immediately after his Jakarta meeting with Prime Minister Manmohan Singh. The arms matter less to him than the legitimacy India has bestowed on him and his not so secret project to turn the clock back to the bad old days of the Panchayat system.

Conclusion

New Delhi will, therefore, be well advised to guard its own steps as it considers helping the Nepalese military forces in combating the kingdom's Maoists in their new identity as terrorists. As India's smaller neighbours, including Nepal, have been confronting the crisis of identity and suffering from the "big-neighbour-small-neighbour syndrome," it is all the more necessary for this country to be extra cautious in extending a helping hand to Nepal lest it be misunderstood as interference in its internal affairs.[41] While trying to persuade the King to restore democracy in Nepal, the Indian establishment must develop discrete contacts across Nepal's political spectrum. Even the Maoists need not be neglected. India can take the cue from China, which has developed an across the board contact with the political class of Nepal. While realigning its stance in Nepal, Indian foreign policy establishment should also undertake initiatives to win the confidence of the Nepalese people directly. This can include low cost options such as opening of primary schools, health care centres or other institutions for providing humanitarian relief, preferably with the help of non-governmental organisations. This will help Nepal to weaken the Maoist appeal and earn the good will of the Nepalese people to India.

The aforesaid policy frame is advisable for India also because of the fact that India's geopolitical interest is to convert Nepal into a terror-free zone in every sense of the term. The reported links between Nepal's Communist extremists and the

People's War Group and other of their ilk in India, or for that matter China, constitute only one facet of worries of the Himalayan kingdom and India. Even more significant concern for India is to prevent an easy access to Nepal of one or more power hostile to India, who can indulge into anti-India terrorist activities such as the hijacking of India's Kathmandu borne plane that took place a few years ago. New Delhi must therefore encourage a process of reconciliation in Nepal to bridge differences among the King, political parties and the Maoists in Nepal.

While India does have a very justifiable need to take a deep interest in internal turmoil afflicting its neighbours like Nepal, it is not India that has the primary responsibility to resolve their problems. It is for the political forces in Nepal to get their act together and deal with the Maoist menace there.

Unfortunately, the Nepalese political system has been a bitter disappointment. The ease with which the King has repeatedly declared emergency, took charge of the Government and maintained control over the Nepalese Army, exposed the weakness of the 1990 Constitution. Without wasting any time, the Nepalese State must therefore embark on multi-pronged course to deal with this grave threat to its very existence. Firstly, the Government must begin with assessing its own strengths while dealing with the Maoists be it on seeking external support or its own negotiating strategy. It is, of course, heartening to note that a gradual change in public perception about the Maoists has pushed them to be defensive. Until a year ago, large sections of the Kathmandu elite, disgusted with corrupt and ineffective politicians and bureaucrats, appeared to see the Maoists in a favourable light, but today they are perceived to be a bunch of criminals, who are hell-bent on dragging the kingdom back to 'hour zero.' Externally, in the changed context of the US war against terror since September 2001, international community has extended strong support to the Nepalese Government in attempts to contain the Maoist menace. Besides, Nepal's 50,000 relatively well-trained and well-equipped Army as compared to rather lackadaisical police has been able to give a good fight to the rebels even though it fell short of expectations.

But the rebels' capacity for mischief must not be underrated. They can be trusted to exploit the divisions within the country's political establishment. It is therefore high time for the King as well as the political parties to understand the need of the hour and work in unionism for the meeting the challenge of the Maoists rebels. As in the case of spread of fire, first priority must be given to extinguishing it, before deliberating about its cause security measures against the rebels need to be vigorously pursued unless they give up arms. They must be totally disarmed to prevent their reappearance in the form of organized crime gangs.

Secondly, the Nepalese State must simultaneously address the long-term causes of the rebellion by initiating radical socio-economic and political transformation programmes directed especially towards removing the grievances of the downtrodden, underprivileged and excluded people and communities. The state must dare to seize the socio-economic agenda of the Maoists and implement it with all seriousness. This alone can prevent the rebels from cashing in on the support of the people on their agenda.

Finally, since it is not possible to wipe out the widespread influence and control that the Maoists had been able to forge in such a large part of the county soon, therefore, failure of the latest round of talks should not prevent the Government from making another attempt for dialogue with them. All the concerned parties must realise that while goal of a negotiated settlement may be distant and the route tortuous, the journey can be accomplished if the signposts are clear and roadman adhere to.

Notes and References

1. Khalid Mahmud, "Maoist Insurgency in Nepal," *Regional Studies* (Islamabad), Vol. 21, No. 1, Winter 2002-03, p. 5. See also, Krishna P. Khanal, "Post-11 September Developments in Nepal: Implications for Curbing the Maoist Insurgency," Dipankar Banerjee, et al. (eds.), *South Asian and the War on Terrorism* (New Delhi: India Research Centre, 2003), pp. 25-37; and Smruti S. Pattanaik, "Maoist Insurgency in Nepal: Examining Socio-Economic Grievances and Political Implications," *Strategic Analysis* (New Delhi), Vol. 26, No. 1, January-March 2002, pp. 119-20.

2. Khanal, ibid., p. 28.
3. Sangeeta Thapliyal, "Maoists in Nepal," *The Hindu* (Madras), 18 December 2001.
4. Prem Jung Thapa, "The Cost-Benefit of Land Reforms," *Himal*, Vol. 14, No. 10, October 2001, p. 30.
5. Study report of a Kathmandu based think-tank, the Nepal South Asia Centre, as cited in Bertil Lintner, "Nepal Struggles to Cope Diehard Maoist Violence," *Jane's Intelligence Review*, June 1999, p. 43.
6. Chitra K. Tewari, "Nepal: Maoist Insurgency," *South Asia Monitor*, no. 31, March 1, 2001, www.csis.org/saprog.
7. In a bizarre game of musical chairs, G.P. Koirala has held the post of prime minister three times, while K.P. Bhattarai and Deuba have had two tenures each.
8. Khanal, No. 1, p. 20. Also see, editorial, "Time to Quell," *Pioneer* (New Delhi), 27 November 2001.
9. Ibid.
10. Deepak Thapa, "Day of the Maoist," *Himal South Asia* (Kathmandu), Vol. 14, No. 5, May 2001.
11. Nirupama Subramanian's report from Kathmandu, "Nepal's Expanding Insurgency," *The Hindu*, 26 July 2004. Also, Tewari, no. 6.
12. Thapliyal, no. 3.
13. *The Kathmandu Post*, 5 December 2001.
14. Rohan Gunaratne, "Nepal's Insurgents Balance Politics and Vio-lence," *Jane's Intelligence Review*, October 2001.
15. Thapa, No. 10.
16. Tewari, No. 6.
17. One the one hand the G.P. Koirala Government allocated US$2.6 million as a developmental package (called the basket fund) for addressing developmental concerns of the poor, offered to the Maoists and announced amnesty of those guerrillas who would give up arms, on the other hand, it created a 15,000 strong armed force for the protection of district headquarter and allocated US$4.72 million for purchase of arms to beef up security against the Maoists. See Tewari, ibid.
18. According to an Indian correspondent, it was the constitutional confusion over 'who controlled Army—the King, the Commander-in-Chief of the Army, or the elected Government, which was exploited by the Army to avoid getting sucked into "civil war type confrontation." See Rita Manchanda, "The Himalayan Thunder,"

Frontline (Madras), 21 December 2001.

19. "Nepal: Not by Force Alone," *Economic and Political Weekly* (Mumbai), Vol. 36, No. 48, 1-7 December 2001, p. 4437.
20. *Ibid.*
21. Manchanda, No. 18.
22. Keshav Pradha's report from Kathmandu, *Hindustan Times* (New Delhi), 25 November 2001.
23. Editorial, "Politics and Terror in Nepal," *The Hindu*, 19 November 2001.
24. Rita Manchanda's dispatch from Kathmandu, "Emergency and the Crisis," *Frontline*, 2 March 2002.
25. John Kifner, "The Power Play in Nepal," *New York Times*, 5 August 2003. Also, Mahmud, n.1, p.13.
26. *Hindustan Times* (New Delhi), 19 January 2002.
27. *Ibid.*, 25 April 2002; *Kantipur* 26 February 2002.
28. A.S. Verma, "Nepal, Maovadi aur America," *Dainik Hindustan* (Patna), 8 May 2003.
29. Kifner, No. 25.
30. *Hindustan Times*, 11 May 2003.
31. *Ibid.*, 22 and 24 March and 26 April 2002, *Samacharpatra* (Kathmandu), 26 April 2002.
32. Khanal, No. 1, pp. 32-33.
33. Inder Malhotra, "Focus Shifts to Nepal," *The Hindu*, 28 November 2002. Also, Farzand Ahmed's dispatch from Kathmandu, "Palace Coup," *India Today* (New Delhi), Vol. 27, No. 42, 15-21 October 2002, p. 41. According to Rohan Gunaratne the Indian organisations with whom the Maoists have links include: ULFA, Northern Bihar Liberation Front, Bhartiya Communist Youth League, Bharat Ekta Samaj, All Nepal Youth Association (Chennai Committee) of India, etc. See his, No. 13, p. 33.
34. Nalini Kant Jha, "India's Security Concerns in a Turbulent World," in Nalini Kant Jha, at. al. (eds.), *India in a Turbulent World: Perspectives on Foreign and Security Policies* (New Delhi: South Asian Publishers, 2003), pp. 31-32.
35. *Ibid.*
36. Editorial, "Cross Border Bonhomie with Nepal," *The Hindu*, 20 March 2002.
37. Gautam Navlakha, "From Battle of Arms to Battle of Ideas," *Economic and Political Weekly*, Vol. 38, No.11, 15-21 March 2003, p. 1033.

38. Dilip Padgonkar, "Nepal Adrift: Constitutional Crisis Looms Large," *Times of India* (Lucknow), 18 July 2002.
39. Prem Shankar Jha, "Follies of the Kingdom," *Outlook* (New Delhi), Vol. 45, No. 9, 7 March, 2005, p. 40.
40. For details concerning causes of volt face in its Nepal policy by the UPA government, see Satish Chandra, "India's Nepal Policy: Dangerous Flip Flop," *The Hindu,* 10 May 2005; Siddharth Varadrajan, "A Policy in Search of a Rationale," *The Hindu*, ibid., 14 May 2005; and V. Sudarshan, "When it Reigns, It Pours," *Outlook*, Vol. 45, No.18, 15 May 2005.
41. Nalini Kant Jha and Pramod Kumar, "India and Nepal: Imperatives of a Good Neighbourliness," in Nalini Kant Jha, (ed.), *South Asia in 21st Century: India, Her Neighbours, and Great Powers* (New Delhi: South Asian Publishers, 2003), pp. 113-24.

22

Quest for Human Security: Rethinking Refugee Problem in Third World Perspective

Vijay Kumar

"Just as in the material realm the plundering of a country's wealth is accomplished by inflating the currency so today one may witness the process of inflation being applied to the realm of rights. The process entails such a growth of newly promulgated rights that people do not notice the fact that the meaning of the concept is being reversed." Ayn Rand[1]

A person who has been forced to flee his or her country out of fear for life and liberty is a refugee. The United Nations Convention Relating to the Status of Refugees 1951, and its 1967 protocol, define "refugee" as a person who "owing to well founded fear of being persecuted for reasons of race, religion, nationality, membership of a particular social group or political opinion, is outside the country of his nationality and is unable or owing to such fear, is unwilling to avail the protection of that country..."[2] This definition of "refugee" is under cloud and is being questioned today by social scientists and human right activists. It is being construed as rather narrow and one-dimensional. Conceived during the two world wars, the conceptualization is Eurocentric and it does not correspond to the today's refugee situations. To quote Justice P.N. Bhagwati: "it is patently narrow and rigid. It provides essentially for the sub-category of individual asylum seekers rather than for the larger categories of refugees in the mass."[3]

No doubt, group of asylum seekers may come under this provision on the basis of an individual determination of their refugee status. But it fails woefully to deal with a situation of movement of refugees in which masses are being displaced from their homelands as has often happened in the post-colonial days. Sponsored by a global organization and replete with universalistic rhetoric, the convention has "functioned within narrow temporal and geographical limits."[4] Parties to the protocol undertook not to send an alien who had entered, by whatever means, back to the country of origin if he or she had the well-founded fear of persecution that defined a refugee under the protocol and the original convention. This is known as rule of non-return, or in the generally used French phrase "non-refoulement". The other norm precluded punishment for illegal entry of persons who had entered in search of asylum. But this norm is qualified in ways that permit sates to follow it in its breach than order.

In assessing their own commitment to assist and protect even those persons who satisfy the protocol, one must enumerate the obligations that states' parties to the protocol have clearly not assumed:

- They are not obligated to refrain from expelling anyone who can find sanctuary elsewhere.
- They may provide only the temporary shelter to those whom they choose or are required to retain.
- They can house the beneficiaries in detention camps and ban them from employment in the local economy.
- They can expel them as soon as their 'fear of persecution ceases to be "credible'. States are not obliged to assist refugees in getting to the point where the doctrine of "non- refoulement" may require the grant of asylum.
- They have not assumed any obligation to accept the advice of the United Nations High Commissioner for Refugees (UNHCR) or any other international agency about how to define the terms in the defi-nition or about the procedures to be employed assessing claims to refugee status.
- They do not take into account "involuntary migrants" who flee their countries of residence because of a

credible fear of imminent death or crippling arising out of (i) personal threat, (ii) generalized condition of intense violence in their home country, or (iii) hunger.[5]

This is why the Organization of African Unity in the OAU Declaration, adopted on September 10, 1969 expanded the definition of term "refugee to cover "every person who, owing to external aggression, occupation, foreign domination or events seriously disturbing public order in either part or whole of his country of origin or nationality is compelled to leave his place of habitual residence in order to seek refuge in another place outside his country of origin or nationality."[6] The Latin American countries have also similarly expanded the definition of the term "refugee" in the Cartagen Declaration Refugee adopted in 1987.[7] As issues of Human Rights had become prominent and promotion of human rights throughout the world became one of the purposes of the United Nations, and realizing that in practice there are massive violations of human rights in many parts of the world, Cartagena Declaration incorporated "serious violation of human rights" as a ground for treating asylum seekers as refugees. The same provision was adopted at the 4th Regional Consultation on Refugees and Migratory Movements in South Asia, held in Dhaka on 10-11 November 1997, when they prepared a Model National Law on Refugees.[8]

It must be mentioned here that although South Asia has over 1.2 million refugees and a highly generous tradition of receiving refugees, none of the countries in the region is a party to the 1951 Convention or its 1967 protocol. They neither have any national law on refugees. The countries of South Asia have not felt the need for setting up legal structure or framework because their refugee policy is based on political solutions reached through bilateral negotiations between the host country and the country of origin. In fact, while the status of refugees and their right not to be forcibly returned are now established part of international law, no corresponding right of asylum is. The grant to refugees of asylums in the way of the right of permanent residence and the right to work and otherwise integrate themselves into the host society, is at the discretion of the receiving state. The various human rights declarations and conventions urge states to grant asylum on humanitarian grounds and all recognize the absolute discretion of states in doing or not doing so.

In sum, the international law of refugees is clear. Every one is free to leave any country, specifically including his or her own because it says, "let those people go", do not send them back where they came from"; and despite a right to stay, it does not say "take those people in". During the Haitian crisis, President Bush, therefore, announced: "we will turn back any refugee that attempts to reach our shore and that message needs to be very clear as well to the Haitian people."[9] This statement of the US President constitutes the first time in more than 50 years that the US has flagrantly rejected the legal and ethical obligations to protect refugees.

Last decade has witnessed a torrent of people in flight from or within Somalia, Rwanda, Iraq, Bosnia, Croatia, Cuba, Haiti, Afghanistan, Tajikistan, Azerbaijan, Armenia, Congo-Kinshasa, Liberia, Sudan, Burundi, Angola etc. During 2003, South Asia remained a tinderbox as rebels, insurgents and governments engaged in military offensives. Afghanistan, Nepal, Bangladesh, India, Bhutan and Sri Lanka remained tense. An estimated 1.1 million Afghan refugees remained in Pakistan and 1.1 million in Iran, some of who have been displaced for decades. Africa, the world's most impoverished continent, saw nearly 3 million Africans turn new refugees or displaced persons within their own countries during 2000. By early 2000, there were more than 13 million people uprooted in this part of the world. Some 3.3 million people were refugees in early 2001 and some 10 million others were internally displaced with in their own countries.[10] Mexico, Central America, the Caribbean had their own share of refugees in Latin America.

The end of cold war and the emerging third world political, economic and social realities demand a fresh look at the refugee problem. These countries have, in the last decade or so, faced mass displacement of millions of people not only due to liberation struggles, revolutions, coups and counter-coups but also due to man-made environmental disasters, natural calamities and short sighted development policies of their own governments. They have been classified as "migrants" or "economic refugees", "environmental refugees" and "refugees of development projects". Legally, they do not qualify to be called refugees because unlike political refugees they are not pushed out of their own states but are compelled to leave their homeland because of economic reasons or weakness of the state to protect their minority rights and economic rights.

In a world population of 5.7 billion in 1995, roughly one in every 130 people on earth had been forced into flight. A majority of them were internally displaced persons. In the 1980s the number of internally displaced increased at an alarming rate: 600,000 in1984, three million in 1985, five to six million in 1988, 24 million in 1992, and 25 million at the beginning of 1994. Norman Myers, an environmental scientist from the University of Oxford, estimates that the number of these so-called environmental refugees which swelled to 25 million in 1995 is expected to rise to 50 million by 2010 and could reach 200 million by the middle of this century.[11] All global climate models predict a further increase in temperature between 2 and 6°C by the end of this century. This would result in rise of sea level about 50 cm by the end of this century. Flooding will endanger low-lying islands and coastal zones. The expected change in atmospheric circulation will lead to a change in the temporal and spatial distribution of rainfall, with direct consequences for agriculture and forestry. The provision of sufficient and clean drinking water will be jeopardized in many parts of the earth. The worst sufferers would be, according to Dr. Wolfgang Seiler, of the Institute of Meteorology and Climate Change, Germany, "the semi-arid countries, which are already suffering considerable climatic stress today..These include in particular the developing and newly industrializing countries in the tropics and sub-tropics which number among the regions with the highest population growth rates'.[12] In these countries the link between climate change and population growth will further aggravate the existing social conflict and destabilizing society giving impetus to mass migration and adding to refugee problem.

Indeed five major factors combine to uproot people:

- Political or religious oppression
- Economic collapse
- Military or civil terror

- War, ethnic violence and
- Ecological disaster

A large number of 'environmental' or 'developmental' refugees are difficult to identify because they are often displaced peoples, i.e., refugees within their own countries. Many of those who live in inhuman conditions in slums that surround almost every city in the developing world have been, in one way or another driven off their homelands. These people become the "rejected people" and "unwanted migrants" because of their weak or failed states. There is a need for the international community to apply its mind to this type of forced displacement. The UNHCR needs to extend its protective umbrella to internally displaced people as it did in November 1991 when the Secretary General asked the UNHCR to assume the role of the lead agency for the United Nations for humanitarian assistance to victims of conflict in former Yugoslavia. In fact, when the convention on status of refugees was being framed there were no refugees who ran away from their own country due to its poverty, economical imbalance or failure to protect its citizen. This is a new phenomenon and it is time now to take up this humanitarian activity in view of its alarming magnitude. These people are, in the words of a UN report "persons who have been forced to flee their homes suddenly or unexpectedly in large numbers, as a result of armed conflict, internal strife, and systematic violations of human rights or natural or man- made disasters."[13]

If these people are not the most "wretched of the wretched,"[14] they are at least the most ignored and least protected. As they fall outside the explicit mandate of the United Nations High Commission for Refugees, the only UN organization with the authority, means and personnel for worldwide day-to-day monitoring and intercession on behalf of the endangered, this institution must be entrusted to look into the affairs of these people and help them. In the Northeast of India alone the displacement figures due to internal violence is quite staggering. A conservative estimate of the displaced in this area at the end of the year 1998 puts the figure between 1,70,000 and 2,30,000 that figure includes 80,000 ethnic Santhals and a small number of ethnic Nepalese 3,500 to 60,000 Bengalis in Assam, more than 20,000 ethnic Paite, Kuki, and Naga in Manipur; 39,000 ethnic Reangs displaced from Mizoram into Tripura; 25,000 Bengalis in Tripura; and 3,000 ethnic Chakmas in Arunachal Pradesh.[15]

In 1996 Bodos of Assam mounted large scale attacks on ethnic Santhals that displaced more than 2,50,000 persons mostly Santhals. In May 1998, further Bodo attacks displaced another 25,000 Santhal. The Bodo-Santhals clash in Assam has resulted in thousands of death while rendering many thousands more homeless. Of the many inmates of refugee campus, more than 57,000 are children in the age of 5-8 years.[16] Evictions or displacements have become a regular feature of urban life in developing countries, especially in the major metropolis. In Mumbai, the largest eviction has been recorded in Sanjay Gandhi National Park where over 70,000 households equivalent to a small-sized township were brutally evicted. In the report on the enquiry of the Indian People's Human Right Commission, Justice V.R. Krishna Iyer stated that it is indeed "amazing that the High Court has deprived so many people of their right to shelter which has been included by the Supreme Court under Article 21 as being part of life and liberty."[17]

Today, nearly every major city in the world has a sizeable immigrant community. Over a hundred million people are living outside the country of their birth and millions earlier generation immigrants maintain their ethnic identities even in remote and far off lands. While Frankfurt has its Turks, Vancouver has its Chinese, Paris has its Algerians, London have its Indians and Pakistanis, New York has its Russian Jews, Bangkok has its Burmese, Tokyo has its Iranians, Dhaka has its Biharis and Dubai, Kuwait, Abu Dhabi have their Indians. In industrialized and developed societies, non-citizens now typically constitute more than 5 per cent of their population. The figure is nearly 9 per cent in US and Germany, over 15 per cent in Canada, 18 per cent in Switzerland and 24 per cent in Australia. In oil producing countries like Saudi Arabia, United Arab Emirates, Oman and Kuwait, non-citizens outnumber natives.[18] But the naturalization rates of these immigrants are very low to an extent of only; one-half of one percent a year-so that even the children and grandchildren of immigrants remain citizens of the countries from which their ancestors came. No attempt is made to assimilate this population, which is discriminated against. For example, the Japanese discriminate against Koreans who have resided Japan for several generations. French educational authorities impose restrictions on immigrants for displaying their religious identity on the campus. Limiting the rights and benefits of the immigrants and their children, creates aggrieved population and disaffected minorities. Even like the desposition of the prime minister of Indian origin in Fiji by local native elements obstruct the role of such ethnic minorities in the development process of the country. They tend to support extremist terrorist or anarchist group of their people.

At a time when the conventional adult workforce in developed countries is dwindling and there is a growing need to import immigrants to maintain their workforce; a liberal immigration policy is needed, instead of making it a politically heated issue.[19] No doubt, coming from different socio-political and cultural settings, the refugees and migrants create different kinds of problem in the host society. They refuse to get assimilated in the larger society, they stick in a group, fail to learn the language and manners of the host, keep their cultural identity intact, create cross-linkages with similar ethnic and religious groups and indulge in underground activities. If they happen to belong to an organized religious order the problem becomes very acute for a democratic and secular host society. For example, a massive invasion of Muslim refugees from Bangladesh to India has changed not only the demographic character of certain areas; their continued presence threatens religious peace and secular credentials of those areas. Though, belonging to a minority religious order, they refuse to behave as on because they are a majority across the border.

Incidentally, in certain cases the illegal presence of refugees becomes extremely difficult to identify. Their kinship and religious ties, especially in the Indian context, where aliens from Bangladesh, Pakistan and Sri Lanka have cross linkages, prevention of refugee's influx, their identification and repatriation has become extremely complicated.[20] The whole of the North-Eastern India is suffering from this problem and Border States like Bihar and Bengal have begun to experience the pinch. This problem is further compounded when there is an explicit complicity between the refugees and underworld dons and politicians of the state. As a consequence, refugees have come to present not a human or social problem; instead they have come to represent a major "security" problem in the host society. Even if a principle on the line of "polluter pays", is evolved, it would be difficult to implement not only on the grounds of national sovereignty, but also on the issue of time frame. How long the country should pay? For the refugees the conditions in their mother country may not improve enough to be repatriated safely. Again, they may like to return to a country where they lost their near and dear ones or to a mother country, which was poorer and devoid of opportunities compared to the host country. Another point that may have to be taken into account is that a host country which is itself poor and not fully able to meet the basic human right needs of its own citizens, additional burden of hosting refugees even under the UNHCR aid may create unmanageable social and political cleavages.

The ideal would be 'one world', 'the global world' or 'world without borders'. In its absence, equal problem sharing is the best solution. At a time when the principal contemporary interest of the developed world is to ensure that the growing global refugee population does not flood their border or tax their treasuries, this is also not an acceptable solution to the developed world. It has been pointed out in various studies that in ten of the world's fifteen most seriously affected refugee receiving countries are among the fifty poorest countries.[21] This type of politically loaded policies has to be reviewed in the interest of all.

Notes and References

1. Ayn Rand: "Man's Rights", in *Capitalism: The Unknown Ideal* New York: Signet, 1970, p. 324. Read this statement in conjunction with Article 13(2) and 14(1) of Universal Declaration of Human Rights, 1948 and Articles 12(2) of International Covenant on Civil and Political Rights. This would justify the use of this quotation here.

2. Article 1(2) of the Protocol signed by the President of the General Assembly and by the Secretary General on 31 January 1967.
3. Justice P.N. Bhagwati: Presidential Address, *Seminar Report on Refugees in the SAARC Region: Building a Legal Framework* New Delhi : UNCHR, 1997, p. 21.
4. Tom Farer: "How the International System Copes with Involuntary Migration: Norms, Institution and State Practice", in Michael S. Tietelbanm and Myron Weiner: *Threatened Peoples, Threatened Borders,* New Delhi: Universal Book Traders, 1997, p. 265.
5. *Ibid.*, p. 266.
6. See Article 1(2) of OAU Convention Governing the Specific Aspects of Refugee Problem in Africa, 1969.
7. See Para II of the conclusions adopted at the Colloquium.
8. I received a copy of the same through UNCHR, 14, Jor Bagh, New Delhi-110003 in 1998.
9. http:/www/refugees.org
10. http://www.refuges.org/news/crisis/aftica_2000htw.
11. Quoted in Nolan Fell: "Outcasts from Eden", *New Scientist,* London, 31 August 1996
12. Wolfgang Seiler, "The Global Climate Change : A Challenge to Society and Science", *Innovation* The Magazine from Carl Zeiss (Germany), No. 11, June 2002.
13. Analytical Report of the Secretary General on Internally Displaced Persons, February 14, 1992, quoted in Tom Farer, *op. cit.,* p. 273.
14. Farer, *ibid.*
15. See Debendra Kumar Nayak and Apresh Patra: "Ethnic conflict and Forced Migration in Assam, India, *Transactions*, Vol. 25, No. 122, January- July 2003, p. 34.
16. *Ibid.*, p. 44.
17. Quoted in Dhurjati Mukherjee: "Stopping Evictions : Upgradation and Relocation the Answer", *Young Indian,* May 10-16, 2003, p. 5.
18. Myron Weiner: "Grave New World: Migration of people, culture has made borders irrelevant", *The Asian Age,* March 24, 1990.
19. See for details Peter Drucker: "The Next Society-A Survey of Near Future", *The Economist,* November 3, 2001.

20. See for details, Aung Phyro and Tapan Bose: "Refugee in South Asia: *An Overview Refugee Watch,* Calcutta, January 1998, pp. 2-5.
21. Sée Barry N. Stein: Refugee Aid and Development: Slow Progress since ICARII in H. Adelmand (ed.) *Refugee policy: Canada and United States,* Toronto, York Lanes press Ltd. 1991, pp. 143-72. The fact is borne out by *World Refugees Survey*, 1997, p.1.

23

Environmental Security in South Asia

Narottam Gaan

The late 1970s witnessed a spurt of activity resulting in a myriad of calls to redefine security in non-military terms that include rising poverty, rapid population growth, spread of infectious diseases, and environmental degradation. The realist understanding and definition of security was state centric connected with state secrecy, nuclear and military power. The realist framework of national security as a function of the successful pursuit of interstate power competition through military means continued right through the cold war. According to Dalby, "cold war versions of security have usually been understood in spatial terms as moves of exclusion and protection is a spatial exercise in distancing and boundary making."[1] This means in geopolitical parlance, the spatial limitation of Soviet political control. During the last half century, security has been primarily a matter of concern for states and their military alliances. The legitimacy of the governments is generally understood in terms of provision of internal security for the inhabitants residing within its territorial jurisdiction. Where stability of the regime has been held synonymous with national security serious inroads into the realm of human rights, and internal repressions have been rationalized in the name of national security. Where political instability has been identified as threat, national security is understood as containing and limiting political change and legitimizing the status quo. The intensification of cold war climaxed in the proliferation of nuclear weapons and in the Reagan administration's Strategic Defense Initiative and Star wars merely exposed the paradox of security where the enhancement of nuclear power does not mean the enhancement of security to the people. The problems plaguing the entire humanity in terms of grinding poverty, burgeoning population growth, spread of diseases, scarcity of resources and environmental degradation could not be comprehended within the realist framework based on state centric military capability. Thus, the dominant realist paradigm to understand the current realities seems to be inadequate. It has "become an anachronism that has lost much of its explanatory and prescriptive power."[2]

Environmental Security

The state-centric and military perspective of security has lost both practical relevance and intellectual credibility in the context of a number of historic forces and events in the contemporary age. These include the end of cold war, global integration of national economies, erosion of national identities and cultures, the shift in priority from military rivalry to economic competition, and the diminishing role of state as the dominant actor in international politics. On the other hand, the emergence of diverse non-traditional and new issues-ranging from poverty to refugees crises, information privacy to cyber-terrorism, environmental problems to natural disasters – which require non-state and non-military policies and strategies, are now being considered a major component of what is christened as comprehensive security. Among these emergent problems replacing the threat of East-West ideological divide, military aggression and struggle for global preponderance is the global environmental crisis. It looms large in terms of global warming, sea level rise, acid rain, greenhouse effect, diminishing capacity of the agricultural system, depletion of earth's finite resources, punching holes in the ozone layer, and biodiversity loss. Simply put, the global agenda has expanded since the demise of cold war, as has the need for urgent attention to these problems for solution. It is thus seen that "welfare not warfare, will shape the rules and global threats like ozone holes and pollution will dictate the agenda."[3] It is within this context that the environmental question has gained worldwide significance as a security issue. In fact, environmental security stands out as perhaps the most widely debated issue, especially due to its all-pervasive nature, cross- national scope and inter generational implications.[4]

While many of the past, present and future causes of conflict and war may seem to have little or no direct connection with the environment or with resources, a strong argument can be made for linking certain resource and environmental problems with the prospects for political frictions and tensions, or even war and peace. At the centre of ongoing debate is the assertion that resource scarcity and certain forms of environmental degradation are important factors contributing to political instability or violent conflict at local, regional and interstate levels. There is a growing perception that local, regional and global environmental deficiencies or resource scarcities will increasingly produce conditions that may lead to conflict.[5] This conceptual shift towards environmental security in the context of collapse of Soviet Union and diminution of security threats associated with cold war, pitch forked into the mainstream security debates urging the policy makers to cast about for a new security focus. Despite contentious debates within the field of environmental security, a wide variety of recent comments by senior diplomats and policy makers are symptomatic of the recognition that issues related to environmental security have ascended to the highest levels.

In 1987, the General Secretary of the Soviet Union, Mikhail Gorbachev stated: "[The World] is not secure in the direct meaning of the word when currents of poison flow along river channels, when poison rains pour down form the sky, when an atmosphere polluted with industrial and transport waste chokes cities and whole regions, when the development of atomic engineering is justified by unacceptable risks. The relationship between man and the environment has become menacing. Problems of ecological security affect all the rich and the poor."[6] In November 1989, Prime Minister Margaret Thatcher gave a speech to the United Nations General Assembly—saying: While the conventional political dangers–the threat of global annihilation, the fact of regional war appears to be receding, we have all recently become aware of other insidious dangers. It is as menacing in its way as these more accustomed perils with which international diplomacy has concerned itself for centuries. It is the prospect of irretrievable damage to the atmosphere, to the oceans, to earth itself.[7] In April 1997, as United States Secretary of state, Ms Albright went on to say: "Not so long ago, many believed that the pursuit of clean air, clean water, and healthy forests was a worthy goal, but not part of our national security. Today environmental issues are part of the mainstream of American foreign policy."[8]

It was in this backdrop of future non-military threats that a number of studies and research institutions undertook works to determine how environmental factors were related to the intra and inter-state conflicts or violence that appeared to be surfacing around the globe.[9] These studies varied in their approach, their terminology, and their specific findings and consistent in their explanations suggested that environmental stress, operating through a set of intervening variables, could contribute to violent conflicts, and thus constituted a threat to national and international security. Furthering this argument that the mounting environmental problems and the associated issues need an attention with which the conventional outlook of national security appears to be incongruent, Jeremy Rifkin points out: "The environmental threats facing the planet are not simply the result of scientific miscalculation. Nor are they merely the consequences of ill-conceived management decisions. Ironically it is the notion of security upon which our entire modern worldview is based that has led us to the verge of ecocide... In less than a century the practice of geopolitics thus pushed the world to the brink of both nuclear Armageddon and environmental catastrophe forcing us to reconsider the basic assumption of security that animates the modern world view."[10]

Similarly, Lodgaard feels that "the concept of environmental security challenges established frames of mind and political conflicts. It conveys a message that environmental problems have a legitimate claim for status as military problems have."[11] Another proponent of environmental security in the same vein opines: "national security is not just about fighting forces and weaponry. It relates to watersheds, croplands, forests, genetic resources, climatic and other factors that rarely figure in the minds of military experts and political leaders, but increasingly deserve in their collectivity to rank along side military approaches as crucial to a nation's security."[12]

The growing significance of environmental security is quite evident in major international forums. Some well-known examples include the UN Conference on Human Environment (1972), Ottawa Conference on Conservation and Development (1986), United Nations Conference on Environment and Development (1992), World Summit for social Development (1995) and UN symposium on the Global Environment in the 21st Century (1997). These conferences and symposia eventually resulted in various international conventions and protocols for environmental protection or security, such as the Vienna Convection for the protection of the Ozone Layer, the convention on Biological Diversity, the Framework convention on climate change, the convention to combat desertification, and the Kyoto protocol. [13] Harking back to as far as 1987, for example, The World Commission on Environmental Development (Brundtland Report) entitled "Our common Future", stresses the factor of environmental degradation causing the violent relationship between states: "environmental stress is both a cause and effect of political tension and military conflict..nations have fought to assist or resist control over raw materials, energy supplies, land, river basin, sea passages and other key environmental resources.

According to the report, such conflicts are likely to increase as these resources became scarcer and competition for them will increase."[14] Environmental security as a concept encompassing non-military aspects was officially mentioned for the first time in the International conference on the Relationship between Disarmament and Development convened by the UN General Assembly in New York from 24 August to 11 September 1987. The final document adopted by consensus states: Recently non-military threats to Security have moved to the forefront of global concern. Underdevelopment and declining prospects for development as well as mismanagement and waste of resources, constitute challenges to security. The degradation of the environment presents a threat to sustainable development...Mass poverty, illiteracy, diseases, squalor and malnutrition affecting a large proportion of world's population often become the cause of social strain, tension and strife.[15]

Two distinct features of environmental security are: First, the environmental causes of conflict, i.e. environmental factors behind potentially violent conflicts; Second, the impact of environmental degradation on overall political economy, health and life of the people. If environmental degradation or deficiencies create the conditions that render conflicts, act as multipliers that aggravate core causes of conflict[16] or act as a catalyst factor in creating conflicts, then environmental degradation or scarcity of resources becomes a national security issue.[17]

Environmental Conflict

In spite of these criticisms, the most influential arguments have concluded that environmental stress is linked to conflict indirectly, but significantly. While the precise character of the linkage varies from case to case, the environmental stress is supposed to overwhelm the adaptive capacity of some societies while simultaneously introducing and reinforcing forms of conflict and instability. While division and debate characterize the field of environmental security, there is a strong degree of theoretical consensus among researchers. The most prominent and dominant thread that runs through the entire environmental security literature is that the environmental stress simultaneously reduces adaptive capacity and engenders conflict.

The dominant paradigm in the environmental security literature harks back to writers like Thomas Malthus, but it has obtained its contemporary influential formulation in the work of Thomas Homer Dixon and Toronto Group. From a myriad of empirical case studies conducted by them on Haiti, Chiapas, Gaza, Pakistan and Bangladesh – India, they concluded that environmental scarcity of renewable resources viz., water, forest, fisheries and cropland give rise to a number of deleterious social effects including economic decline, social segmentation and human migration – these social effects in interaction with other political, economic and social factors, can generate conflict and instability. Central to their model was the notion of supply of ingenuity gap or a disparity between the solutions required to cope with environmental scarcity and the human, social and institutional capital that could be mustered to provide these solutions. This ingenuity gap essentially undermines human adaptive responses. That means, according to their studies, resource scarcity and limited or inadequate adaptive capacity coalesce together to generate violent conflicts in various regions.[18]

Dominant Paradigm

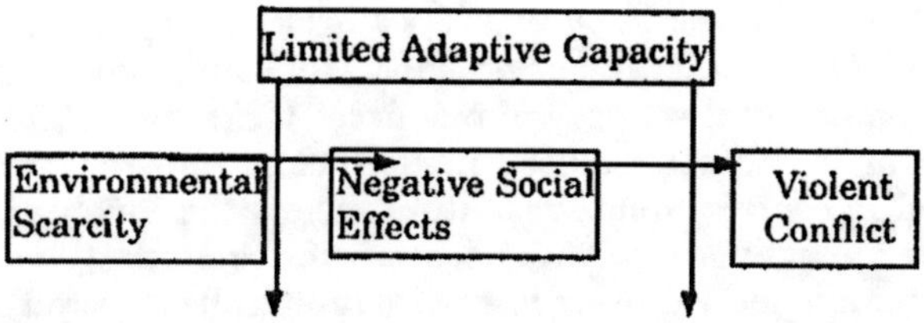

A theoretical representation is made in this figure[19] to understand the linkage between environmental stress and conflict. On theoretical ground it is criticized that even if resource scarcity plays a causal role in conflict, there are other more convincing explanations for conflict. Further, the prospects for adaptation, cooperation or resolution are not as completely bleak as is often presented. At the very prospects of an unlikely nuclear war, the fear of destructibility by the use of nuclear weapons has not any way diminished the universality of nuclear weapon as a main national security issue. It is that fear of destruction, which may have brought many nuclear powers to negotiating table for cooperation or disarmament. The resultant cooperation should not be cited to under-rate the holistic perception of nuclear weapons as being a national security concern. Similarly, environmental scarcity of resources with its disastrous social effects may not be everywhere a direct cause of violent conflict, sometimes in combination with other factors causes conflict. For example, sea level rise a consequence of global warming due to North's mindless pursuit of industrialization based on fossil fuel technology will affect low-lying areas such as Bangladesh turning millions of refugees fleeing to Indian territories that is likely to exacerbate the already infested ethnic conflict in North-Eastern states. The consequences of environmental scarcity of resources on political, economic and social life of a state or states may prompt states or nations to cooperate to avoid the negative effects of war on environment. So the environmental co-operation syndrome as argued by some should not be overrated to diminish the role of environmental scarcity of resources causing conflict or violence. No nuclear war has ever been fought in this world after American's dropping of hydrogen bombs on Japan's Herosima and Nagasaki during the course of Second World War. This would be as preposterous to say that nuclear weapon lack the potential or prospects for conflict as to say that the environmental scarcity of resources lacks the potential for conflict as it has not resulted in conflict in some areas or has resulted in cooperation. Adaptation means the involvement of all state apparatus, institutions, scientific community, even the social system and value structure including the affected to take steps that would obviate the negative effects of environmental scarcity. The poor developing countries may not have the economic and scientific wherewithal as argued by Dixon to cope with the situation. Even the developed countries will not find it a smooth sailing while responding to the environmental crisis. For example, in regard to stabilization of CO_2 in the atmosphere American steps to renege on its commitment agreed to at Kyoto were a capitulation to the petroleum, coal industrial lobby. What has threatened the world is the Western inordinate life style and pattern of development causing global warming, sea level rise and ozone layer depletion. To ensure environmental security what it requires is to make an overhaul of its pattern of life and development, which is not possible with strong protestations from high-class people. So Bush, American President caving in to the pressure of the industrial class justified his rejection of Kyoto protocol on the ground that countenancing the Kyoto commitment would hamper its economy and life style of its people.[20] Environmental security means overhauling the entire economic development pattern and existing social values related to liberal capitalism that is not possible without politico-socio-economic disruption. So the potential for conflict lies as much in the environmental scarcity of resources as in the very remedies and adaptive measures – a part of fulfillment of environmental security.

In spite of the criticisms, the main thrust of the studies showing the linkage between environment and conflict, remains paramount: the environmental scarcity operates through a set of intervening variables, contexts or ideational factors that directly cause conflict, and that environmental social effects and stress, as such outstrips attempts to cope with the crisis. Another study undertaken by Swiss Peace Institute's Environment and Conflicts Project (ENCOP) was in the direction of what the Toronto group suggests. Gunther Bachler belonging to this group in his study used the term transformation by which he meant "the introduction of a heuristic concept in recording those interactions between the three levels – nature, human beings and the economy in a regional context which have led to conflicts between human communities and will ..increasingly lead to such conflicts."[21] Degradation is used in this context as an indicator of the degree of environmental transformation. In the words of Kates et al, "the biosphere has accumulated or is on its way to accumulating such a magnitude and variety of changes that it may be said to be transformed."[22] In other words, "transformation conflicts are caused by fundamental anthropogenic changes in the environmental media and by the interactions between the processes of change and their consequences in the eco-regional context."[23]

Another authority Stephan Libiszewski belonging to ENCOP, making a distinction between traditional resource wars and environmental causes of conflict is of the view that 'an environmental conflict is a conflict caused by the environmental scarcity of a resource, that means: caused by a human made disturbance of its normal regeneration rate. Environmental scarcity can result from the overuse of a renewable resource or from the overstrain of the ecosystem's sink capacity, that is pollution. Both can reach the stage of destruction of space of living. Conflicts caused by physical, geopolitical or socio-economic resource scarcity are not environmental conflicts but traditional conflicts of resource distribution."[24] As found in the Toronto Group's research the ENCOP also walks on the same furrow that scarcity gives rise to conflict. Also it is alleged to be silent about human adaptation to resource scarcity. In these studies, it is mal- development, a condition similar to Homer Dixon's ingenuity gap that undermines human responses and enhances conflicts.[25] Though the ENCOP model is more complex than the Toronto Group's general model, but the theoretical argument presented by both is very similar.[26]

In a 1999 NATO pilot study this dominant environmental conflict paradigm was found in the line with the other studies.[27] According to this study, "it is not environmental stress in isolation that characterizes the nature of the conflict between groups but other factors."[28] Here too political, economic and social factors intervene between environmental stress and conflict. The State Failure Task Force (SFTF), another research group marking the same dominant paradigm as with the preceding studies, reiterates the causal weight of environmental stress through intervening variables.[29] While the researches did find that massive environmental damage in a short time frame could directly cause political collapse, the far more common scenario was that environmental stress operates through the intervening variable of quality of life to generate conflict. Though highly critical of Toronto group, recent work by Gleditsch and de Soysa appears to have been co-opted by the dominant paradigm. According to their studies, resource scarcity the one component of a multifaceted development problem that they call "poverty" reduces agricultural production that in turn leads to conflict. That is, scarcity leads to a negative social outcome that becomes the proximate cause of conflict.[30] Beyond this; however, the Gleditsch and de Soyasa model is similar to the Toronto Group and there is little room for human adaptation to conditions of scarcity. Indeed, their key independent variable, poverty, is defined by a lack of social and human capital. "Like Homer Dixon's ingenuity gap, Gleditsch and de Soyasa's explanatory variable appears to lock in negative social outcomes, leaving little room for human adaptation."[31] There is some variation in these models and term presented by these research groups. But in each case the general theory linking resource scarcity and conflict is the same. Homer Dixon focuses on an "ingenuity gap", ENCOP on "mal development" and Gleditsch and de Soysa on "poverty". Nevertheless, all these phrases describe a similar process–a limited capacity to respond to scarcity.

The model, which is critical of all the above models adopted by Richard A Matthew et al, finds flaws in current theory in environmental security on two counts. "First, it focuses on too short a time frame. Second, and relatedly, it underestimates human adaptive capacity."[32] They were averse to accepting the two extremes, Homer Dixon's lack of adaptive capacity in the poor countries, and Julian Simon and Herman Kahn's faith in the infinite capacity of individuals to adopt. To them, human adaptive capacity lies somewhere between these two extremes. Julian Simon writes, "there is no physical or economic reason why human resourcefulness and enterprise cannot forever continue to respond to impending shortages and existing problems with new expedients that, after an adjustment period, leave us better off than before the problem arose."[33] Homer Dixon responds to this saying, "while I acknowledge the extraordinary potential of human resourcefulness and enterprise, I nonetheless argue that some societies – especially poor societies – will not be able to supply the unprecedented amounts of ingenuity they will need to solve their emerging scarcity problems."[34] This clearly demonstrates, Homer Dixon never maintains that all societies will not be able to cope with the situation. It is some poor societies because of various factors that will be in dearth of required supply of ingenuity to adapt to the situation. This brings Homer Dixon closer to the position taken by Richard A. Matthew and his associates. If adaptation is a dynamic and continuous process, then there may be adoption failure in some and adoption success in others visited with trauma, travails and hardships. When such individual trauma, travails and ordeals while adapting to the environmental stress becomes a collective or group phenomena in a particular political context or in the face of growing incapability of state, the potential for violent conflict exists. Taking a departure from this, Matthew group holds that from a longer time perspective even if the adaptive failures through feedback will result in adaptive success, thus avoiding the prospects for environmental conflicts. Contrary to what Neo-Malthusians such as Paul Ehrlich, Robert Kaplan, and Thomas Homer Dixon contend, "adaptive mechanisms do not simply stall or become overwhelmed while levels of environmental stress continue to escalate."[35] To quote Richard A Matthew further: "This is not to say that all forms of adaptation are socially desirable. Adaptation can mean people of the developing world going further and further into the hinterland to gather fuel, wood and water; parents sending their children to work in factories because of crop failure; and simple belt-tightening people eating less,"[36] or as happened in Klahanie district of Orissa people eating the dried up Kernel of ripen mangoes died while adopting to food scarcity, or people in these tribal areas of Orissa are forced to sell their children as bonded labourers as a mark of adaptation to the environmental scarcity of crop land and food. These latter examples are certainly unsettling and portent of potential for violent behaviour in an organized form depending on the nature of political system prevailing. If to use the language of Matthew, these starvation, death, or going without food, or half fed situations are the genuine form of adoption, then conflict arising out of these situations created by environmental scarcity in the form of collective or group behaviour or response can be a genuine version of adoption with a view to develop new legitimate and representative political authority and institution and new value structure that would reinvent the political-economic thinking which so far has contributed to environmental scarcity. As Walker argues, conflict is a normal and important aspect of social development.[37] Then the portrayal of environmental crisis as an environmental conflict paradigm from a broader perspective does not lose its significance or acceptability, as a theoretical framework as argued by Richard Matthew and his group. The conclusion that this group arrived at is not to deny the linkage between environmental scarcity and conflict but stresses on "longer term studies" that "might provide deeper understanding of the ways in which concerns about environmental stress and degradation are relevant not only to those concerned with international security, but also those worried about human rights, social justice and sustainable development.[38]

On the one side the economic deprivation, decreased agricultural production, health hazards, poverty, starvation or half fed or even death situation due to pollution and water scarcity- part of the adoptive success as propounded by Matthew – may cause indirect conflict in association with other factors as nuanced by Volker Boge[39] or Homer Dixon[40]. The other side is the situation of direct conflict or violence arising out of the environmental scarcity of resources–a case of adaptive failure. Hence the conflict emanates directly from the overuse and or pollution/destruction of a renewable natural resources. For example, if a downstream riparian threatens to go to war against an upstream riparian, because the latter pollutes river water so gravely that it cannot be used by the inhabitants of the downstream riparian, who are highly dependent on this water, then the environmental character of conflict is evident.[41] An array of evidences can be cited to show such threats of conflict over environmental scarcity of water all over the globe. [42] That in some cases it has led to cooperation to avoid war does not divest the environmental conflict of its theoretical appeal. Another example of direct violent conflict over environmental scarcity of resources like fish can be cited. The decline in fish catch due to environmental degradation all over the globe and in South Asian regions in particular could result in a series of violent conflict between Tamil Nadu fishermen of India, and Sri Lanka over fishing in waters of Kachchativu Island ceded by India to Sri Lanka as a gesture of friendship and good will in 1974.[43]

Environmental Security in South Asian Context

As the new millennium begins, global concerns about sustainable economic development have brought the concept of environmental security into sharp focus. Nations in all regions of the world, if they are to provide for the long-term well being of their citizens, must find the means to protect the environment in order to ensure continued access to natural resources and the health of their citizens. But national sovereignty and regulatory policy at the level of individual nations cannot guarantee success in matters related to environmental security. It is now quite apparent that threats to a nation's environmental well-being may not only arise outside its borders, but may prove beyond the reach of corrective measures at the national level. To steer a course of sustainable development requires that nations find the means and mechanisms to take collective action to protect the land, water, air, and bio-resources through policies that are cooperatively defined and implemented. This brief review summarizes the scope of national environmental concerns in the region, and identifies those problems that have clear trans-boundary effects such as acid rain, deforestation, siltation, soil degradation, the migration of toxic or hazardous wastes, marine pollution, and climate change. Significant trans-boundary impacts in most of these areas of concern point to an urgent need for regional cooperation to complement individual national responses if environmental security for the region is to become a reality. The status of current plans to achieve such cooperation is reviewed here and the urgent need for an agenda for implementation is highlighted. Though the countries in the region share many concerns, environmental priorities are not necessarily the same in every case. Table1 summarizes the key environmental concerns of South Asian economies.

Table 1 Environmental Priorities for South Asian Countries

Country	*Land Degradation*	*Water Scarcity*	*Water quality*	*Air Pollution*		*Urbanisation*	*Marine environment*	*Deforestation*
				In door	*Out door*			
Bangladesh	High	Med.	-	High	Med.	Med.	High	Med.
Bhutan	-	-	Low	High	-	-	-	Med.
India	High	Med.	Med.	High	Med.	Med.	Low	Med.
Nepal	Med.	-		-	High	High	-	-
Maldives	-	Low	-	-	-	-	-	High
Pakistan	High	Low	Med.	High	-	Med.	Low	Med.
Sri Lanka	-	Med.	-	-	-	-	-	High

Though the table shows some diversity in the ranking of specific issues, an analysis of any specific area of concern immediately suggests that regional–as opposed to exclusively national–actions may be required to tackle them. Regional and trans-boundary dimensions of the issues are evident in all cases.

Regional Issues

Air Pollution

The surge in energy demand, characterized by the region's dependence on coal (particularly in India), has manifested itself in major increases in airborne pollution. Urban air quality has deteriorated largely on account of growth in industrial activity, transportation needs, and energy production. Fly ash, combined with emissions from the increased use of coal, has emerged as a major environmental concern. It is estimated that about 35-40 million tons of fly ash is generated by thermal power plants each year in India, of which a mere 2 to 3 per cent is recycled. In 1990, areas with acid loads in excess of the critical levels were in parts of northern India and Bangladesh. The effects of burning coal and the resultant air pollution tend to spread over large areas, resulting in acid deposition in areas near the coal-burning plants as well as further away. Recent evidence from atmospheric studies of the Indian Ocean shows high concentrations of small particles, known as aerosols, consisting primarily of soot, sulfates, nitrates, organic particles, fly ash, and mineral dust suspended over a very large area of the northern Indian Ocean, including the Arabian Sea and much of the Bay of Bengal. The studies indicate that the long-term impact of air pollution on climate through radical changes in the hydrological cycle will be widely felt throughout the region.

Water Resources

Experience from all regions of the world points to the potential for both regional conflict and cooperation in matters related to the protection and use of water resources: the deterioration of the Danube in Europe, the out-take from the Nile in Africa and the Colorado and Rio Grande in North America, and the development and destruction of the Amazon in South America are some examples. The major northern watersheds of the Indian subcontinent are no exception. The effects of land-use, deforestation, and discharges of contaminated water on aquifers, rivers, and streams reach across national boundaries and bear the potential for major conflicts between countries. The rapid growth of both agriculture and urbanization has imposed growing pressure on the region's already strained water resources in terms of both quantity and quality. This is evident in the gradual decline in per capita availability of water throughout the region. In India, for instance, the per capita water availability fell from 6000 cubic meters in 1947 to 2300 cubic meters in 1998. Estimates for the year 2050 predict acute shortage of water in India. Countries in the arid zone, such as Iran and Afghanistan, suffer from chronic water deficits. Use of groundwater for irrigation has emerged as a key area of concern on account of the depleting underground aquifers in several parts of the region. In some pockets in the Indian states of Rajasthan, Haryana, Punjab, and Gujarat, the extent of over-exploitation ranges from cent per cent to 260 per cent compared to the critical level of 85 per cent. It is estimated that by 2015, 36 percent of the blocks in India will be over exploited. In Bangladesh, excessive withdrawals of water have led to waterlogging and salinity and to land subsidence in cities such as Dhaka. Declining water quality is also a common feature in the region due to contamination from both untreated sewage and industrial effluents. In India, the total sewage treatment capacity is a mere 10 per cent of the present waste-water generation. On an average, less than three-fourths of municipal solid waste is collected and the rest finds its way into sewers or is burnt in the open. A survey of some of the major Indian rivers showed that while most can support aquatic life, the water they provide is totally unfit for drinking or even for bathing. In Pakistan, chemical pollution of the Ravi results in an annual estimated loss of Rs 10 million in income from fisheries. Since the causes of declining water quality are common to all the countries in the region, there are significant opportunities for cooperation in the search for remedial and regulatory responses within the region. Regional cooperation could also benefit from lessons learned in other regions of the world.

Land Degradation

In the continuing struggle to provide food and other basic needs of the region's burgeoning populace, land degradation has emerged as an important issue. Soil suffers from varying degrees of degradation on account of rapid deforestation, poor irrigation and drainage practices, and overgrazing. The depletion of land resources through desertification and the loss of nutrient-rich topsoil through water and wind erosion threaten the livelihood of countless millions throughout the region. In India alone, as much as 27 per cent of soil cover suffers from severe erosion. The Thar region of Pakistan and India, and selected watersheds in the Himalayan regions of India and Nepal, are among the worst affected. Another cause of land degradation common to the countries in the region is mining, which is typically unorganized and unscientific, without any defined environmental management and land reclamation plans. In some cases there are clear trans-boundary impacts. Poor mining practices in the dolomite mining areas of Bhutan, adjoining the state of West Bengal in India, have resulted in increased landslides and soil erosion. The Indian foothills have taken the burden of landslide debris. Little is known about the impacts on groundwater and the pollution of aquifers in the region as a whole, but they are likely to be significant.

Deforestation

On account of industrial and agricultural expansion as well as trade in forestry products, deforestation remains a major concern in South Asia. Bangladesh and Pakistan are the countries with the highest rates of deforestation. In Nepal too, over 75 per cent of population depends on fuel wood for energy needs, which puts tremendous pressure on the country's forest resources. Landslides and soil erosion increase the sediment loads in rivers and cause sedimentation and flooding downstream.

Marine Ecology

Untreated effluents from industries and cities in coastal regions have contaminated large areas of the Indian Ocean, with obvious transborder impacts on marine life and fisheries. In particular, the chemical, paper, and sugar industries are major polluters of the marine environment. Agricultural run-off has also contributed to ocean pollution. An estimated 1800 tons of pesticides enter the Bay of Bengal annually and increased use of pesticides in some areas has resulted in contamination of mollusks and fish species. The depletion of mangroves in estuaries, lagoons, and bays, encouraged in part by shrimp breeding in coastal swamps, threatens such important natural processes as soil binding, nutrient recycling, and the prevention of soil erosion and silt accretion.

Oil spills are yet another major threat to ocean resources. Approximately 5 million tons of oil is deposited in the Arabian Sea every year; another 4,00,000 tons is added to the Bay of Bengal. With the growth of tanker traffic in the Indian Ocean and increased offshore exploration and development, the threat of oil spills will undoubtedly increase.

Loss of Biodiversity

Within the Asia-Pacific region, overall habitat losses have been the most acute in the Indian subcontinent. The underlying causes are international trade in timber, introduction of non-native species, improper use of agro-chemicals, excessive hunting and poaching, etc. In Pakistan, hunting is still pursued as a popular sport. Falcons are smuggled to the Middle East and lizards and snakes are killed for their skins. Marine and coastal environments are also vulnerable to tourism, exemplified by the destruction of coral reefs along the Maldives coast. In the Sunderbans, an ecosystem common to India and Bangladesh, increasing population pressure together with industrial activity has led to the loss of diversity of both plant and animal species.

Trans-boundary Movement of Hazardous Wastes

Trans-boundary movement of hazardous wastes is emerging as a critical issue, which countries in this region have not been able to address fully. Although seven out of nine countries in South Asia have signed the Basle Convention, the region lacks a common approach to the import of hazardous wastes. In Bhutan, where cheap labor and power are available, recycling is emerging as an important economic activity. The same is true of other countries, the most dramatic being the ship-breaking industry in the coastal regions of India and Pakistan. The impact of these trends in the context of trans-boundary issues is as yet uncertain, but it is clear that the institutional and regulatory capacity of the countries in this region for surveillance of the import of hazardous wastes is limited and may need to be addressed cooperatively.

Climate Change

Climate change in tropical Asia is projected to have significant impacts on ecosystems (both land and coastal), water resources, and agriculture; apart from its implications for human health. Studies suggest an annual increase of 0.7°C and 1°C respectively in annual mean maximum and minimum surface air temperatures over land regions of the Indian subcontinent in the 2040s compared to the temperatures in the 1980s. Further, this projected warming is likely to be lower than that over the adjoining ocean, which could lead to a decline in mean summer monsoon rainfall of about 0.5 mm/day over the region. The problem of climate change quite clearly necessitates a coordinated policy response from the South Asian countries. This review serves to illustrate the range of local and trans-boundary environmental problems that have emerged in the process of development in the region. It is clear that much remains to be done to quantify current trends, assess the scope for remedies, evaluate their costs, and define mechanisms for region-wide intervention.

Response Strategies

Recent years have witnessed the emergence of a number of national and local responses to environmental problems in countries of the Indian subcontinent. These initiatives have taken the form of development of national environmental action plans, environmental regulation, and some effort to seek market-based remedies. In some countries, intervention has taken the form of decentralization and devolution of power to local/provincial governments for environment planning and management, as well as increased support for grass roots organizations such as associations of water-users in the design and implementation of solutions. Among the institutional mechanisms for regional cooperation on the environment, the most significant one is SACEP (South Asia Cooperative Environment Programme), established in 1982 under the aegis of the United Nations. Its membership consists of nine countries: seven member nations of SAARC (South Asian Association for Regional Cooperation), Afghanistan, and Iran. SACEP's Council, consisting of the ministers of environment and forests in member countries, meets once in two years. Its secretariat is in Colombo, Sri Lanka. The organization implements projects funded by the UN and other multilateral or bilateral agencies.

Although it has no formal link with SAARC, SACEP is responsible for the implementation of a regional project resulting from the SAARC meeting of environmental ministers held in Malé, Maldives, in October 1997. The Male Declaration enunciated a need for a regional environmental action plan and adopted a common position on climate change. The absence, however, of a formal affiliation with SAARC probably limits SACEP's ability to mobilize resources and to implement regional actions.

The SACEP strategy and programme (1992-96) incorporates the following key features:

- Capacty-building and raising awareness.
- Information exchange and technology transfer.
- Training in environmental management and institutional development.
- Cooperative management of mountain ecosystems.
- Conservation of wildlife and their habitat.

The action plan relating to environmental cooperation within the region developed proposals for (1) assessment of the environment, (2) development and revision of national environmental plans, (3) development of legal instruments, and (4) awareness building. The meeting also discussed the ways and means of organizing institutional and financial support for the plan.

In contrast to these rather general statements of principles, a more targeted regional approach within SACEP has been formulated with respect to action on a regional response to atmospheric pollution. The Malé Declaration on Control and Prevention of Air Pollution was signed in April 1998 at a meeting of SACEP's governing council. This declaration seeks to conduct baseline studies and implement an action plan for reducing air pollution. As part of the implementation process, the declaration aims at the following:

- Creating an air pollution.
- Raising regional awareness on acidification.
- Knowledge-sharing and improvements in pollution monitoring systems.
- Review of policy.
- Preparation of national and sub.

The Way Forward

Given the gravity of common concerns in the region, there

is an urgent need for an agenda to implement remedial action among countries of the region. The establishment of SACEP and efforts within the framework of SAARC are clearly steps in the right direction. However, translating broad principles into concrete action will need the coordinated efforts of many institutions within governments, public sector organizations, and private institutions. While efforts within SACEP and SAARC may take some time before they lead to any action, there are other avenues for regional cooperation to be explored. Programmes for regional action will need to have answers that can be addressed through collaborative research and analysis. The questions include the following:

- To what degree can the point sources and origins of regional environmental stress be identified and where should the responses to be target?
- Can regional impacts of specific environmental problems be attributed to market failure, to specific failures of policy, or simply to a lack of awareness?
- Which of a myriad of existing institutions are capable of being mobilized to implement cooperative programmes of action and what appropriate.
- To what degree can the trends be reversed through legal and institutional reforms in the prevailing property rights regimes?
- How can the potential for conflict due to social or economic interests be reduced between neighboring countries?

Cooperation to address these questions is imperative for very pragmatic reasons: it is likely that if the necessary resources are to be found for regional programmes for mitigation, monitoring, and intervention, a consensus on the priorities for common action must also be found. A cooperative approach to answering these questions can be the foundation for cooperative action—environmental security can have little meaning in the absence of such an effort. In the words of Adil Najam "The prospect of interstate violence in South Asia over environmental issues is slim. However, given the region's history of distrust and dispute, environmental differences could add to existing tensions and apprehensions and perpetuate the general sense of insecurity that pervades interstate relations in the region."[44] The environment has the potential to become an entry point for wider regional cooperation based on mutual trust, harmony, and cooperation rather than on legacies of distrust and dispute.

Notes and References

1. S. Dalby: American Security Discourse: The Persistence of Geopolitics, *Political Geography Quarterly*, 9, 1990, pp. 171-88.
2. O.R. Holsti: *International Systems, Systems Change and Foreign Policy,* Diplomatic History, 15, 1991, p. 94.
3. J. Joffe: Entangled for ever, in C.W. Kegley Jr. and E.R. Wittkoff, (eds.), *The Future of American Foreign Policy* (New York: St. Martin's Press, 1992), p. 35.
4. M. Shamsul Haque: Non-Traditional Security and the Environment in North East Asia, *Work in Progress* Vol.16, No. 3, Summer 2002, p. 24.
5. Peter H. Gleick: World's Water: *The Biennial Report on Fresh Water Resources* (Washington D.C.: California: Island Press, 1998), pp. 105-06.
6. M. Gorbachev: Reality and guarantees for a secure world. *Moscow News*, No. 39, 1987, p. 3287.
7. Quoted in Peter H. Gleick, World's Water, *op.cit,* p. 106.
8. US Department of State, "Environmental Diplomacy: The Environment and US Foreign Policy", *US Department of State,* Washington, D.C.: 1997.
9. Ted Gurr: *Minorities at Risk: A Global View of Ethnopolitical Conflicts* (Washington DC: US Institute of Peace Press, 1993).
10. J. Rifkin: *Biospheric Politics: A New Consciousness for a New Century* (New York: Crown, 1991), p. 2.
11. Sverre Lodgaard: Environmental Conflict Resolution, paper presented at the UNEP meeting on *Environmental Conflict Resolution*, Nairobi, 30 March 1990, p. 18.
12. Norman Myers: The Environmental Dimension to Security Issues, *The Environmentalist* Vol. 6, Winter 1986, p. 251.

13. M. Shamsul Haque: The Fate of Sustainable Development Under the Neoliberal Regimes in Developing Countries, *International Political Science Review,* 20/2 (1999), pp.199-222.
14. World Commission on Environment and Development, *Our Common Future* (Brundtland Report (New York/London: Oxford University Press, 1987) p. 290.
15. Quoted in Dietrich Fisher, Nonmilitary Aspects of Security: A System's Approach, United Nations Institute for Disarmament and Research (UNIDIR), (Aldershot: Dartmouth Publishing Company Ltd., 1993), p. 10.
16. Norman Myers: The Environmental Dimension to Security Issues, *The Environmentalist* Vol. 6, Winter 1986, p. 253.
17. Gareth Porter: Environmental Security as National Security Issue. *Current History,* May 1995, p. 218.
18. Thomas F. Homer Dixon: *Environment, Scarcity, and Violence* (Princeton, New Jersy: Princeton University Press, 1999); Thomas F. Homer Dixon and Jessica Blitt, Evidences: *Links Among Environment, Population, and Security* (New York: Rowman and Littlefield, 1998); Thomas F. Homer Dixon: Environmental Scarcities and Violent Conflict: Evidence from Cases, *International Security,* Vol.19, 1994, pp. 5-40.
19. Thomas F. Homer Dixon: Environment, Scarcity, and Violence, p. 7 and Daniel Esty et. al.: *The State Failure Task Force Report: Phase II Findings* Environmental Change and Security Project Report 5, 1999, p. 63; S.C. Lonergan, (ed.), *Environmental Change, Adaptation and Security,* (Boston: Klewer, 1999); David Dessler, "Review of Environmental Scarcity and Violence", *Environmental Change and Security Project Report* 5 (1999), pp.100-01.
20. David L. Levy and Daniel Egan: Capital Contests: National and Transnational Channels of Corporate Influence on the gions of Climate Change Negotiations, *Politics and Society* Vol. 26, No. 3, September 1998, pp. 337-61. See also N. Gaan: Politics of Governance of Global Climate change: Not on Equity but on North's Interests. *India Quarterly,* Vol. LVIII, No. 4, October-December 2001, pp. 89-112.
21. Gunther Bachler: Conflict and Cooperation in the Light of Global Human-Ecological Transformation, *ENCOP, Occasional Paper* 9

October 1993, p. 5.

22. Robert W. Kates and B.L. Turner II and William Clark: *The Great Transformation.* In B.L. Turner II, and William C.Clark, Robert W. Kates, John F. Richards, Jessica T. Matthews, William B. Mayer, (eds.) *The Earth as Transformed by Human Action: Global and Regional Changes in the Biosphere over the Past 300 years* (Cambridge: Cambridge University Press with Clark University, 1990), p. 1.
23. Gunther Bachler, Conflict and Cooperation, ibid., p. 16.
24. Stephan Libiszewski, What is an Environmental Conflict? *ENCOP, Occasional Paper* No. I, July 1992, p. 6.
25. Richard A. Matthew, Ted Gaulin, and Bryan McDonald, "The Elusive Quest: Linking Environmental Change and Conflict" submitted to *Canadian Journal of Political Science*, Revised Manuscript submitted; Dec. 21, 2001, File Number: 01-12, p. 7.
26. See for details Nancy Peluso and Michael Watts (ed.): *Violent Environments* (Ithaca: Cornell University Press, 2001), pp.15-24.
27. Committee on the challenges of Modern Society, NATO: *Environment and Security in an International Context*, NATO Report 232, 1999.
28. *Ibid.*, p. 22.
29. Daniel Esty et.al.: *The State Failure Task Force Report: Phase II Findings*. Environmental Change and Security Project Report 5, 1999.
30. Ted Gaulin: To Cultivate a New Model: Where do Soyasa and Gleditsch Fall Short. *Environmental Change and Security Project Report* 6 2000, pp. 104-07.
31. Richard A. Matthew, et al., "The Elusive Quest", *op.cit*, p. 9.
32. *Ibid.*, p. 25.
33. Julian Simon: *The Ultimate Resources* (Princeton, N.J.: Princeton University Press, 1981), p. 345; and Julian Simon, *The Ultimate Resource 2* (Princeton, N.J.: Princeton University Press, 1996).
34. Thomas F. Homer Dixon, Environment, Scarcity and Violence, p. 114.
35. Richard A. Matthew, et. al., *The Elusive Quest*, p. 21.
36. Ibid., p.16

37. Michael Walzer: *Just and Unjust Wars: A Moral Argument with Historical Illustrations* (New York: Basic Books, 1992); Michael Walzer: *Spheres of Justice: A Defence of Pluralism and Equality* (Oxford: M. Robertson, 1993); Michael Walzer: *Thick and Thin: A Moral Argument at Home and Abroad* (Notre Dame: University of Notre Dam Press, 1994); and Michael Walzer: The politics of Rescuse. *Social Research 62*, 1995, pp. 53-67.
38. Richard A. Matthew, et.-al, "*Elusive Quest*, p. 24.
39. Volker Boge: Proposal for an Analytical framework to grasp environmental conflict. ENCOP, occasional Paper No. I, July 1992, *Swiss Peace Foundation*. p. 5.
40. Homer Dixon, Environment, Scarcity and Violence, *op. cit*
41. Volker Boge, *op. cit.*
42. Peter H. Gleick: *World's Water: The Biennial Report on Fresh Water Resources* (Washington D.C.: Covels, California, Island Press, 1998); Haleh Hatami and Peter H. Gleick: Chronology of Conflict over Water in the Legends, Myths and History of the Ancient Middle East Report of the Pacific Institutes of the Studies in Development, Environment, and Security. Oakland, California, October 1992; Helga Haftendorn: Water and International Conflict. *Third World Quarterly* Vol. 21, No. 1, 2000, pp. 51-68; Marq De Villiers,Water Wars, London: Weidenfeld and Nicolson, 1999); World in Transition: Ways towards Sustainable Management of Fresh Water Resources, German Advisory Council on Global Change, Annual Report 1997 (Heidelberg: Springer-Verlag Berlin, 1999)
43. N. Gaan, Environmental Scarcity of Fish and Conflict: The Case of India and Sri Lanka over Kachchativu Waters. *International Studies Notes* Vol. 22, No. 3, Fall 1997, pp. 17-23.
44. Adil Najam: The human dimensions of environmental insecurity: some insights From South Asia. In *Environmental Change and Security Project Report*, No. 9, 2003, p. 70.

24

The Task of Good Corporate Governance

T.K. Mishra

Good governance may be described as one, which entails establishment of institutions in the organization on principles that are universal, values that are eternal and with practices that are democratic, ethical as well as transparent. It is a collective action that is continuous in process, futuristic in application and most satisfactory to the citizenry. Deep down every human nature is divine and ethical. It is only element of ethics, which brings the difference in managerial style. Otherwise it is same. High standards of corporate governance are not only significant for the sustenance of companies but also for making the success ever lasting. Values combined with vision can help companies not only to weather storms of changes but also charge them adequately to scale new heights. They can serve a strong anchor in a turbulent sea of changes. An attempt to introduce good governance is made here to replace price-based governance to value based one. A cooperative environment based on mutual-trust and in tune with clear benchmarks of values synthesizes good governance. It is about ensuring fairness to all the stakeholders' i.e. customers, employees, investors, the government of the land, and finally, the society at large. It is about not creating asymmetry in benefits amongst them. It is definitely value based and normative in perspective.

UNDP has recently characterized good governance as one that is participative, transparent, promotes equity and equality, able to develop resources and methods of governance, tolerates and accepts diverse perspectives, able to mobilize resources for social purposes, strengthen indigenous mechanism, operate by rule of law, efficient and effective in the use of resources, commands respect and trust, accountable, enabling and facilitative, regulatory rather than controlling and service oriented. A study of the impact of value-based culture can reveal whether or not the top management's value related targets have permeated to the shop floor. Value-based culture echoes the extent of the permeation of value consciousness across the organization.

Corporate Governance

Previous decade has been a shake up period of public out cry for corporate governance. The LPG (Liberalization, Privatization, Globalization) has fired the competitive spirit among the corporate people of India. With modern companies increasingly concentrating on the objectives of productivity, efficiency, professionalism and growth; elements like character building, moral values, ethics, patriotism, discipline, brotherhood etc. in the work culture are getting into oblivion. While in developed economies institutional investors and investors associations activism has been playing a powerful role in forcing the companies to adopt good corporate governance, these mechanism have remained weak in India. Similar weaknesses apply to enforcing existing legal and regulatory regime. Similarly, with life style and work-culture being increasingly mediated by market, extravaganzas and to a great extent media, the individual as a worker and part of household is slowly turning into mechanistic, diluted and faceless humanity. Somewhere young generation of executives and workers have lost out on the simplicity of life. Missed out on the joys of having meals together, satisfaction of saying prayer together. Value systems are fast eroding, perspectives are getting lost and business ethics, rarely fashioned. Basic values are neglected in business dealings. Competition fueled by technological revolution is compelling them to move towards mergers and takeovers to obtain readymade access to market, technology and infrastructure. Hire and fire system (Job-insecurity) is increasingly being used as weapon to extract desired level of performance. Supremacy of monetary or materialistic aspiration and lack of loyalty or commitment amongst employees towards company gets reflected in their frequent and quick switchovers. Selfish career goals are becoming sole driving force; eroding elements of respect for the superiors, love for the fellowmen, and trust in the subordinates. Talents and abilities of workers in the absence of integrity and dependability prove to be a liability for the organizations. Many do not know how to cope with such a scenario. Governance is posing for itself a rather complex task than ever. Not with standing the considerable research work underway on corporate governance in official and non-official circles, there is no unanimity on good or right governance so far. Several committees were set up to look into existing norms for good corporate governance. Apart from Parliamentary committees, Department of Company Affairs constituted a committee headed by Naresh Chandra, SEBI set up a committee headed by N.R. Narayan Murthy and another headed by Kumar Manglam Birla. All have submitted reports and recommendations, codes and principles, regulations and legislations on the subject. Industry and trade associations such as FICCI, ASSOCHAM, CII etc. have also not lagged behind to profess their outlook on corporate governance. While most of the findings of these official or non-official bodies revolve around their inter-relationship with shareholders, clients, workers and government departments, they touch only the fringe of the problem. Hardly these studies look at the problem from point of view of day-to-day functioning or strategically long-term philosophy. What distresses even more, however, is that vessel of corporate governance is yet to find its ethical rudder in the absence of which it is buffeted by gales of self-interest, indifference, opportunism and worst of all arrogance on the part of corporate people towards stakeholders, including the workers. In any society, one of the primary concerns of the workers is that their company organization must be good. For a company to be good, it is essential that the systems and sub-systems of governance must be efficient, effective, ethical and equitable. In addition, the governance process must also be just, fair, caring. For these and other qualities of good governance, the machinery of governance must also be transparent, accountable and responsive. The expectations of the workers and society to have good governance are in no way based on fragile doctrines and dogmas. Instead, these have their civilization base that goes to the roots of the very existence, legitimacy and credibility of any corporate organization. In promoting the culture of good governance, how far corporate statutes and value-based principles are utilized in building sound inter and intra relationships need to be ascertained. With the purpose of facilitating the organization to institutionalize a system of Good Governance, we have developed a Core Mark framework of Governance. This could make a positive impact on the literature related to devising a value-based action plan and executing it in the context of Governance.

The Core Mark Framework

Corporate Governance has, by and large, acquired connotation of policing the thieves. Major reason for 'confrontanistic undertone is that managers remain unconvinced that Corporate Governance is a powerful tool for transparent, prudent and participative management that could be fair to all stakeholders and still enhance value of an enterprise as well as reward them commensurate with performance. Contrary to such negative connotation, while developing Core Mark framework of Governance, we have tried to depict some of the requisite principles of modern corporate person and integrate such principles of competitive management into actual practice. It may also provide a structure of benchmarks to judge and measure quality and standards of governance practiced in the organization. Perhaps, one could use this as a model to evolve a path for corporate development! Recognizing that the problem lay substantially in the weakness afflicting the sphere of human values, it provides a framework for the policy makers to bring about attitudinal reforms at different levels of organization. An attempt has been made in the context of Governance to design a normative code of conduct and devise a value-oriented action plan for the organization. True to the parameters of high quality governance, the core fulcrum in the framework is conscience-driven orientation, both within and outside. For the gap between conscience and action is source of pure stress. How does one govern firm with thousands of persons with thousands of consciences, each with their own conscience-action gaps? Letting people tune in to conscience is the primary task of Governance. Then, each person becomes a custodian of firm's ethics. Yes, it could indeed be an uphill and challenging task. But then, who said Governance is easy? Is it not an art that needs constant honing?

The Core Mark framework explores a fine-tuning between the task of attitudinal reforms and institutional outcomes for the organization. It further seeks a self-inspired network of corporate people who are able to self-actualize a high level of emotional satisfaction, meet deep-down spiritual aspiration, and attain self-worth realization. Self-worth realized people are able to comprehend the transient nature of the world and remain established in the Self while the ordinary people due to ignorance suffer in associating themselves with ups and downs of corporate or worldly life. Lord Krishna taught the eternal and worthy nature of the Self to Arjuna in the battlefield to get over the fear of death. Lord Krishna thought that as a warrior if Arjuna died he would attain heaven as reward and if he won he would stand to rule the world. But if he refrained from war he would only incur infamy and also commit a sin for dereliction of duty. Such inspiration enables achievement of bondage-free pursuits (Karma) and finally a royal perspective in life.

Core and Mark of values in the organization are levered in an interactive mode with corporate persons and also among themselves. Deviation from or dilution in any of the Core values affects quality of the Mark and therefore the final outcome for the organization. The Core values are-compliance, conscientious decision-making, courage to withstand pressures; objectivity in approach, output orientation, ombudsman-driven; respect for traditional values, responsiveness, responsibility-guided; enrichment focused, ethical, educative and Mark of values as outcomes are- motherhood truths and principles sensitized, architect of Guru-Shisya parampara, role model of relationships and Karma concept in vogue. Core values are hard facts that need to be understood in the most relevant perspective for governance to be effective. The framework prescribed here could act as a mirror for the effectiveness of its value-based culture. It could also represent an evolution of the value systems across the organization.

The primary task for any company, while introducing Core Mark framework, is to shake off the rigidity of the work culture norm, which, over time, has acquired mechanistic airtight compartmentalization of jobs. The perforce has to acquire an integrated and multi-faceted outlook. Among the various factors that can drive business leadership, Core values are most significant. Development of such pursuits calls for long-term investments in self-inspired, skilled and committed professionals of the organization. The framework prescribes for attaining conscience-driven growth or Good Governance on sustained basis in the following manner.

C=Compliance of laws; Conscientious decision-making; Courage to withstand pressures:- Voluntary compliance of law in letter and spirit is one of the essential ingredients of Good Corporate Governance. Majority of the companies have only complied with the norms in letter. Compliance in spirit is not quite pronounced. Areas where new processes and technologies are involved, the law may not offer guidance. In such situation, one needs to tune in to one's conscience, to deep values substituting the law. 'Legality establishes minimum standards, whereas ethics and values go beyond those standards. Ethics and values are about fairness and justice. It is about respecting people's needs and rights' says Shiv Khera, a management guru. Instead of seeking legal opinions, perhaps, one needs to probe inside oneself. It should also be ensured that the norms adopted are coherent across all levels, functions and geographies. Our commitments in the organization and the manner in which we treat our shareholders, employees, and customers, as also the stakeholders including the society in which we operate should consistently reflect conscientious decision-making and the courage on part of leadership to withstand pressures of any kind. 'The tenets of Good Corporate Governance, says M.S. Zaheed of HMT, should be triggered from within and cannot succeed when imposed from without'. For Venu Srinivasan's TVS, the values on which any TVS company is built are: trust, value and service. Trust is one of the most fragile things on earth, once it breaks, one cannot mend it because it instantly disappears. Conscience as a vibrant machinery of the soul should bring reasons and judgment into all human relations. Courage is the dominant factor that creates leadership and helpfulness.

O=Objectivity in approach; Output orientation; Om budsman-driven:- Leadership styles with content of subjectivity, prejudices, whims and fancies will not find any place in Governance. Objectivity as used here in decision-making sense is interchangeable with mission, vision, core competence and basic values. Currently, the goals of governance are not intrinsically motivating. With regard to output, it could be observed that wherever system takes care of the output and task that it delivers the system survives. It is important not merely to produce and sell products, but to produce and sell quality products. Output in the form of a product is a package of information, which the customer interprets in his mind while going through the process of consumption. Therefore, the concept of any product must start with the customer in mind, and end with his total satisfaction. Such organizational objective must be explicitly stated. Generally we are seen putting more emphasis on economizing the cost of inputs rather than the quality and composition of output that are produced or task that are performed. Such cost effectiveness focus, apart from increasing future task of the society, amounts to damaging the core values of neo managerial culture. Further, corporate persons are generally seen to be obsessed with production or market orientation. They, in fact, need to be process oriented. Such orientation would help them innovate and diversify. This has been the philosophy as well as secret behind the success of Japanese. 'Corporate Governance is not just about ethics and moral responsibility. It is also concerned with ensuring profitability, dividend growth, and enhancing shareholder value on a sustained basis' says Deepak S. Parekh of HDFC. However, one should not get confused profitability guided with objective of profiteering or profit/wealth maximization. With regard to ombudsman-driven pursuits, even, so to say, a thief is required to be careful about the watchdog. Likewise a master can get sound sleep only when he is quite sure of the fact that his conduct has been as per the prescribed norms. Every corporate person needs to be conscious that there is always some om budsman or invisible agency keeping an eye over whatever is being pursued in the organization. This will always keep one deterred doing the wrong things. Such concept as that of having Private Ombudsman is gaining much ground in some of the developed countries.

R=Respect for traditional values; Responsiveness; Responsibility-guided:- Modern education gives you sharpness and analytical skill but not subtleness of mind. How this subtleness is obtained? Our traditional scriptures would suggest, through Yagna and Upasana. 'The need of the hour is to create a climate of opinion which says respect is more important than wealth. It is time to make traditional values like honesty, integrity and decency fashionable again' says Narayan Murty of Infosys. These may sound old values but have certainly not gone obsolete. They have stood test of the time immemorial and thus, should remain in fashion forever. Respect and commitment to value-driven growth should get reflected in each pursuits of the organization. 'Governance is an attitude of the mind, binding core values, beliefs and ethics, molding themselves into the culture of an organization. It is far beyond Company Law. A regime of Corporate Governance acquires special luster when it is self-prescriptive' opines Keshab Mahindra. It is about application of best management practices. Effort should be made to project an environmentally responsible public image. The efficiency Krishna talks of, in Gita, is actually dual efficiency: Efficiency within, in personality terms, and efficiency without, in terms of productive work. Just remember the wheel. Rapidly moving outer rim represents the restlessness of the outer world. The center of the wheel is one's internal stability that integrates and controls. Befriend the Self and the Self will save you. There is no other savior than your Self. When one is overwhelmed by thoughts, emotions or events, one needs to withdraw oneself into one's centered calm. The center can be a mantra, an awareness of breathing or any other reference point. One needs to go through the activities of the day by being aware of the hub and not the rim.

E=Enrichment focused; Ethical; Educative: Enrichment of qualities is not for judging your self with your contemporaries but judging and comparing yourself with your own feedback that you receive. When profits are generated through economics where does honesty and integrity come in? Quite simply in sustenance and growth. In the long run no transaction can survive on dishonesty. Retrenchment of people or hire and fire practice cannot be accepted for maximizing profits of the organization. They are myopic, negative and non-creative response to the problem of economizing costs and improving productivity. 'Corporate Governance is a mechanism by which the values, principles, management policies and procedures of a corporation are inculcated and manifest. The essence of Corporate Governance lies in promoting and maintaining integrity, transparency and accountability in the higher echelons of management' says M.S. Ramachandran of IBP Co. 'Corporate Governance is not merely about enhancing legislation but about establishing a climate of trust and confidence among various constituents. Maintaining high quality standards in all sectors of business and industry is a sine-qua-non for increased competitiveness and growth, says Thomas Doering of Thomas Cook. Some of the techniques for improving the educative horizon of employees and thereby quality of decisions could be: process consultation, job-rotation, scenario building, in-house refresher and training programmes, and spiritual discourses and Yoga orientation programmes. It opens the door for employees to look beyond the usual routine response, and create an environment where they voluntarily come up with innovative solutions for seemingly intractable problems. Leaders who will meditate on the Bhagwad Gita will derive fresh joy and new meanings from it every day in their corporate life. There is not a single managerial tangle, which the Gita cannot unravel.

It is said that Good Governance means institutionalizing the principles that are universal, values that are eternal and practices that are democratic, ethical as well as transparent. Mark of values, as institutions, that forms an outcome of the attitudinal reforms in the organization can be summarized as below.

M=Mother-hood truths and principles sensitized: Corporations basically are artificial being, invisible, intangible and existing only in contemplation of law. People act within the corporation as corporate people created not by God but by law and humans. Presumably, they have only the ends given to them by their creators and the ends given to them by this structure are to maximize stock price and shareholder value. Mother in a household occupies best example of an ideal manager. The glory of our tradition is such that women derive their power by virtue of their infinite patience and the ability to sustain themselves during hardships for the ultimate triumph of virtue over vice. Such element was the overriding feature that could be seen in Ramayana. Rama was apprised of the aspersions being cast on Sita and about Him taking Her back after Ravana kept her captive. Rama without losing a moment sent for Laxmana and commanded him to leave Sita in the vicinity of Balmiki's hermitage. When he escorted Her much against his wish Sita was unaware of what had transpired and She went with him happily. One can imagine Her plight when Laxmana broke the news to Her that Her Lord had abandoned Her. Sita, the manifestation of the Divine Mother, pathetically told Laxmana, 'I was born to be unhappy. The spirit of sorrow is incarnate in Me.' She declares that Her conduct had been pure and did not deserve this but could not give up Her life as She was carrying Rama's progeny. A more heart-rending situation cannot be even imagined. Corporate persons, in order to practice Good Governance, should treat their company as their natural mother and themselves as voluntarily adopted children. No mother would like the ward to behave immorally or act unethically or even irresponsibly. Such motherhood personification would also help in molding others to the desired standards or benchmarks of performance. Kiran Mazumdar, Chairman of India's biggest bio-technology venture. The Bicon India Group, said in an interview 'I may be worth millions on a piece of paper. That doesn't mean anything to me. I am so happy that I have created this organization with such good people. That is the pleasure I get. It is not the money I get.' Management principles based on motherhood truths can prove to be most successful. Narayan Murthy, traces his love for people to his childhood days when he grew up in an environment of affection. He believes that these 'family' values have been carried through in Infosys. Corporations have no mechanism called systems or beliefs. The result is that corporations are able to act without morality or accountability for they are formed for that one purpose to maximize pecuniary shareholder value.

A=Architect of Guru-Shisya Parampara: Management gurus have spoken much about styles and qualities of leadership but nobody has ever spoken about true follower ship, as Gita does. Shisya has the intrinsic and relentless aspiration of seeking with qualities of devotion towards the cause, humility and a deep sense of gratitude towards the guru. All such qualities are catalytic to the prosperity of any institution. Lord Krishna would have failed to guide Arjuna at the war field of Mahabharata had Arjuna not obeyed his instructions as ardent follower. Guru, as a preceptor, provides enlightenment to shisyas. As a storehouse and dispenser of knowledge, wisdom, experience and spiritual energy, he is much more than a formal teacher or instructor. He helps the seekers purify the inner self and let the light of truth and wisdom emanate from the conscience. According to Deepak Parekh, Chairman-HDFC group, these phenomena appear similar to the situation of Guru-Shisya parampara or Prophet and Apostles transposed to the business world. Manager is neither an executor nor instructor. He actually needs to act as illustrious guide, motivator or inspirer of people. The shloka; 'Gurur Brahma, Gurur Vishnu, Gurur Deo Maheshwara, Gurur Sakshat Parambrahma, Tamsaye Shri Guruvai Namah' typifies Guru with the trinity of Gods – Brahma, Vishnu and Maheshwara i.e. creation (of good qualities), sustenance (of higher nature) and destruction (of negative qualities). Even avtars like Krishna and Ram subjected themselves to worthy gurus like Sandipani and Vashistha. Manager needs to behave more as a coach or a guru than captain of the team, for he learns more than a teacher every day. Until and unless learning solutions relate to real life situations and motivate the learner to acquire and apply the knowledge the whole process will remain superficial. Apart from dispelling ignorance, skill of a guru is about creating a vision, communicating that vision to one's followers, and exhorting them to move towards that vision. The most important aspect of a leader, however, is building trust and credibility. The crucial issue before a company is not about deciding what system of governance to adopt, what actually important is how to build a band of learners in the organization. Managers would be quite successful in transmitting their skill and wisdom down below if, some how, respondents are transformed into true learners, or shisyas. Here true learner is one who's learning is based on doing things and not merely knowing things. Transmission of desired skill and knowledge can be best effected if guru-shisya system is brought into vogue.

R=Role model of Relationships: Our entire civilization was based on relationships. Our knowledge was holistic as we tried to explain man's relationship with his environment and himself. It had a great balance of spiritual, emotional, physical and intellectual capacities. What we must realize is that we stand together as a human race because of the honesty and integrity that still exist in our lives. In our own lives, our families will cease to exist if parents are dishonest or lack integrity in their relationships with their children. The bedrock of our existence is relationships, which are mutually honest and respectful. This is what maintains the integrity and long- term viability of any business. Suppliers, bankers, investors, employees, government, collaborators, transporters, and distributors do have a stake in the firm's well being and therefore have to be treated as key resources. An interactive, mutually reinforcing, and firm relationship between the stakeholders and firms is quite necessary. 'Good Corporate Governance is not just about following the listing norms and meeting the statutory requirements but also truly believing in being socially responsible and behaving ethically in all that we do' says Ratan N. Tata. Azim Premji says almost the same thing: 'to meet the challenges of the future, we are prepared to change every thing about ourselves except our beliefs, as they alone guide, govern and bind us together as an organization. If we fail to honor beliefs, we will lose cre dibility, not only as individuals, but also as an organization'. Mukesh Ambani mentions nine core values that have been the guiding principles for Reliance. These are: Honesty, Integrity, Respect, Fairness, Purpose-fullness, Trust, Responsibility, Citizenship and Caring. A distinction needs to be drawn between eternal values and yuga dharma. Eternal values, enshrined in Gita, must control yuga dharma i.e. transitory. Corporate managers have to take enough lessons from Gita while building philosophy and work culture in their organization, more so, for combating the challenge offered by contemporary developments. Philosophy based on sacred Gita can continue to prove most relevant and successful for a manager.

K=Karma concept in Vogue:- As a professional manager one can find lot in the Bhagwad Gita to make oneself a better practitioner of the art and craft of management. In this, Krishna explains the virtues of detached action. The essence of Gita: 'You have the right only to action, never to the fruits there of; let not the fruit of your action be your motive; nor let there be any attachment to inaction.' We are embodiments of God; therefore every act of ours is an act of God. With such belief in mind when one approaches to a task one could miraculously find that the particular task already got done. To experiment for once, one can wilfully select to do any one good act one day, say, one chooses to work honestly in the work place a particular day. At the end of that day, back home, one can feel himself the unmatched relaxation and satisfaction. Our source of anxiety is seldom the work itself. Instead, it is neglecting or avoiding the work. Even if one fails some times in one's work, one should have faith that it is not him but God alone who would weather out the consequence as He initiated the action. It essentially tells one to focus on what needs to be done here and now. And if the end result falls short of expectations, it gives one the energy to go ahead and try something else. Seen thus, even failures can be handled effectively. Detachment at work place is supposed to translate into greater focus and efficiency. It can improve manager's faculty of thinking and judgment, give better control over anxieties and emotions, cultivate determination and self-esteem and provide inner peace. In a way, to promote efficiency, attain selfless creative calm and liberate oneself from pride and prejudices, Karma concept has to be brought into vogue. To be detached in the workplace, one needs to become meditative in action. Meditation here does not refer to certain naval-gazing exercise. It refers to achieving an all-round excellence or multi-dimensional and multi-faceted efficiency through creating a distance between that entire one thinks, feels and one's own Self. In today's competitive world, generally, we observe managers working for personal gains or satisfaction, which is basically a selfish motive. Selfish actions dissipate moral energy and don't promote healthy development of the individual. Karma yoga is a system of ethics focused on efficiency and unselfish action. Swami Vivekananda says 'activity which is selfish is immoral, and that which is unselfish is moral. Work is never the cause of misery, selfishness is'.

Governance Parameters: Corporate Governance must include volatile attitudinal measures described in the above framework towards accomplishing stable institutional outcomes in the form of reforms. In such, it may be noted that the Core and Mark of values are not only volatile, interrelated, but also overlapping. On the basis of synergies developed, the task of the corporate people is to strike a 'fit' between the various volatile and stable components appropriate to the organizational values and strategic requirements of the times. The successful corporate person is a combination of such mutually dependent attributes. Rahul Bajaj says 'Indians are neither comfortable with what they are, nor with what they want to be. They are also loud and shallow'.

When one examines the interned records of one's national past, one may acquire 'a certain depth of feeling and understanding'. Our country, apart from having offered to the world unique illustration of upholding human values at the cost of national boundary and obtaining political sovereignty through peace and non-violence, is illustrious of having sustained worthy cultural heritage. Nowhere in the world gurus and priests, parents and elders, brothers and sisters, friends and natives, fellows and peers command as much of love, respect, care and concern as in our country. Perhaps, nowhere in the world, as that of our country, even animals are worshiped and symbolized as embodiment of God. This is why, unlike India, species of such animals are eloping and becoming subject confined to museums in most of the developed nations of the world like Japan, USA, UK etc. Our country; known as country of temples, sages and seers, epics and scriptures, art and architecture, celebrities and festivals, is illustrious of enriched joint-family culture (including business) and strong marital bonds.

In the name of LPG (Liberalization, Privatization, Globalization) or openness if we merely imitate, it cannot promote a genuine and enduring development capable of earning respect and admiration for India in the world. China and other Budhist economies, which have emerged as economic might, are the testimony to above contention. Openness should precede respectful openness to our own roots. Gandhiji had said about the relationship between Indians and Indian culture, "we have not known it; we have been made even to deprecate its study and depreciate its value. We have almost ceased to live it. An academic grasp without practice behind it is like an embalmed corpse, perhaps lovely to look at but nothing to inspire or ennoble". While delivering convocation address at Jamia Millia Islamia, our President APJ Kalam very aptly quoted Maculay's 1835 speech in British Parliament, "I do not think we would ever conquer this country (India), unless we break the very backbone of this nation, which is her spiritual and cultural heritage, and therefore, I propose that we replace her old and ancient education system, her culture, for if the Indians think that all that is foreign and English is good and greater than their own, they will lose their self-esteem, their native self-culture and they will become what we want them, a truly dominated nation." The President concluded by urging that our system must produce creative leaders who should not command but coach, not be managers but mentors, not directors but dedicators and not command respect but facilitate self-respect.

Realization of our worthy culture and the spiritual insights may drive us to progressive attainment of the task of conscience driven and value based Corporate Governance. Traditional instructions seem to be dominated by fact-based knowledge. However, real life requires us to do things rather than know things. Today, strong macro-economic fundamentals, good growth rate, low interest rate, low inflation, burgeoning forex reserves, global recognition of India's potential and up gradation of country ratings, encouraging Indo-Pak relations, surging secondary markets and rising confidence level of investors all these augur well for the country. As complementarities, let the Indian corporate governance standard also be rated high. In the absence of an ethical underpinning, let the Governance not become, somewhat, an opportunity for a new form of colonial managerialism.

Acknowledgement

The present study is undertaken with the guidance and support of Professor Y.P. Singh, Delhi School of Economics and Dr. C.L. Bansal, Delhi University.

Notes and References

1. Manab Adhikary: *'Global Business Management'* Macmilan India Ltd., 2001.
2. Sanjiv Agarwal: *'Corporate Excellence a product of Good Corporate Governance'*; Souvenir-2nd ICSI National Award For Excellence in Corporate Governance, New Delhi, 2003.
3. N.E. Bowie: *'Business Ethics and Cultural Relativism'*, in P. Madsen and J.M. Shafritz (eds.) *'Essentials of Business Ethics'*, Meridian, New York, 1990.
4. F.N. Brady: *'Ethical Managing: Rules and Results'*, Macmillan, 1990.
5. S.K. Chakraborty: *'Management by Values: Towards Cultural congruence'*, Oxford University Press, New Delhi, 2003.
6. Ashok A. Desai: *'Towards Meaningful Corporate Governance'*, Chartered Secretary, August 2003.
7. O.C. Ferrel: *'International Business Ethics'*, in Business ethics-Ethical decision-making and cases, Houghton Mifflin Co., Boston, 1991.
8. Robert E. Fredric: *'A Companion to Business Ethics'*, Blackwell Publishers, Massachusetts, USA.
9. Y.S. Hegde and Rajeshwari Krishna, *'The A to Z of Management Skills'* UBS Publishers Ltd.
10. G. Hofstede: *Culture's consequences: International differences in work related values'*, Sage Publications, Bavery Hills, 1980.
11. D.M. Izraili, and Y Zeira: *'Women Managers in International Business: A Research and Appraisal'*, Business and contemporary World, Summer, 1993.
12. Shiv Khera: *'Ethics and Values; Learn the Difference between Old and Obsolete Values'*, Sterling Publishers Pvt. Ltd., 2004.
13. Kumarmangalam Birla Committee Report on Corporate Governance.
14. Karuna, Mishra: *'Para Vidya'* (Spiritual Knowledge) Bhavna Prakashan, Delhi, 2003.
15. G. Oddou, and M. Mendenhall: *'Succession Planning for the 21st 000000000000Century: How well we are Grooming Our Future Business Leaders?'*, Business Horizons, 1994.

16. H.V. Perlmutter: 'Building the Symbiotic Societal Enterprise: A Social Architecture for the Future', World Futures, 1984.
17. M.E. Porter: 'Competitive Advantage: Creating and Sustaining superior performance', Free Press, New York, 1985.
18. C.K. Prahlad and Y.I. Doz: 'The Multinational Mission: Balancing Local demands and Global Vision', Free Press, New York, 1987.
19. D.K. Rao, Prahlada: *Emerging Trends in Corporate Governance'*, Chartered Secretary, August 2003.
20. Report of the Naresh Chandra Committee on Auditor Company Relationship, 2003.
21. V.P. Sharma, and M.A.Joseph: *'Business Ethics, Professionalism and Corporate Governance'* Backgrounder, 31st National Convention of Company Secretaries on Corporate Excellence and Professional Accountability, ICSI, September 2003.
22. S.S. Singh: *'Distilling Contribution of Administrative Law in Promoting the Culture of Good Governance'*, IJPA, Vol. XLIV, July-Sept., 1998.
23. K.M. Talreja: *'Philosophy of Vedas'* Talreja Publications, Bombay, 1982.
24. Amit K. Vyas: *'Corporate Governance in India-Much Celebrated but hardly implemented'*, Chartered Secretary, August 2003.

Index